BRAUNSWEG'S BALLET SCANDALS

BRAUNSWEG'S BALLET SCANDALS

THE LIFE OF AN IMPRESARIO
AND THE STORY OF
FESTIVAL BALLET

———————

JULIAN BRAUNSWEG

AS TOLD TO

JAMES KELSEY

READERS UNION
Group of Book Clubs
Newton Abbot 1974

ACKNOWLEDGEMENTS

In the preparation of *Braunsweg's Ballet Scandals*, James Kelsey would like to acknowledge the help and kind co-operation given to him by the following people and organisations:

Nigel Abercrombie, The Arts Council, Stuart L. Bacon, J. D. Ball, Irina Baronova, Cyril Beaumont, Caryl Brahms, Oleg Briansky, British Actors' Equity, Frederick Bromwich, Peter Brownlee, Reg Cooper, Gerald Croasdell, Gertrude Crocker, Kathleen Crofton, Mike Davis, Donmar Productions Limited, Angela Ellis, Alfred Francis, Greater London Council, Val Gielgud, Beryl Grey, Pamela Hart, Victor Hochhauser, J. D. Kessler, Anita Landa, Alec Leaver, Henry Legerton, Ken Levison, London's Festival Ballet, Susan Marlys, Norman McDowell, Beatrice Meyer, Peter Plouviez, Polish Embassy, Dianne Richards, Roy Rosekilly, Helen Salaman, Coral Samuel, S. John Roper, Gerry Sevastianov, Molly Sole, Zinka Solomons, Erling Sunde, Bridget Taylor, Benn Toff and Vivien Wallace.

CONTENTS

ILLUSTRATIONS

Illustrations

Illustrations

Illustrations

CHAPTER 1

THE BRAUNSWEG CARNATION

I am in my seventies, five foot two and rather portly. I speak English with what my detractors say is a heavy mid-European accent. I speak my native Polish and Russian perfectly. And in any language I can get hold of, French, German, Italian, Spanish, I talk irrepressibly. Slow down, slow down, I keep telling myself. Don't rush yourself, but I do. Talking is one of the questionable assets essential for my profession. I am an impresario.

An impresario is, in essence, a versatile cultural juggler. For over fifty years I have juggled with personalities, talent and money; crises, scandals and money; temperaments, intrigues and money. Inevitably I have lost a fortune. My proudest achievement was the founding and fostering of London's Festival Ballet, when for sixteen years my juggling was almost exclusively concerned with crises and money.

Luckily I recognised very early in my career the importance of cigars and whisky and the ability to work out percentages. Impresarios are reputed to be immune to disappointments. They have to be. They endure so many. So, they just juggle a little faster, smoke more cigars and down a few more whiskies. My years of experience in the theatre did not give me immunity to the biggest disappointment in my life – the loss of Festival Ballet. However, all that comes many crises, scandals and thousands of pounds later.

My twin and I were born in Warsaw in 1897, when Poland was occupied by the Russians who were hated by everyone. We were a well-to-do Jewish family, the kind that is not irreligious but simply pays no attention to religion. Besides my twin brother, Marian, I had another brother, Stanislav, four years older, and a sister, Eugene, one year older. We lived in a spacious eight-roomed flat with lots of room to study and play.

My father made and sold artificial flowers of every kind as well as elegant feather decorations which were used to adorn ladies' hats and trim dresses. The business had been founded by my grandfather. In the large factory which adjoined the shop, over a hundred workers spent their lives creating flowers indistinguishable from natural blooms, and fashioning exotic ornamentations from feathers imported from Africa. Father imported special paper from Japan to make carnations. Their craftsmanship made them appear genuine, but the final subterfuge was the carnation perfume from Paris with which they were impregnated. At one time, no well-dressed man in Warsaw would be seen without a Braunsweg carnation.

Mother and father worked hard: a characteristic I inherited. Mother supervised the shop while father saw to exports and organised production. There were very few firms of our kind and we sold a lot of merchandise to Russia. Artificial flowers were in great demand there. Every Russian house possessed an ikon which had to be decorated with flowers, and ours went everywhere – even as far as Vladivostock. It was a profitable business. Every Thursday the railway inspector came to lunch and afterwards he and father filled in masses of forms for whole train-loads of man-made flowers to be transported to Moscow.

The shop was open six-and-a-half days a week and it was a long working day. As a very small boy I remember both the shop and factory workers going on strike for better conditions. They won their fight and their working day was reduced from fourteen to twelve hours.

As a family we had a stable, secure home life. Our parents didn't entertain much. They didn't have time even though we had servants. As children we were taught by tutors who gave us, among other things, a grounding in languages. Besides Polish and Russian, they taught us the rudiments of French, German and English. Literature was an important subject in our studies. Shakespeare, Sir Walter Scott, H. G. Wells and Rudyard Kipling were the authors we read.

Talents have I none, nor any outstanding characteristic, except one – stubbornness. To me, it is not a fault. In fact, in later years, it proved to be an ideal qualification for my profession. Whenever someone told me not to do something, I immediately did it. To achieve the impossible delighted me. With Festival Ballet, it was always the impossible that had to be achieved.

We had a magnificent Bechstein grand which my older brother, Stanislav, played brilliantly. He excelled in Chopin, Liszt and Bach and we had regular evening concerts which delighted the whole family. While still in his teens he began giving recitals and it was his enthusiasm for music and my parents' love of the theatre that first stimulated my interest in the arts.

Marian and I were sent to separate schools where we continued to study languages. Mathematics was one of my favourite subjects and I quickly learned how to work out percentages. This skill was a blessing in later years in quick-fire discussions about money with artists and managers. When presented with a figure I knew immediately how much I was likely to get out of the deal.

Providing I liked the teacher, I worked hard at my studies, but my German mistress was a small, miserable woman who disliked me as much as I disliked her. Consequently my German was so bad that I remained for two years in the same grade until I made some progress in the language. Sports never interested me, although I did play football and tennis. Marian and I concentrated on tennis one year, playing it every day throughout the summer. Eventually we became so proficient that we won the junior championship at the Polish spa town of Ciechocinek. We were thirteen.

At that time Warsaw was popular with famous Russian musicians, singers and dancers, en route to engagements elsewhere in Europe. From the age of ten I was permitted the luxury of a season ticket for the Philharmonic Hall, where such artists as Kreisler, Chaliapin and Paderewski performed. The Warsaw Philharmonic gave regular concerts under the baton of Grigory Fitelberg and guest conductors included Mengleberg, Weingartner and Toscanini.

I saw my first ballet at the age of eleven. It was *Pan Twardovsky*, the Polish version of the Faust legend. The dancers interested me less than the marvellous drama of the story. There were two Russian Imperial Theatres in Warsaw which we visited regularly on family outings – one where drama was played and the other opera and ballet. I preferred the dramas. Ibsen, Pirandello and Molière were popular. We also went to the Polski Theatre, which had been built and was directed by Arnold Szyffmann, a pupil of Max Reinhardt. It was the first theatre in the country to have a revolving stage.

Around that time my sister became friendly with a girl called Appolonia Chalupek. She came from a working-class family and had gleaming blonde hair and beautiful, arresting blue eyes. Impressed by her looks, Szyffmann took her into his company and re-named her Pola Negri. She was fourteen. We went to see her, although I cannot remember whether she was good or bad. She became the toast of the town and we enjoyed being able to say that we knew the young actress. Later, Szyffmann took her to Germany where she made a tremendous impact in a pantomime directed by Reinhardt, called *Sumurun*.

Although my brother and I looked alike, we were completely dissimilar in temperament. But I realised quite early in life that there was a great advantage in being one of twins. Whenever we found ourselves in difficult circumstances, we pretended to be each other. As junior students we were not allowed to go to the operetta, one of the most popular and daring entertainments in the capital. As we dressed alike, in smart military-type uniforms, it was difficult to tell us apart. Consequently I often appeared at the operetta and was quite frequently stopped by masters from my school.

'Mr Braunsweg,' they would say, 'You know you have no right to be here. What do you have to say?' I would confidently reply: 'Sir, I am sorry, but I don't know you.' They immediately thought I was my brother and often apologised.

And I fell in love with a picture in a magazine. The group included Mathilde Kchessinskaya, Anna Pavlova and, for me, the greatest beauty of them all, Tamara Karsavina. I cut the picture out and had it framed. I paid homage to Karsavina's beauty every day until the paper turned brown with age. Years later I told her of my youthful passion. She gave me one of her dazzling smiles. 'What a beautiful compliment,' she said.

To a student in his early teens, Warsaw offered a romantic, leisured life – money, friends and the constant heartbreaks of adolescent love. My consuming interest in the theatre dominated my life but there was a new entertainment too – the cinema. Chaplin and slapstick comedies were the rage of the silent screen, but I, like my family and the majority of my friends, preferred live, flesh-and-blood performances. Everyone thought the cinema was just a flash in the pan. As I attended so many plays, concerts, operas and operettas – the ballet was appalling in Warsaw at that time – I considered myself an authority on the theatre. I tended to express opinions in that forceful, authoritative manner which is so presumptuous in the young.

However, this life was soon to end. Like many of my countrymen I had paid little attention to what was happening in Europe and war came as a shock. By September 1914, it was a reality, with the Germans advancing on the city. The schools Marian and I attended were evacuated to Moscow and, since half my father's fortune and property were there, it was decided that the family should split up. Father, Marian and I would go to Moscow while Mother, Eugene and Stanislav – who by this time had decided to become a solicitor rather than a pianist – would remain in Warsaw to take care of the business.

At sixteen, I, like many of my countrymen and women, looked to England as the land of freedom and democracy. For elegance and chic perfumes, France was supreme; for efficiency and aggression, our neighbour Germany was pre-eminent. Every day we read about England in our newspapers and, as far as I was concerned, British Parliamentary rule, locomotives and cars were the best in the world.

Russia was the unknown. We packed our things in high spirits and without any regrets or emotion at leaving the rest of the family we set off for Moscow by train. We were excited, we were going to a new city, a new way of life. Even father, who tended to be more pessimistic than the rest of us, was convinced that the war would be over within twelve months.

CHAPTER 2

'QUITE THE IMPRESARIO'

Moscow was a revelation. It was vast, a mixture of wealth and elegance and utter poverty. Compared with the cultured environment of Warsaw, the city had an undefinable Asiatic atmosphere. Although there was no evidence that the country was at war, there was a great feeling of dissatisfaction and unrest among the poorer classes.

My father was a member of the First Class Guild of Merchants of Moscow, and we were given an enormous eleven-room flat which overlooked two streets – on one side Loubianka and on the other, the elegant Kuznetsky Most. Kuznetsky Most was a thoroughfare for the rich aristocrats and their horse-drawn carriages. Loubianka was an unprepossessing thoroughfare which later gave its name to the notorious prison when the Bolsheviks seized power.

The modern building where we lived housed the Russian Imperial Insurance Company. 'Imperial' was a grandiose title which really meant nothing at all. It simply divided society's sheep from society's goats. The sheep were the peasants. The goats were the rich aristocrats who pursued a life of dinners, theatre parties and balls.

My father, who had brought various materials from home, began a work room in the flat and we settled in and continued our education. What delighted Marian and me most of all was the variety and high standard of the theatre. We were overawed when we first saw the Bolshoi with its imposing colonnaded entrance thronged with carriages and beautifully dressed Muscovites. Opposite stood the Maly, or Little Theatre, where drama was played. Elsewhere in the city were the Moscow Arts Theatre and the Gorki, as well as a number of smaller theatres with full-time companies. Tickets were at a premium and to us it appeared that all Moscow's wealthy aristocrats and business people went to the theatre every night.

The Moscow Arts Theatre imposed an unusual booking system readily exploited by the brighter students. Every seventh member of the queue was allowed to purchase seven pairs of tickets. The remainder were limited to one pair. As students we had more time than anyone else, so we made sure that we were always the seventh to be served at the box office. We then resold the tickets, often at black market prices.

I had discovered another method of seeing all the productions that interested me. Our apartment had formerly been occupied by Herr Fischer, a German who had been official photographer to the Russian Imperial Theatres in Moscow. Like all Germans, he had been dispossessed at short notice by the authorities. Investigating the vast apartment, I found a tiny darkroom, stocked with hundreds of negatives of dancers, singers, actors and actresses appearing in the Imperial Theatres. Herr Fischer had left so quickly that he had had no time to take his valuable negatives. Buying the necessary paper, I began printing them. They were to become my season ticket to the city's theatres.

One of my first negatives I printed was of Catherine Geltzer, an ugly prima ballerina at the Bolshoi who was better seen from a distance. It showed her in one of her most successful ballets, *La Bayadere*. I visited her in her dressing-room and presented her with the picture. She was delighted by my kindness and gave me two complimentary tickets for her next performance. Her interest gave me confidence and I began distributing pictures to all the leading artists in Moscow. When they could not give me tickets they invariably allowed me to watch performances from the wings.

Some encounters did not begin well. When I knocked on Fedor Chaliapin's dressing-room door, a deep base voice shouted 'Come in' cordially enough. On seeing his pictures in my hand he jumped up from his chair and snatched them from me.

'Where did you get these? What do you want, money?'

'I don't want anything,' I replied, somewhat nervous of the

towering singer. 'I can produce these pictures for you, any number, I have the negatives. You can have them.'

A great smile spread across his face and his aggressive manner vanished in an instant. He thanked me, autographed one of the pictures and invited me to his next performance.

During the following two years I saw every new production of drama, opera and ballet in Moscow, always checking my photographic supply against the announcements of forthcoming programmes. My first opera production at the Bolshoi was Glinka's *A Life for the Czar*, an opulent spectacle with a mazurka danced by 120 couples. The enormous stage gave the dancers plenty of room for movement and I have never seen the mazurka danced with such fire.

Every day there was news from the front, but the war seemed remote and far away, something that did not touch our lives at all. While Moscow society flocked to the Bolshoi to see *A Life for the Czar*, the real Czar, destined to be the last of the Romanovs, was leading his armies against the Germans miles away in the west.

All the Bolshoi productions were spectacular. When the Bolshoi Company made its debut in London some forty years later, it was as if the clock had been turned back to the Moscow of the First World War. The costumes and scenery had not changed at all. Only the technique of the dancers was outstanding. In cutting themselves off from the Western world, the Soviet authorities paralysed all artistic development and set the ballet back fifty years.

In 1916, I left school and enrolled at the Moskovsky Komerscheski Institut, a college specialising in commercial subjects, where I studied economics. We students wore magnificent officer-style uniforms, including a short, ceremonial, but nevertheless lethal dagger. The uniform was topped by a superb plumed hat. Being somewhat self-conscious of my shortness, I ensured that the crown of mine was made deeper to make me appear taller.

It was as a student that I first became conscious of the political unrest in the country. At the Institut discussions went on endlessly about Russia's critical situation, but we remained loyal to the Czar.

In all the arguments and discussions none of us realised just how serious the situation was. Of Russia's 180 million population, over 100 million were illiterate. Students enjoyed a privileged position and were treated with deference by all. As we went through the city streets to our studies we were frequently saluted by the troops, whom we regarded as our friends.

Meanwhile at the Maryinsky in St Petersburg, Tamara Karsavina danced the *Water Lily* while Mathilde Kchessinskaya, the former mistress of the Czar, appeared in *Pharaoh's Daughter*. Nicholas and his Czarina, Alexandra, visited the theatre to meet one of the brilliant young soloists, George Balanchine. But a wave of anti-monarchist feeling was sweeping the country. While Nicholas served with his armies, Alexandra, influenced and guided by the notorious Rasputin, took to governing in her husband's absence from the Alexandra Palace at Tsarskoe Selo. A constant procession of Government ministers came and went on Rasputin's recommendation. Alexandra's interference in state affairs became a public scandal. Despite increasing criticism she refused to hear anything against her peasant counsellor, whom she regarded as a saint.

And father went on happily making money. He imported ostrich feathers and very soon the flamboyant decorations became the vogue, adorning the hats of every fashionable lady. Moscow stimulated his creative talents and he was very soon importing materials from France and Britain and manufacturing smart accessories to dazzle the eyes of his feminine clients.

Although I received a generous allowance, I frequently found myself without money. Every third or fourth day I visited my father's cashier to ask for money to buy books for my studies. After examining the accounts, Father questioned me about the number of books I needed and expressed surprise that none of them were in evidence. I told him I kept them all at the Institut. He looked at me knowingly.

'Books, Julian? It must be an entire library.'

The news from St Petersburg was more and more unsettling. Rioting had become a regular occurrence and the riots turned to insurrection. Rasputin's murder at the end of the year was greeted with jubilation, but after the St Petersburg bread riots in March, the Czar lost all authority in the country. The news of his abdication was hardly to be believed – Russia without the Czar was like a ship without a captain.

Alexander Kerensky quickly established himself as head of the Government, but the struggle for power between his so-called Social Democrats, other political self-seekers and the Bolsheviks resulted in further outbreaks of rioting and violence throughout Russia. Many of the students supported Kerensky, who was anti-Bolshevik, while the rest of us remained loyal to the Czar. Like the aristocracy, we were not affected by food shortages or rising prices. Most of us were convinced that by the end of the summer General Denikin would have restored Nicholas and Alexandra to the throne and everything would return to normal.

It was fashionable to holiday in the Caucasus watering town of Kislovodsk. In the summer of 1917, like ostriches burying their heads in the sand, the élite of Moscow and St Petersburg society thronged the resort for their annual summer holiday. Kislovodsk was expensive. When I asked my father if I could go, he suggested the adjacent but less fashionable town of Essentouki, ten minutes by train from Kislovodsk.

The main resort was packed with visitors. Mathilde Kchessinskaya, who had fled from the beginnings of the revolution in St Petersburg, had rented a house. Michel Fokine and his wife Vera were there and many of the artists from Moscow's Imperial Theatres could be seen nightly at the casino. We students gathered regularly at a cafe. There was little to do except argue about politics but as communications were disrupted throughout Russia it was difficult to find out what was happening. We had heard that the Czar and his family had been imprisoned at Tobolsk and there were constant arguments about his abdication, the war with the Germans and the pacification of the country.

It was suggested that we should form a students' union with the aim of making student opinion known throughout Russia. Most of the students were the sons of aristocrats. At the first meeting it was decided we could not operate without money. A fund-raising concert must be arranged. As I had frequently boasted of my close friendships with the artists of the Moscow theatres, the responsibility for organising the event fell to me. It was one thing to be friendly and sociable with the performers, but I was a little apprehensive about asking them to give their services free for a somewhat dubious student movement.

The train that linked Kislovodsk with Essentouki was always packed with people. Most of the passengers had to stand for the journey. Travelling back one evening I discovered the famous Russian comedian, Borisoff. He was standing with his back jammed against the window at the other end of the compartment and I plucked up enough courage to tackle him about my concert. Because I was acutely nervous and had to shout across the carriage to explain what I wanted, Borisoff got the impression that I had already asked Chaliapin, Michel and Vera Fokine, Lydia Lipkovska – a leading soprano who often sang with Chaliapin – and Leonid Sobinoff, a distinguished tenor, and they had all agreed to give their services.

'I'll be glad to appear if they have all said yes,' he yelled back to me. 'I wouldn't want to be left out of such a distinguished gathering.'

They hadn't, but having succeeded with Borisoff, I visited all the other artists in Kislovodsk telling them quite blatantly that all I needed was their names to complete my all-star bill. They all agreed to give their services free. The one exception was Kchessinskaya who, presumably still in a state of shock from having her St Petersburg home used as the headquarters for the revolution, resolutely refused to have anything to do with me.

I thought the most difficult part of the assignment had been accomplished. However, having got the performers, I needed a theatre and an orchestra. The Kursaal in Kislovodsk agreed to provide me with all I required and for two weeks I worked as I had never worked before. I organised the programme, engaged a rehearsal pianist, got the artists together for rehearsals and attended to the hundred-and-one other things necessary for a public performance.

On the day of this event I was convinced that none of the artists would turn up. Why should they, they were not being paid? I had worked so hard that I was very near collapse and I promised myself, faithfully, that I would never, under any circumstances, undertake such a venture again.

The performance was sold out, people were standing in the aisles. The operatic arias were a great success, but the triumph of the evening was Michel and Vera Fokine dancing the pas de deux from *Chopiniana*, which later became *Les Sylphides*. It was being seen by the majority of the audience for the first time and the romantic wistfulness of the dance caused a furore. The audience were elated and the artists were delighted with their enthusiastic reception, and the sumptuous dinner I had arranged for them after the performance.

The students were more than pleased with the money raised and I was voted honorary president of the union. I was proud of this distinction and quite forgot the agonies I had endured in arranging the entertainment.

'Quite the impresario,' said one of my student colleagues on the way back to Essentouki. It was the first time I had ever heard the word. It sounded important. Flushed with success, I decided it was something I would quite like to be.

On my return to Moscow, my father told me that the invading German army was approaching Riga. Kerensky and his Commander-in-Chief, Kornilov, were engaged in a power conflict which eventually resulted in Kornilov's arrest. The Bolsheviks had openly proclaimed revolution.

Every morning at the Institut the students assembled in the main hall. One day we had hardly taken our places when the doors burst open and a group of Bolsheviks rushed in brandishing revolvers. Pushing the teachers from the rostrum, their leader addressed us. We would remain there until we all agreed to sign a paper pledging our allegiance to the Lenin–Trotsky revolution. No one wanted to sign and we stood there hour after hour, whispering to each other and getting more and more frightened. Our captors constantly harangued us with slogans and propaganda. Some of us, eventually all of us, wanted to go to the lavatory, but we were not allowed to leave the hall. At the end of twenty-four hours, exhausted and suffering from claustrophobia and more embarrassing discomforts, we realised that the only way to escape was to sign. None of us thought the Bolsheviks would retain power. General Denikin's army was active in the Ukraine and it was only a matter of time before he restored law and order in Moscow.

Russia's peace treaty with Germany was announced a few days later, but my father had grave doubts about me remaining in Moscow.

'When the Denikin army returns, the Communists will be ousted and everyone who has given them support, such as the signing of that document, will be in trouble. It would be better for you to leave,' he said.

Without any ceremony I packed a bag, bade my father goodbye and along with a good many other students left the capital for Rostov-on-Don, where Marian was studying at the university.

Trotsky seized all the country's railway terminals and ousted Kerensky who escaped to lead the fight against the Bolsheviks elsewhere. Food was short and riots were commonplace. Although Rostov was a long way from the Bolshevik centre of activities in Moscow, it was eventually taken by the Communists. The revolution had disrupted all communications throughout the country. Trains were few and overcrowded. We had no news from Moscow or Warsaw and no money. We decided that I would return to Moscow to find out what was happening and get some cash. But no one could travel without a permit and administration in Rostov was in chaos. I presented myself at the appropriate office and asked for permission to make the journey.

Leaving Moscow, I had changed the year on my student's card from one to four. I thought this would safeguard me against inquiring officials. Fourth-year students were considered much more knowledgeable and responsible than those in their first year and had authority which, I thought, befitted a travelling young student.

Instead of being given permission to make the journey which I presumed was a mere formality, I was ushered into the Commissar's office. The uniformed officer introduced himself.

'I am Commissar Wojciechowsky. I see you, like me, come from Warsaw.' He spoke in Polish and as I sat down I could see my papers on the desk in front of him.

'I have a job for you to do here.'

With some surprise and apprehension, I asked what job. 'I'm a student. I've come to ask permission to visit my father in Moscow.'

Ignoring my request, the Commissar looked at my student's card.

'Fourth year at the Commercial Institut. You know about banking, you must do. I am appointing you Commissar of the Rostov Bank immediately.'

His statement was such a surprise I sprang to my feet. 'The Rostov Bank!' I cried incredulously. 'I know nothing about banking!' I was just about to blurt out that I was only a first-year student, but caution checked me.

'You must know something about banking. Being a fourth-year student you certainly know far more about it than any of the party members here. Your permission to leave Rostov is refused. It is in the national interest for you to remain here. I expect you at the bank next Monday. I'll be waiting for you.'

He curtly dismissed me. I rushed back to my brother and told him of the extraordinary interview. We called in our friends to discuss the situation. It was agreed that whatever I did, it looked like the end of the road for me. If I refused to accept the appointment, the Communists would most probably execute me. If I accepted, I would either be executed by Denikin's army when they recaptured the town or by the revolutionaries when they discovered, as they must do sooner or later, that I knew absolutely nothing about banking and had forged my student's card.

The only solution was escape. I changed my student's uniform for a worker's blouse and trousers and boarded a train carrying refugees to Kharkov. Most of the journey was spent under the seats as the train was constantly being machine-gunned by revolutionaries, counter-revolutionaries, bands of insurgents and, at one point, a gang of peasants. On arrival in Kharkov, I went to see clients of my father and they took care of me for some weeks.

In the meantime, Marian, not bothering to seek permission from anyone, had returned to Moscow to find that my father had been arrested and thrown into prison. As there were constant arrests of the intelligentsia in Moscow, he fled to Kiev, where I joined him. For the next few months we had the time of our lives. We had money from my father's clients in the city and spent it freely. There was no studying to be done and Kiev was full of people like ourselves, seeking temporary sanctuary from the revolution. We spent most of our time at the theatre or in night clubs. It was in Kiev that I developed my taste for drink and cigars.

One day an acquaintance from Warsaw asked me if we would be interested in financing a new business venture. He told us he was importing Army surplus underwear by boat to Kiev and hadn't the money to continue the transactions. As the amount he needed was small, we gave it to him. A month later the ship arrived. The underwear, which was warm and of excellent quality, was sold by our business partner at a high profit to the retail shops. We made a much larger investment for another shipment. This deal was even more lucrative so, confident we could not lose, we financed an even bigger transaction.

The morning the boat was due, Marian and I went down to the docks. We were a little disconcerted to see the police swarming everywhere. Immediately the ship docked, they went aboard and returned almost immediately down the gangplank with the officers and crew. We beat a hasty retreat. We learned afterwards that our friend had also been arrested. The underwear was stolen property. Such offences were punishable by death.

There was other news far more devastating – news that seemed to silence the city. At first we heard that the Czar had been murdered by the Bolsheviks at Ekaterinburg, later that the whole Romanov family had been massacred.

Without any money or papers and only the clothes on our backs, Marian and I left for Warsaw. The journey was spent largely in cattle trucks. Whenever we were discovered, we changed our story to suit the circumstances. We were everything to everyone and avoided being arrested. We were Bolsheviks joining some vague fighting force, we were Polish or Russian refugees, we were students returning to Moscow. After eight days of scrambling from one cattle truck to another, we arrived in the goods yard outside Warsaw. Begging the price of a telephone call from a passer-by, we called my brother Stanislav, who came to collect us.

The reunion was dramatic for all of us. At home the factory had been closed and my mother was attempting to run two small shops with little success. My sister and brother had married and my sister had one child. A few days after our return my father was sent back to Warsaw on a Red Cross train. He was seriously ill. In Moscow, the Bolsheviks had confiscated all his property and possessions, including a quantity of diamonds. He had been so badly beaten and tortured in prison that he died a few weeks later at the age of forty-six.

Sorting through what remained of father's business papers we discovered that he had made a deposit of £10,000 in London. He had always done business with English companies, buying large quantities of batiste to make leaves for artificial flowers. He also sold the material in bulk for light summer shirts and dresses. The money had always been sent through the bank and during the First World War, the material was imported through Archangel. A few weeks before his arrest he had sent the £10,000 to London for another order, but when the Communists began arresting the leading businessmen of Moscow, he telegraphed the firm cancelling the order and advising them to hold the money until further notice. Years later, when I arrived in London, I tried to track down the agents to whom the money had been sent. Search as I might, I had no success.

At my father's funeral, I found myself reflecting on his life. He had worked hard, establishing thriving businesses in Russia and Poland. He had amassed a sizeable fortune, but had never enjoyed it. The revolution had destroyed everything he had and he died a broken man. I made a resolution which I have always kept. I would work hard, live as comfortably as possible, but I would never save a penny.

CHAPTER 3

HELP FROM LADY WINDERMERE

———

After life in Moscow and Kiev, Marian and I found Warsaw drab and provincial. I resumed my studies at the Polish Polytechnic and concentrated on learning languages, particularly English. But neither of us could settle down. The family business had contracted so we sold a large apartment block my grandmother owned and divided the proceeds among us. Marian was already thinking of returning to Moscow, which to me seemed quite extraordinary. I planned to leave Poland altogether for America where my mother's brother had a business in New York. Being a student of military age, I was not permitted to leave the country, so I had to depart illegally.

A local freight agent who had worked for my father introduced me to a guide who promised to take me across the frontier to Germany. Money changed hands and he gave me a rendezvous where he would guide me across the border under cover of darkness.

Unused to crossing frontiers and being bound ultimately for America, I dressed myself in my most elegant suit, filled a large suitcase with suits and silk shirts and presented myself at the appointed hour. Carrying a suitcase and slithering about in the mud of 'no-man's-land' between the Polish and German frontiers, I soon fell behind the party. In a fit of panic I shouted to the guide to wait for me. Convinced that I was a soldier shouting, he fled, leaving us all to muddle through as best we could. We hadn't gone many steps before we were arrested by a German border patrol and after being roughly handled we were put into gaol. I was very worried about my suit. It was covered in mud.

My three companions were dressed as workers and carried no luggage. After being interrogated, they were released and sent back to Poland. The border police obviously thought that I, in my sartorial finery and with my suitcase stuffed with everything a travelling gentleman should have, was a wealthy refugee who might earn them some money. After an uncomfortable night, I was visited by a senior NCO of the German Field Army and asked if I could afford to stay in a hotel.

We proceeded to the best hotel, where I entertained him to lunch. As the wine flowed, I made it quite clear that he would stand to gain financially if he would get me to Berlin. I was carrying a small amount of dollars. I have always found them to be the most persuasive currency for an impresario. He left promising to intercede on my behalf after I had given him a hundred dollar bill. He said he would change it for me.

I sat in the hotel for eight hours until he returned. No mention was made of the money, but he told me the Commandant wanted to see me straight away.

With due ceremony I was shown into an office to be greeted by a handsome young Commandant. He asked me if I were a Communist.

'Do I look like one,' I replied, laughing.

My German was very poor and in preparing for my trip to the promised land of America, I had spent a lot of time before leaving Warsaw studying and reciting aloud Oscar Wilde's *Lady Windermere's Fan*. When the Commandant asked me if I spoke English, the Wildean dialogue flooded my brain. For the next hour I replied to his questions with phrases, however inappropriate, that I had learned parrot fashion from the play. His English was very good, but I am certain that at the end of the evening he was wondering if he had mastered the language at all.

After I had convinced him that I was not a Communist or a secret agent, he agreed to help me reach Berlin. He told me that he was a student of economics. The only thing I had with me that might be of interest to a student of economics was a solid gold Gillette razor in an ivory case which my father had bought me as a birthday present from Cartier's in Moscow. I showed it to the Commandant and asked him if he would like it.

He gazed at the gleaming gold for a moment.

'I will look it over. You can leave it here. Return to your hotel, get a good night's sleep and all will be well in the morning.'

At nine the next day the hundred-dollar NCO arrived, told me to pack and took me to the railway station. The Commandant kept his word. I was given a first-class ticket to Berlin and a travel document authorising the journey. I was ceremoniously put aboard the train and settled in my compartment. With great relief I left the border town of Deutsch-Eylam. I had not paid my hotel bill or my train fare – and I could not shave.

So I arrived in the German capital, ostensibly en route for America. I needed more money for the trip and, as my papers stated that I was a native of Deutsch-Eylam, I also needed new documents. These were quickly provided by a Russian refugee organisation specialising in issuing émigrés like myself with everything from passports to birth certificates. A student group arranged for me to meet officials of the YMCA, who were instrumental in getting me a scholarship to the Handelshochschule to continue my studies. For the moment I gave up the idea of America. But my tutorials were spasmodic as I spent most of my time at the Theatre des Westens, a cellar where a Russian cabaret were performing. The compere was Gregory Ratoff, the amiable charmer who eventually became a leading character actor and producer in Hollywood.

I asked Ratoff if he needed any help in running the cabaret. He didn't, but suggested I might like to sell programmes. Looking through them I noticed they carried no advertising, so I began selling space to local tradesmen and was soon making a profit. Later the cashier fell ill, so I deputised. Business was not as brisk as we would have liked, but quite by chance I met a friend of my father's who agreed to invest some money. I introduced him to Ratoff and the three of us formed a company. I was administrator, but Ratoff's sociability combined with my inexperienced administration quickly exhausted our finances. After a few months the company collapsed and Ratoff departed for fame and fortune in America.

Russian singers, dancers and musicians thronged Berlin and I was soon organising concerts and recitals for them. I collaborated with a rich young Russian girl called Mary Bran, and launched a series of literary evenings at which young, unknown writers and poets read from their works. One was a tall, fair-haired, handsome young man, the son of the editor of a Russian newspaper in Berlin. He was a frequent guest until, like many other Russian émigrés, he left for America. I heard nothing more of Vladimir Nabokov until his book, *Lolita*, was published many years later.

I had always enjoyed a good life and Berlin in the early twenties suited me very well. I soon forgot all about America. I was renting my own office, earning enough money to pay for my studies and enjoying myself. I juggled well enough, had become phenomenally quick at working out percentages and had learned how to persuade artists to do what I wanted them to do.

Among the Russian companies I brought to Berlin were the Alexandrinsky Theatre from Petrograd for a season of drama. I also brought singers such as Leonid Sobinoff, Alexander Smirnoff and Antonia Nazhdanova, comedians Vronsky and Kutznetsov, and the Bolshoi dancers, Reisen and Jukov. These two enjoyed a great success and agreed to continue their tour to Prague. Very happy, I rushed off to book their theatre and arrange advance publicity for their appearance. As I was to find out later, dancers, like many artists, are extremely selfish. Immediately I had left Berlin, Reisen and her partner departed for Moscow without even leaving a message.

I also toured a ballet group throughout Germany led by two other Russian dancers, Gamskurdia and her husband, Demidoff. During the Second World War I met Demidoff in London. He was no longer a dancer but chief medical officer to General de Gaulle and the senior officers of de Gaulle's Free French Army. After years of touring he had decided that there was little future in being a dancer. He enrolled at the Sorbonne as a medical student and after hard study graduated with honours. His wife had also retired and was associated with a leading French fashion house. In his new role as de Gaulle's medic, he did not want his former occupation revealed. Whenever we met, we would find a quiet corner away from Demidoff's military colleagues, to reminisce about his dancing days.

One day I was feeling unwell. I had overeaten. Demidoff was very concerned. 'I'll give you a thorough check up,' he said. 'Come and see me at South Kensington tomorrow.'

The Free French Army had their headquarters at South Kensington. I presented myself to the white-coated Demidoff who gave me a thorough examination, took X-rays, and samples of my blood and urine.

A few days later he telephoned me to say he wanted to see me urgently. Fearing the worst, I went immediately to South Kensington. He sat me down in his consulting room.

'I have some bad news for you. Your heart is in a very delicate condition, the aorta is twisted. You must take things very carefully, take life gently, don't rush about. Otherwise things might be serious for you.'

I was a bit overwhelmed by this news for a few days, but I have come to the conclusion that Demidoff was a better dancer than doctor. I've never had any trouble with my heart, and I've never been able to stop myself from rushing about.

Leon Leonidoff, the impresario, brought the Moscow Arts Theatre, directed by Stanislavsky, to the German capital, where they played to packed houses. I organised literary recitals for two of the company, Boris Katchalov and Olga Knieper, Chekhov's widow, at Reinhardt's Kurfürstendamm Theatre. They were so popular that the younger members of the company asked Mary Bran and me to arrange a tour for them. This group included Alexandra Gretch, Pavel Pavlov, Mikhail Chekhov and Nina Tarassova. When the company was due to leave for home these artists remained to play at Zopot for one week. Leonidoff was furious and ordered the actors and actresses to return home with the rest of the players. To appear under the management of a young, inexperienced boy like myself, he said, would be a catastrophe. Fortunately the youngsters ignored the warning. The performances were a great artistic and financial success.

Elated with our share of the box office takings, I went to the Casino on the last night and lost everything I had, including the company's rail fares back to Berlin. Among the players at the

Casino was Leon Mostovoj, the Russian comedian whose jokes made everyone laugh so uproariously that his sleight of hand when dealing the cards went unnoticed. Seeing the look of appalling misery on my face, he asked me if he could help. I explained my problem and he took my place at the gaming table.

Laughing and joking, he quickly regained all I had lost and then took me to breakfast, where he delivered a stern lecture on the stupidity of gambling with other people's money. That experience and his words of wisdom have stayed with me all my life. Years later, when I met him in Paris, he asked me if I had any money and then we played cards. He won from me all that he had won for me in Zopot and he made a very successful career in Hollywood. He died of a heart attack still joking at the card table.

A telephone call from Walter Nouvel brought me into association with Diaghilev's Ballets Russes. Nouvel, Diaghilev's administrator, asked me to arrange performances for the company in Berlin. The Deutsches Künstler Theatre were keen to have them. I would receive 10 per cent of the takings, for which I was to act as impresario and publicist for the four-week season.

Anton Dolin, Serge Lifar, Lubov Tchernicheva and her husband, Serge Grigorieff were with the company and during the four weeks we became good friends. I saw Diaghilev, a tall, distinguished figure, always immaculately dressed, watching rehearsals with Lifar on one side and Dolin on the other. He was in the process of educating these talented dancers in the arts. When they were not dancing they were usually visiting art galleries and places of historic interest in the city.

The Ballets Russes opened with *Petrouchka* which was an enormous success. The company had a varied repertoire, but subsequent performances were not popular. I was constantly at the theatre trying, unsuccessfully, to see Nouvel to get my share of the takings. He was a careful and punctilious man always preoccupied with details, so I was rather surprised that he had not given me my fee. When I did manage to see him, he fobbed me off with a promise that he would pay me the following day.

At the end of three weeks I went to see Diaghilev. He had a lazy grace which put you immediately at ease and he received me cordially. I told him of the work I had done for the company.

'Yes, the publicity has been excellent. Do you like the ballet?'

The repertoire and the dancing had been excellent and I told him so.

'For ballet you need the *crème de la crème* of dancing, music and painting. It is only when you have the best of these three arts that you can succeed, and it is a very expensive business.'

I thought it an ideal moment to mention that I had not been paid.

'Not paid! But that is terrible. What has happened?' he asked Nouvel, who was hovering nervously in the background.

'There is not enough money to pay everyone,' said the administrator, shaking his head sadly.

Diaghilev looked concerned. 'This ballet business, it's very bad, very bad.' Suddenly, as he was talking, he turned both feet upwards towards me. His highly polished shoes had enormous holes in the soles. You could see his socks which were just beginning to wear through.

'Never become a ballet impresario, young man. It never pays.'

He made Nouvel empty his pockets. 'This is on account,' he said, giving me a few coins. 'The rest of the money will be paid later.'

Leaving the office, I met Dolin and Lifar. They had been in the office next door, eavesdropping. To them the whole conversation was a joke. The money I received was just enough to buy us all coffee at a nearby cafe. When the season ended, the legendary Ballets Russes departed, leaving me unpaid, but a little wiser.

In between playing the impresario, I was continuing, in a dilatory way, to study at the Handelshochschule. I was resigned to the fact that I would never learn enough about economics to qualify for my degree, but I was not unduly perturbed. One day I was introduced to two Soviet professors of economics – Nikolai Potiechin and Alexander Kluchnikoff – who were in Berlin attempting to lecture on post-revolutionary Russia and its expanding economy. They wanted me to arrange lectures for them. It was a propaganda mission and they were prepared to pay extremely well.

I was reluctant to get involved in politics and refused. They went on talking, emphasising that they only wished to pinpoint Russia's development in relation to the rest of Europe. Eventually they persuaded me to help them.

Talking to them, I realised that they might be able to help me. I refused their handsome fee and asked, in exchange for me arranging their tour, if they would tutor me on Russian economic affairs. After the revolution, the banks in Russia had been nationalised. A few years later a National Economic Policy was launched giving the banks greater freedom in making loans to factories and merchants. This was in keeping with the general policy of expansion and economic development and my two instructors painted a very rosy picture of Bolshevik achievement.

We worked together for some weeks before their lectures began, and at the end of these tutorials I had collected enough material to write a knowledgeable thesis of some hundred pages. I submitted a shortened version to the Handelshochschule for my degree. The faculty immediately accused me of copying it from Russian newspapers.

I was arraigned before a board of twenty professors, who questioned me at length. My Russian tutors had taught me well and I was able to discourse non-stop on all aspects of Russia's economic policy. The scholarly gentlemen were obviously impressed by my newly acquired and authoritative knowledge and awarded me a Doctorate of Economic and Political Science – Dr Rerum Politicarum.

With the degree, I knew I would have no difficulty in making a career in banking or commerce. But I had already been spoilt. Working six days a week at a dull office job would bring me less financial reward than organising one concert a month, and my life was anything but dull. So, my degree has remained a memento, not of my mental brilliance, but the brilliant performances of those two Russian propagandists who achieved for me my only academic distinction. Their lecture tour was a disaster.

CHAPTER 4

LESSONS IN GAMBLING

The Russian Romantic Ballet was financed by Mr Gutchoff, a German millionaire who made his fortune from Jasmatzi cigarettes. His interest in the company was not entirely cultural, but centred on a rather handsome lady called Elsa Krueger, a variety dancer whose speciality was an Amazonian pas seul but whose ambition was to administer a classical ballet company. Gutchoff had given her the company, which had some fifty dancers led by Boris Romanoff, Anatole Obouhkoff and Alexandra Smirnova from the Russian Imperial Theatre at St Petersburg.

The company had been in existence in Berlin for about a year and were appearing at the Apollo Theatre in Vienna when Gutchoff asked me if I could help them. He offered me a handsome fee with all expenses paid, including a five-star hotel, if I would go to Vienna for one week and try and sort out the company's finances. I agreed and began my lifelong association with the ballet.

Arriving in Vienna, I found that everything was running smoothly. The publicity was good, the houses were full every night and the performances were excellent. But there was no money for the artists' salaries.

I went to see Max Rosener, the agent handling the season. He told me that after the cost of publicity, the cost of the theatre and running expenses had been deducted from the takings, there was nothing left. To prove his point he showed me the accounts. They included an astronomical figure for publicity. I asked a few pertinent questions, including how much he paid for newspaper advertising. His answers were vague, but when he saw that I could not be bluffed, he stated quite baldly that all the expenses had been multiplied by ten.

'I understand your desire to make money, M. Rosener, but this is ridiculous. I suggest you would make enough by merely doubling your expenses.'

There was a pause as he looked at me inquiringly.

'Otherwise,' I said quite calmly, 'I will be compelled to go to the police.'

The remainder of the three weeks' season was played to capacity audiences and the company received the gross box office takings. Even after expenses had been paid there was still a substantial profit.

Gutchoff was very pleased and offered me the job of company administrator at a large salary. So began my very happy and highly rewarding association with the Russian Romantic Ballet. What I learned in administering the company has helped me throughout my career and certainly enabled me to juggle successfully in keeping Festival Ballet together during the sixteen years I ran the company.

The repertoire included *Giselle*, in which Miss Krueger played Bathilde with two enormous Borzois: *L'Arlesienne* to Bizet's music, *Quattro Cento* to Mozart and a number of short works choreographed by Romanoff.

Just before we left Vienna it was necessary to get refugee Nansen passports for the Russian members of the company. All dancers look much younger than they are, but in filling in the application for the travel document, Miss Krueger showed a particular reluctance to give her age. I tackled her on the subject.

'What would you say I was?' she asked.

Always diplomatic on such occasions, I said 'Thirty-one.'

'An ideal age. Now will you be able to persuade the passport official? He's coming here this afternoon and if we offered him two tickets for the performance, I'm sure he would agree to me being thirty-one.'

'But isn't that your age?'

'I'm forty-one, but no one must know, particularly Gutchoff.'

When the passport official arrived at the theatre, I tactfully explained the situation. I offered him two complimentary tickets for the evening's performance and Miss Krueger lost ten years of her life.

The more I discovered how the company operated, the more I was able to economise. Freight and transportation costs were particularly high, so I arranged them myself, cutting the outgoings by nearly 50 per cent.

I had signed a contract for the company to appear in Warsaw at the end of 1923. Everything had been arranged and it only remained for the visas to be issued by the Polish consulate. After protracted discussions, the Poles refused permission for us to appear. No argument could persuade them to change their minds.

Gutchoff asked me to go to Warsaw and ask the German Ambassador to intercede on our behalf. I always enjoyed visiting my home city, as it enabled me to see my family who were still in business and reasonably prosperous. Armed with a letter of introduction, I presented myself at the German Embassy in Warsaw. The Ambassador expressed concern, but said although the company was German-owned, our title was a major stumbling block. Poland's long occupation by the Russians and the Bolshevik revolution, during which many Poles had been persecuted, made it unlikely for any Russian company to be given a welcome in Warsaw.

'I will do what I can for you, but I don't hold out much hope,' said the Ambassador. 'However, Paderewski is coming here to lunch next week. You could come too and have a talk with him. I'm certain he could use his influence to get you your visas.'

On the appointed day I went to the Embassy and was introduced to the distinguished musician who was also Poland's Prime Minister. We talked on general topics until I brought up the subject of the visas. I described the Russian Romantic Ballet and its repertoire, but Paderewski showed only polite interest. The only way to appeal to him, I thought, was as an artist, not as a politician. I suggested that as ballet, opera, music and drama were responsible for fostering closer relations between countries, a visit by the company to Warsaw could only contribute to friendship and understanding.

'After all,' I concluded, 'art is international.'

'Ah yes,' he replied, 'but ballet, Dr Braunsweg, is not art.'

We did not go to Warsaw. In 1941, Paderewski died in Poland.

It was rather ironic that I should be asked to arrange memorial concerts in Glasgow, Edinburgh and other Scottish cities to raise funds for the Polish Red Cross.

Before leaving for Warsaw, Gutchoff had provided me with the equivalent of £1,000 for the visas for the company's visit. After carrying the money in my pocket for about two months, I found that £400 had just disappeared on day-to-day expenses. Feeling somewhat guilty, I sought the advice of a Russian lawyer friend of mine, Adam Adamoff, an émigré in Berlin.

He was a cheery fellow with a wicked sense of humour.

'I'll tell you a better story. Just before I left Moscow another friend of mine, a cashier in a bank, came to see me on a Saturday night after losing 5,000 roubles at the races. He had "borrowed" it from the bank that morning, convinced he was going to win. He was contemplating suicide. I asked him if he could still get into the bank. Yes, he had the keys. "Then go back and take another 45,000 roubles," I told him. He was unwilling to do it, but I said it was his only salvation. Eventually he brought me the money.

'On Monday morning I went to his bank manager and told him that his cashier had stolen 50,000 roubles and lost it at the races. In a fit of remorse he had sought my help. I had gone to his relatives who were very shocked at the news. Between them they had raised 45,000 roubles. They were willing to return this amount to the bank providing nothing was said about the misdemeanour and the cashier kept his job.

'The bank manager was only too happy to agree. What I suggest you do is go to Gutchoff and tell him you've spent the whole thousand. Say you'll repay it out of your salary. They cannot do without you and if they sack you, you'll at least have a nest egg to start life again.'

I took his advice and confessed all to Gutchoff. He said that I could repay the debt with monthly deductions from my salary. I did make an attempt to reimburse the management, but after two months I was told to forget it.

At the beginning of 1924 I signed a contract with Oswald Stoll for a seven-week engagement at the London Coliseum. Distinguished, elegant and charming, Stoll was a man of the theatre who loved ballet.

Travelling to London from Berlin, I made a £100 wager with Elsa Krueger that I would make the journey without a ticket. There were fifty people in the company and myself. I bought fifty tickets and always accompanied the ticket inspector along the train, and on the boat, to count the dancers and stage staff. The inspectors were so concerned with counting, not one of them asked me for my ticket.

When we arrived at Dover, catastrophe. There was a railway strike. Fortunately our scenery and costumes had been shipped two days before our arrival, but once through immigration we found ourselves marooned on a station without trains. Each member of the company had a trunk with 'Russian Romantic Ballet' emblazoned large in red lettering. The dozens of unoccupied porters regarded us with curiosity and eventually, in sheer desperation, I decided to air my fractured English. I approached a group of them and summoning up what I remembered of *Lady Windermere's Fan*, and acting out my speech with wild gesticulations, I tried to explain it was essential for the Russian company to get to London. They showed a flicker of interest when I mentioned Russia and workers, so I peppered my conversation with the two words until they agreed to help.

An engine, baggage waggon and carriage were produced from nowhere. Fifty porters, for £1 each, loaded the fifty trunks. Our arrival at Victoria was a sensation. The station was packed with would-be travellers, but our small train was the only one into the terminal that day. The press coverage was enormous.

The Coliseum's stage manager was Henry Crocker, a willing and capable worker. With our own stage manager, Mischa Shklovsky, he worked through the night on the sets for the ballets. As I was the only person in the company who spoke English, I sat up all night with a dictionary, translating instructions. At six o'clock in the morning they and I were exhausted. Something went wrong with one of the tabs and Mischa gave vent to his feelings by cursing loud and long in Yiddish. Mr Crocker responded in the same language. I need not have sat up all night after all.

The Coliseum bill was a mixture of dancing, drama and knock-about variety. It changed continually. We opened with the first act of *Giselle*, in which Smirnova danced the title role partnered by Obouhkoff as Albrecht. The ballet was set in Scotland with lots of tartan costumes and a backcloth of misty blue Highland mountains. Miss Krueger managed to attract attention with two of the biggest Borzois I ever saw, accompanying her in the hunting scene. The following week we gave the second act of the ballet, in which Smirnova really excelled. As the programme changed, so we changed our ballets. We performed *Harlequinade*, choreographed by Petipa to Drigo's music, and *Andalusia*, the original *L'Arlesienne*, renamed for the London season. This was a Spanish divertissement which gave Miss Krueger another opportunity for her character dancing – this time without the dogs.

Among the acts sharing the bill was Bransby Williams playing characters from Dickens, and Style and Sonny manipulating hoops. We performed Romanoff's *The Feast of Prince Gudal* from Lermontoff's *Demon*, to Rubinstein's music, and *A Robberess and the Dancer* to Mozart. The drama spot changed to the tall, statuesque Margaret Halston in G. B. Shaw's *How He Lied To Her Husband*, and in between the acts we had Geaiks and Geaiks, humorous imitations and whistling and Mme Loyal and her fifty beautiful pigeons. They made a terrible mess on the stage. The cinema was already a strong competitor to the theatre, so every show ended with *Moving Moments on the Screen*.

The theatre was always full and played continuously from noon until midnight. I could not understand where the audiences came from. One of the stage hands told me that the English middle classes did not work. Their income came from the Empire! I believed him.

After life in Europe we found London very grey and very dull. The twenties have the reputation for being bright, brassy and exciting. I found the British capital cold and dreary, and Sundays were intolerable. I was staying at the Piccadilly Hotel and on Sundays all the staff were given the day off. There was no food except stale sandwiches which had been prepared the day before. The company were in digs in Russell Square and I joined them on their first morning for breakfast. Porridge, fish, steak, eggs and bacon, coffee and marmalade – food in abundance. The dancers, who always ate a lot, did ample justice to this marvellous meal and expressed approval of British eating habits. Full board was £2, but the dancers' complaints came later. At lunch they were offered soup, meat and cheese. At supper time, after three performances, they were given sandwiches. Everyone appealed to me to have the menu reversed, but try as I might with the theatrical landladies, nothing could be done.

The corps de ballet received £5 a week and the principals between £10 and £25. The fee of £700 from the Coliseum enabled us to show profit.

Moss Empires invited me to make a nine weeks' tour of the provinces. I would receive 50 per cent of the gross box office receipts, but had to pay for the variety acts who made up the programme. The tour opened in Lewisham. After the Coliseum's house-full notices we expected our popularity to continue. In Britain at that time, there was no demand for ballet outside London. Even with the variety acts the business at Lewisham was catastrophic and we did not earn enough to pay salaries. I telegraphed Gutchoff in Berlin, who sent us enough money to pay our bills. Moss Empires agreed to cancel the rest of the tour with one exception, the King's Theatre, Hammersmith. Gutchoff was not pleased and said if there were no customers, he would only pay the dancers and not the variety acts accompanying us. Ever optimistic, I suggested that as the theatre was close to London, we might even make a profit. The reply came back from Berlin that this was unlikely. Gutchoff rashly promised that any profit we might make would be mine. I gave the manager at the King's £20 and told him to get to work publicising the company. At the final accounting at the end of the week, after paying all our expenses, I had a profit of £300. Full of bonhomie, I threw a party for the company and the management of the theatre. It lasted until the early hours of Sunday morning and the station master at Victoria had to hold the Paris train for ten minutes to allow me, and other late-night revellers, to get aboard.

By this time I was getting to know the dancers and knew how to get the best out of them. Dancers are children, obsessed with their own problems. Some are more eccentric than others, but generally they are all selfish and slightly mad. I think you have to have a slight madness to be anything in the ballet. It is a mad world. The disciplining of the body, which is the dancer's life, and the continual struggle to achieve perfection, breed a narcissism which creates neurosis and encourages introversion. I learned how to cope with temperaments, scandals, hysterics and a variety of dramas, some real, the majority imagined. They only exist in ballet companies. The best way to operate as an impresario is to say 'yes' to everything and then go your own way. It is a practice I have been following for years and, combined with a little juggling and the palliatives of tobacco and drink, it has always worked.

In the hot, humid June of 1924, we opened with *Giselle* in Madrid, with King Alfonso, Queen Victoria Eugenia and the royal children in the audience. During the first interval the King's aide came backstage and invited me to introduce four of the company's principal artists to the royal family. I chose Smirnova, Krueger, Obouhkoff and Romanoff. Pleased with the compliments paid to the company, I hurried backstage confident that our success in the Spanish capital was assured. At that time the second ballerina in our company was Claudia Pavlova, a good dancer but no relation to the famous Anna – although her name certainly drew people to the box office. *Giselle* was being danced by Claudia Pavlova and I heard her before I saw her – screaming!

Wearing her second-act costume and make-up, she rushed at me. 'How dare you, what do you think I am? How dare you not introduce me to the King! Me, I'm dancing the leading role. It's an outrage, a deliberate insult.'

Knowing that no amount of reasoning would placate her, I stood silent while she stamped up and down the stage. I looked at my watch. The curtain was due to go up at that moment. The corps de ballet were crowded in the wings and the other principals looked on as Pavlova rushed off stage. A few seconds later she returned. Trembling with anger, she stood in front of me.

'I am not dancing the second act.'

I knew that my future relations with the company depended entirely on how I dealt with this public display of indiscipline.

'You are dismissed.'

She fell back as if I had struck her. Calling to her understudy, I told her to get ready. I then arranged for Pavlova and her husband, Chaikievitch, the company's Artistic Director, to be given tickets for their return to Paris. I don't think anyone noticed that it was a different ballerina dancing the second act.

The Spanish royal family attended each change of programme, but the boxes which on opening night had been filled with the aristocracy were empty. The stalls were filled. After one performance the King again summoned me to his box and told me that he was concerned as he knew we must be losing money.

'All the people in the stalls are not paying customers. They are secret police,' he said. 'You see, I love the theatre, and my family and I go whenever we can so it is no novelty for the audience to see us.' Shaking his head sadly he added, 'I have no box office appeal.'

He was due to meet Italy's King Victor Emmanuel in Barcelona and suggested that I should try to arrange a season there. 'If I bring Victor Emmanuel, your theatre will be full and perhaps you can recoup your losses.'

Knowing that two kings are better than one, I immediately travelled to Barcelona. The only available theatre which coincided with the visit of the two monarchs was the Teatro Catalana, and I booked it. The hot weather continued. On opening night in Barcelona there was not a monarch to be seen in the empty auditorium. After three days playing to empty houses, the King's adjutant came to see me. He apologised for the King's absence and explained that owing to the hostility that existed between the Government and the Catalans, it would be impolitic for the King to visit the Teatro Catalana. It might lead to revolution!

The company lost money and when we returned to Paris, Gutchoff decided we must economise. The company's strength was reduced from fifty to thirty and we rehearsed new, modern ballets. Everyone was exploiting Gershwin's *Rhapsody in Blue*, so we included it in our repertoire and toured the French spas with moderate success.

When holiday time came, a few of us rented a villa at Neuilly-sur-Seine, just outside Paris. It was a beautiful spot, and I prepared to spend a month doing nothing. It is something I cannot do, but at that time, I thought I could. Among the guests invited by Elsa Krueger was Serge Prokofieff, whom she had asked to prepare a ballet score from his opera, *Love of Three Oranges*.

Every minute of every day he spent hammering the piano giving us different interpretations of his music.

'What do you think of this?' he would ask, as he played a number of strident chords. 'Is it better than this?' followed by another atonal clash on the keys. In the ballet world, I had perfected an amazing collection of complimentary adjectives, but at the end of three days they were completely exhausted. I had also developed a terrible headache. With Prokofieff's music assailing my ears, I decided to flee. I never heard what became of the ballet score, but whenever I hear the opera, I remember the 'holiday' I spent with the composer.

When the company re-assembled in Berlin for the autumn season, Elsa Krueger told me that I was to share my duties with an old friend of hers from Russia, Michel Martoff. As the company was smaller, I thought another administrator unnecessary and after some argument, I resigned.

I had arranged for the company to appear in Turin and they left with their new administrator. Their ten-day season was a disaster and they were forced to abandon scenery and costumes and return to Berlin, where the company disbanded. Gutchoff, who had already poured £100,000 into the Russian Romantic Ballet, may well have come to the conclusion that he could no longer afford Miss Krueger. For me it was very sad. After three years of building a repertoire, creating a team of artists who complimented each other and enjoyed performing together, the company was allowed to disintegrate.

Eugene Grunberg, co-editor of a Russian publishing house in Berlin, was presenting Tamara Karsavina at the Scala Theatre. All her performances were sold out. Karsavina was giving performances at 5 o'clock in the afternoon, but she was so popular that she was also asked to dance at lunchtime. Having been in love with the ballerina since boyhood, I was very keen to work with her and proposed a tour of Europe for her and her two partners, Laurent Novikoff and Pierre Vladimiroff, who danced with her alternate weeks. She gladly agreed and so began a very happy association.

Karsavina was thirty-nine, and at the height of her career. She still appeared with the Diaghilev company, but they were not performing, so she had decided to give concert performances. Her programme included pas de deux from the *Sleeping Beauty*, *Swan Lake* and *Giselle* and a beautiful short work, which, I think, she had choreographed herself to the *Eine Kleine Nachtmusik*.

Her husband, H. J. Bruce, was Britain's representative in Bulgaria. Karsavina worked very hard, doing classes every day with either Novikoff or Vladimiroff. As a dancer she was technically strong, but it was her dark beauty, expressive eyes and arms and her warmth of personality that captivated everyone who saw her.

On the tour I was to pay her a fixed fee for each performance plus cost of transportation and first-class hotel accommodation. She was very economical with money. At the beginning of our travels, she explained to me that in order to save, she preferred not to eat in the hotels we stayed at, but at cheap restaurants close to the theatre. I was also entrusted to send as much of her salary as possible to her savings account in London. She was always saving, and yet she found herself without money in old age.

Over the many meals we had together she gave me an education in the dance. She recounted her days in St Petersburg, talked enthusiastically about the Diaghilev company, and about the history of the ballet. She was alive, vital and full of energy.

Inevitably there were times when all was not harmony and light. Karsavina always peeped through the curtain every night before the performance to see how many people were in the audience. In Hamburg, she saw the theatre packed to the roof. Immediately she must have thought that I was making a fortune. The same thing happened at other towns we visited and although she was far too

49

much of a lady to mention the fact, I felt our relationship was not as friendly as it had been.

We were booked to appear in a hall at Karlsruhe which seated 5,000 people. When I arrived, I found that only half the house had been sold. The local agent asked if he should give complimentary tickets to the students to fill the hall. Seizing my opportunity, I told him not to issue one free ticket.

When Karsavina peeped through the curtain, she saw the auditorium half empty. She turned to me and with her enormous eyes full of alarm said: 'Where are the public? Why are they not coming to see me?'

'No complimentary tickets have been issued tonight, Tamara,' I said, letting her absorb the full significance of my remark. 'You must remember, all that glitters is not gold.'

She took the point immediately. From then on she was always well satisfied with the fee.

Just before we arrived in Kemnitz, I was surprised to get our full fee in advance from the agent. When we got there, there was a red carpet rolled out at the station and a carriage drawn by white horses to carry Karsavina to her hotel. Posters advertising her appearance were everywhere and the theatre was sold out.

During the interval the agent was nowhere to be found. At the end of the performance there was a succession of knocks on my door. all from gentlemen presenting me with bills. There was the printer with a bill for the posters and programmes; the man who had arranged the triumphal procession through the town; the theatre manager who wanted his rent. Everyone, in fact, who should have been paid by the agent. He had disappeared with the takings. I asked them all to wait. I hastened to Karsavina and her partner, told them to get out of the theatre as quickly as possible. After paying the hotel bill, we caught the night train to our next engagement.

The pianist on the tour was Efrem Kurtz and when we reached Breslau, the manager insisted that his orchestra must be used. We had to provide a conductor. Efrem had never conducted in his life, but he agreed to try. There was practically no rehearsal and the sounds that spluttered from the orchestra pit that night bore little resemblance to anything the composers had written. What Efrem wanted, and what the orchestra played, were two quite different things. But Karsavina carried the day. Some years later, I was able to arrange a series of concerts for Efrem, who by then was a world-famous conductor.

While I was touring with Karsavina, Max Reinhardt and his brother Edmund offered me a job as administrator of a new company – Internationale Pantomime Gesellschaft – which I could not accept. Reinhardt was producing his first ballet, *Die Grüne Flöte*, for the Salzburg Festival, and asked me for advice. Choreographed by Ernst Matray, the ballet had music commissioned from Richard Strauss, a libretto based on a Chinese legend by Hugo von Hofmannsthal and decor by Ernst Stern. It was an unusual production with the ballet's thirty scenes depicted on a roll of richly embroidered gold and black cloth which unrolled as the ballet progressed.

On my recommendation Reinhardt engaged a number of dancers and the stage manager from the extinct Russian Romantic Ballet. I also selected Katta Sterna, Maria Solveig and an English dancer called Tilly Losch.

My return to Berlin at the end of the Karsavina tour coincided with the premiere of *Die Grüne Flöte*. Again Reinhardt asked me to

Internationale Pantomimen-Gesellschaft
m. b. H.
Künstlerische Oberleitung: Professor Max Reinhardt

Direktion: Ernst Matray, Heinz Herald,
Dr. J. Braunschweig

Aufsichtsrat:

Rechtsanwalt Dr. Apfel, Vorsitzender,
Rechtsanwalt Artur Wolff, stellv. Vorsitzender,
Dr. Richard Otto Frankfurter,
Hugo v. Hofmannsthal,
Professor Max Reinhardt,
Generalmusikdirektor Dr. Richard Strauß

administer the company. He had lost something in the region of 200,000 Deutschmarks on the new production and the dancers had no further engagements.

I was given a free hand. I set about reorganising not the artists, but the top-heavy administration. To economise, I asked Reinhardt to dismiss four directors and their secretaries. I did their work with one assistant. We toured successfully through Germany, Austria and Czechoslovakia and I was able to recoup the 200,000 Deutschmark deficit and make a profit. When I left, Reinhardt, at a farewell party, told the assembly that it had taken a bloody foreigner to come and teach a German ballet company how to make a profit on tour.

In 1926, I was back in Berlin, unoccupied, with a very good bank balance – something that was very unusual. The Russian impresario, Eugene Iskoldoff, was running a troupe called Carousel a pot pourri of singers, dancers and musicians. He asked me to go into partnership with him and arrange a tour.

We opened in an enormous cinema in Dresden, where we were to receive 50 per cent of the gross takings. We started in the middle of a heat-wave which persisted throughout the month of September. The cinema remained empty.

We travelled to Vienna. The finale of the first act was a number performed by four very tall boys, all over six feet, dressed in loud check suits, who sang an Italian song and executed a comic dance. On opening night the theatre, surprisingly enough, was full, but one of the boys was so ill he could not perform. In those days we never had understudies. Everyone was trying to find a suitable deputy, but apart from myself and the stage hands, who were required to change the scenery, there was no one to take his place. Iskoldoff was the only person quite unperturbed and as he looked at me, I knew his thoughts before he voiced them.

'You'll have to go on,' he said airily. 'You've had lots of experience.'

I had never been on stage in my life. The three boys literally pushed me into the check suit which cloaked me like a tent, put a wig on what could be seen of my head, and a moustache which could not be seen at all. As the curtain went up, one of them whispered, 'Mime the words.'

Clutched firmly between two of the singers, I was manipulated like a puppet. I tried to do what they did, but was always two or three beats behind the music. When it came to the dance, I must have looked particularly ridiculous. Not only was I tiny in comparison with my partners, but hampered by the costume, and confused by the whispered instructions, I got everything wrong. I bumped into them at every move and, dazzled by the brightness of the lights, became increasingly confused. I was quite unconscious of the roars of laughter from the audience. I felt terribly embarrassed and could not wait for the dance to end. Next morning the critics hailed me as a new Chaplin. The number was changed and the artist for whom I had so inadequately deputised, imitated my confused antics with enormous success.

The tour included Zagreb, where we were to get 50 per cent of the gross takings after tax deduction. This was my first experience in the Balkans and I assumed that the tax would be as in other European countries, around 15 per cent. We played to capacity, but at the end of the first week when I went to collect our earnings, there was not enough to pay for the company's accommodation. The statement I was given showed 10 per cent had been deducted for government tax, 10 per cent town tax, 10 per cent Red Cross, 10 per cent union benevolent fund, 10 per cent author's royalties, 10 per cent music royalties. Other unremembered taxes brought the total to 90 per cent of the takings.

Knowing that I had been robbed, I created a scene. The manager pointed out that I should have asked about taxes before signing the contract. Finally, he agreed to pay board and lodging for the company for the run of the show.

When we ended in Zagreb there was not enough money to travel to Belgrade. Our travel agent came to our aid and we felt we were set for success at the luxurious Belgrade cinema, which seated several thousand people. Again, at the end of a week playing to full houses, I received a pittance. This time there was no mention of taxes, but the evil manager, gazing beadily at me across his desk, said my contract stated that I would receive 50 per cent of the gross box office takings from the Luxor cinema at such-and-such a street. The cinema constituted an entire block with four separate entrances. There were four box offices. Only one was named in the contract. Argue as I did, I could only get hold of 50 per cent of the takings from that particular office.

Furious at this demonstration of sharp practice, I consulted a lawyer who told me that nothing could be done. As I was travelling on a Polish passport, I appealed to the Polish consul, who lost no time in telling me that as we were largely a Russian company, it would be politically inadvisable to make trouble. He gave me my railway fare back to Berlin and told me to make myself scarce. I had been staying at the city's best hotel, the Moskva, but unable to pay the bill, I was compelled to steal away leaving everything I possessed. The company managed to struggle on, eking out their earnings by performing in night clubs.

Returning to Berlin with only the well-travelled suit I stood up in, I went to visit a close friend of mine, impresario Julius Borkon. He was from Riga and I had worked with him when he first arrived in the city, introducing him to various theatre directors. He had become successful and wealthy.

Sitting in his luxurious flat, I made fun of my disastrous tour, quite confident that he would at least offer me some food and a bed for the night.

'Where are you staying?' he asked me when I had related my story. Thinking he was joking, I replied, 'The Adlon, of course, where else?'

Sometime later, looking at his watch, he said: 'It's getting late. If you don't mind, I've got a busy day tomorrow, so I'll let you get back to your hotel.'

It was many years before I could bring myself to speak to him again.

My former landlady gave me a bed in her kitchen. She pressed my suit and washed and ironed my shirt while I slept, then woke me up the next morning with breakfast and a cheery smile. I was somewhat depressed. I had practically juggled myself out of existence.

CHAPTER 5

PAVLOVA'S WARDROBE

The Bühne und Film Club in the Hardenburgstrasse was patronised exclusively by Berlin's theatre and film fraternity. You could get an excellent dinner there for one mark and have the pleasure of talking to people like Ernst Lubitsch, Alexander Korda and his wife Maria, Emil Jannings and Conrad Veidt. All, in turn, had to listen to my account of the tour in the Balkans.

Among these notables was a handsome Italian actor, Angelo Ferrari, who played opposite Lya de Putti in silent movies. He used to invite me to his flat, where we ate spaghetti when we could not afford dinner at the club. His first film had been a great success and on the strength of it he had signed a contract with a studio to make two films with a minimum guarantee of thirty days work at 200 Deutschmarks a day. His second film with de Putti had been a stinker and he had received a letter from the studio cancelling the contract. Appointing myself his manager, on condition he gave me 20 per cent of anything I might squeeze out of the studio bosses, I took the letter and went to see them.

I had persuaded my landlady to sponge and clean my threadbare suit. With a flower in my buttonhole, and looking as debonair as possible, I presented myself for interview with Messrs Milakovsky and Horozetsky. At first they thought I had come for work and treated me somwhat casually.

'Gentlemen, you must have misinterpreted the reason for my being here. I am Angelo Ferrari's manager. I want to know when he should report for work on his new film?'

Both men denied Ferrari was under contract to them.

'But I assure you he is, gentlmen. I have his contract here. If it is not honoured, my client will be forced to sue.'

I was asked to return a few days later, when the two film magnates paid 3,000 Deutschmarks compensation. Angelo was quite delighted to get the money and pay me my cut. That night at the club, he told everyone how I had succeeded in extracting a proportion of his fee from the studio directors. Before the evening was out, I was in a new business.

One of my first clients was a movie star called Olga Tchekova, who was enormously popular at the box office but was still being paid a very low salary by her studio. Her chief was Josef Somlo, who, after the Nazis came to power, made many films in Britain. At our interview, I pointed out that Miss Tchekova earned a great deal of money for him, and that it was only fair for him to raise her salary.

He had me thrown out of his office. The next day he took a full page advertisement in the *Film Courier*, warning all directors and producers to close their doors against me, as I was deliberately increasing the cost of film-making by trying to negotiate higher fees for artists. Far from achieving his aim, he increased my popularity and many more film stars asked me to act for them.

I became a film manager although neither I nor anyone else was exactly sure what the title meant. I was not an agent, as I did not take a percentage of the artists' earnings. I provided the actors and actresses individually, or in groups, for studios where cheap films were being made as quickly as possible. I paid the artists and received my fee from the studio.

I soon found myself with a good deal of power. Most of the stars were under contract to me and the studios invariably had to negotiate for anyone they wanted to employ. I had cornered the market. At the end of six months I had three hundred actors and actresses on my books. For two years all went well. I brought in international stars, ran an office with three secretaries and had a chauffeur-driven Citroen. On a visit to Frankfurt, I went to a show and saw an English beauty dancing with the Tiller girls. I mentioned her to Richard Eichberg, the producer, and at the second performance he engaged her on the spot. Lilian Harvey was an overnight sensation in her first film and became the toast of the thirties.

The Nazis were already influential in Germany and one day I was summoned to the Police President's office in Berlin.

'I've been having a lot of complaints about you, Dr Braunsweg,' he said. 'It appears you're monopolising the market as far as artists are concerned and the studios and agents don't like it. Being a foreigner you cannot be an agent. As a manager, you will have to limit your clientele to five principal and ten supporting players. You do understand, Dr Braunsweg. I have no alternative but to warn you that if you don't follow my suggestion, I may have to withdraw your papers.'

The implied threat in the President's speech was far more ominous than his determination to put me out of business. I knew I could not continue with such a small number of artists so, in the spring of 1929, I liquidated the company and left Berlin. When I was passing through the city in 1937, Max Pfeiffer, Director of the Neu Blabelsberg Studios, took me to see the place where I had worked so profitably. A complete English town had been built on the lot. It had been constructed, I was told, for an anti-British propaganda film made by Dr Goebbels. It was so bad it didn't get out of the cutting room.

I don't like holidays. Like my mother and father I just cannot stop working. When I left Berlin, I thought I needed a rest and went to the spa town of Zopot. For the first, and perhaps only, time in my life, I enjoyed myself. Understandably, because the holiday ended in marriage.

Vera Kitajeff was the daughter of a Russian timber merchant. I had met her briefly in Berlin. From the moment we met again we enjoyed each other's company. She was intelligent and considerate, and interested in me and all the things I had done. Very soon, what began as a friendship developed into love. In October 1929, after a brief courtship, we were married at a registry office in Danzig. We had already decided to make our home in Paris.

My wife's family never really approved of my profession and when I began touring a troupe of German dancers as the 'Casino de Paris', they voiced their disapproval to Vera. But she was fascinated by the theatre and accompanied me everywhere. She encouraged me, revelled in our successes, made light of our misfortunes and, apart from a miserable separation during the Second World War, has sustained me throughout my juggling career.

Back in Paris, I brought the Kamerny operetta theatre from Russia and, shortly afterwards, became friendly with Arnold Meckel, the impresario for La Argentina. She had appeared all over the world, but never with a company. I suggested to Meckel that a season should be staged in Paris by a Spanish company with La Argentina as its star. He thought it an excellent idea, but said it was impossible. First of all we could never find a suitable theatre, and the cost of getting a company together and La Argentina's fee would make the whole venture prohibitive.

I went out and hired the Femina Theatre on the Champs-Elysees for a month. It was a 600-seat theatre, small and beautiful. I told Meckel to talk to La Argentina and ask her to accept a smaller fee. She was enthusiastic about appearing with a company. Meckel, however, still had to be convinced that we would make money.

To reassure the doubter I took over the entire financial responsibility for the season, and we left for Madrid and Barcelona to recruit dancers. We found none of the high calibre we needed, but were directed to the small night clubs and cabarets of Malaga, Seville and Granada. Here we found an immense amount of talent – brilliant young girls and boys who were natural dancers. But no girl in Spain went anywhere without her mother, father, brothers and sisters. In engaging a corps of twenty boys and girls, we were obliged to transport sixty people to Paris.

Family life proved to be one of the major problems of the Paris season. None of the newly recruited dancers had ever been out of their own village or town. They would not be parted from their parents, so each family occupied one hotel room in which they washed, slept, and Mama cooked. As there were no facilities for family cooking in the rooms, the hotel proprietor was convinced that his establishment would be burned to the ground. And he objected strongly to the smell of garlic which permeated the entire hotel and even reached the end of the street.

I saw very little of La Argentina. Every evening I was referee in passionate arguments between the irate hotel manager and paella-cooking Mamas who machine-gunned us both in rapid Spanish, which neither of us understood. The Mamas won every argument and remained impervious to the hotelier's daily demand that they should vacate their rooms.

Before we opened, I calculated that even if we played to capacity audiences throughout the season, there would still be no profit. Paris was full of Americans and South Americans and since the dollar was a highly respected currency, I arranged for half the house to be sold at the box office at the usual prices. The remaining tickets were sold by the concierge of the exclusive hotel which adjoined the theatre. They were sold at exorbitant prices, sometimes five or six times more than their value. Concierges are adept at such transactions. Provided you grease their palms you cannot lose. We didn't.

La Argentina was forty-two, and had no equal in Spanish dancing. During the month we premiered *El Amor Brujo*. It was a great success but the critics began to pay particular attention to a little spitfire in the corps de ballet. Lolita Mas was a beautiful 15-year-old who danced with such temperament and fire that she captured everyone's attention. At times she appeared so possessed she was quite oblivious to anyone around her – she seemed to be dancing for herself alone. However, she did wake up one night when she fell into the orchestra pit in the middle of her solo.

The Director of the Casino de Paris, Marcel Varna, asked me if he could use Lolita in his next show. He gave her a twelve-month contract, arranged for a special Spanish dance to be choreographed for her and spent a small fortune on costumes. Lolita was rehearsed, rehearsed and rehearsed, and on opening night was a complete fiasco. All the vibrant spontaneity of her dancing had disappeared and her unsuccessful attempts to imitate La Argentina were hopeless. In the corps de ballet she had been outstanding; as a soloist she simply did not project. Lolita and her inevitable family returned to Spain where they disappeared into oblivion.

Ballet was still my dominant interest, and when I was asked by

Anna Pavlova's representative, Alexander Levitoff, to arrange a tour for her, I jumped at the chance.

Pavlova was no longer technically perfect and, although I did not know it, was nearing the end of her life. In the past thirty years, only one dancer has had her lightness and that was Markova. In her late forties, Pavlova had the body of a 16-year-old girl and looked like a beautiful, young adolescent. Her company were an odd assortment of dancers, the majority of them English, some tall, some short. They were chosen, I think, for their imperfections. Each member of this unprepossessing corps de ballet emphasised Pavlova's perfect physique and unique talent as a dancer.

She had the fanaticism of the perfectionist. In class, gazing into the mirror, she would rehearse a movement of the hand, arm, leg or head over and over again until she was satisfied. The next day you would see her rehearsing exactly the same movement.

Her death was mourned universally, but I do not think she would have been happy in retirement. Dancing was her life and touring an essential part of it. Nothing mattered but the performance, and once one was over, preparation began for the next. She had an obsession about her point shoes, her costumes had to be perfect and she rehearsed the company to exhaustion. She herself was as bright and fresh at the end of a long, tiring rehearsal as she was at the beginning.

With the exception of *The Swan*, her solos were trite little pieces unworthy of her, but she delighted in dancing them and so delighted her audience. Pavlova had a wonderful, lyrical quality, incredible speed and, in the famous pas seul, *The Swan*, an ability to drift on the stage as if blown by a gentle breeze.

The repertoire included *The Fairy Doll*, in which Pavlova wore an awful blonde wig; *La flute Enchante*; *Valse Caprice*; *L'Automne*; *Bacchanal*; *California Poppy*; *Dragonfly*, in which she displayed her lightning speed; and *The Swan*.

In any programme she only appeared for fifteen to twenty minutes. The corps de ballet knew that their only purpose was to prepare the audience for Pavlova's entrance and that was timed with great precision. Pavlova knew exactly the moment when the audience would wait no longer. Whether her dances were of gaiety, happiness or sadness, she cast an emotional spell and the audience identified with her.

We visited Lyons, Cannes, Lausanne, Geneva, Frankfurt, Dortmund, Hanover and Berlin. In Hanover, at the Stadthalle, the stage was erected in the centre of the auditorium which held 6,000 people. I stood at one of the exits to watch Pavlova dance *The Swan*. As the tiny figure bourreed so smoothly into the spotlight to the mournful Saint-Saëns melody, it seemed to me that the audience, in one concerted movement, reached for its handkerchief.

Pavlova's husband, Victor Dandre, was ten years her senior. He was a father figure who indulged her every whim and spent his life sorting out her problems, making her comfortable and trying to keep her happy. Dandre looked like a handsome, immaculately dressed, middle-aged, doting father. Pavlova, his vivacious, beautiful daughter.

Occasionally I would sit and talk to Pavlova in her dressing-room or hotel, where she painted or did embroidery. 'And I don't do either to calm my nerves,' she told me. 'It's just that I cannot sit still.'

Towards the end of the tour we appeared in Halle, near Berlin. After the show, Anna, Victor and I had dinner and then Pavlova retired leaving her husband and me to discuss the accounts. Even Pavlova did not make money although she played to capacity audiences everywhere she went. Passing her bedroom door hours later, we heard noises. Dandre opened the door. Pavlova, looking diminutive in a white nightgown, was moving an enormous wardrobe to the other side of the room.

'Anna, what are you doing?' asked Dandre.

She paused in her task and looking up at us with her enormous, dark eyes, said: 'I could not sleep with this wardrobe here. Its lines are aesthetically unpleasing in relation to the lines of the other furniture in the room. You know my room must be artistic.'

CHAPTER 6

BUTTERFLY THROUGH EUROPE

———

In Paris, I arranged a concert for the violinist, Fritz Kreisler, and a
tour, which began in Berlin, for Chaliapin. He was still a star
attraction, although by this time his voice had lost much of its
richness and beauty. An hour before the Berlin concert, he came to
me backstage.

'I cannot sing. I have a throat ailment. I just cannot make a
sound.'

Immediately I thought of the financial loss and the awful prospect
of telling the packed house that the concert was cancelled. I decided
to be diplomatic.

'Obviously your voice is your life, Feodor. If you cannot sing
tonight we must cancel the performance straight away. I would not
want it any other way,' I said, moving towards the stage manager's
office.

'It is terrible. Of course you will lose a great deal of money.'

Bearing in mind his other engagements, I said: 'So will you,
Feodor, but we must conserve your voice for your next concert.
We must cancel.' I turned away but he called me back.

'No, I'll sing. I cannot place you in such an embarrassing position.
Do not worry, I will sing.'

He told me quite happily afterwards that if I had insisted on him
performing he would have refused. Because I had his interests at
heart, he felt he could not let me down.

When I first met Johann Strauss, he was playing waltzes on his
violin in a small night club in Budapest. He was tall with a mane of
grey, wavy hair and a long, grey beard. Pinned to his chest was an
enormous medal. He was the leader of the citerazenekar, and as

listened to him, I was impressed with his musicianship. His bowing added a sparkle to the lilting melodies. I told the waiter that I would like to meet him.

After introducing myself, I asked his name.

'Johann Strauss,' he replied.

At first I thought he was joking, but he reassured me that that was his name and had been for seventy-eight years.

JULIAN BRAUNSZWEIG
12, RUE DE CIVRY
PARIS (16ᵉ)

IMPRESARIO

Theatre d'Art de Moscou
Petersb. Akademie Theatre
Prof. Max Reinhardt

———

Ballets Russes Romantiques
Ballets de Monte Carlo
Ballets Polonais
(Polski Balet Reprezentacyjny)

———

Anna PAWLOWA
Tamara KARSAWINA
Nyota YNIOKA
Manuela DEL RIO

———

Fritz KREISLER

———

Fedor CHALIAPINE
Teiko KIWA
Georges DUBROWSKI
Georges THILL

———

MISTINGUETTE
Maurice CHEVALIER

———

63

'Have you ever been to Vienna?'

'Yes, I used to work there. This medal was presented to me by Emperor Franz Josef when I retired from conducting. I was the Kapellmeister of the Hofkapelle.'

'Can you conduct an orchestra?'

'Mm, well, I'm better playing by myself.'

I asked him if he would consider doing a series of concerts for me.

'I don't do the business any more. My daughter handles it all. If she says yes, then I'll do them. She is in Berlin.'

I went to Berlin to negotiate a contract with his daughter. The concerts opened at the Salle Pleyel in Paris. Johann Strauss had died in 1899. The public, like me, would be surprised to find him still playing. I engaged the Concert Pasdeloup Orchestra and rehearsals began.

Posters went up all over Paris. 'Johann Strauss conducts music by the Strauss family.' Everyone was intrigued and the concert was sold out. Johann played and conducted well. Next day, the Paris critics did not question which Strauss this was, but one of them did say that although he played the waltzes beautifully, as a conductor he was not so good. Other successful concerts followed in Warsaw, Knock and Ostend, but Johann was already failing. He asked for a rest and went to stay with his daughter. A few weeks later, an agent for Columbia Artists contacted me with a 5,000 dollar contract for Strauss. His daughter opened the door when I arrived at her apartment in Berlin to tell her the good news.

'What a pity,' she said. 'He died last week.'

Vera's family had mounted a nagging campaign to persuade me to leave the theatre. They wanted me to embark on a business career. Trade was so much more secure and dignified. After a good deal of argument, they decided I should spend some months learning the grocery business from a friend of the family who owned a large grocery store. I merely determined to prove, once and for all, that trade was not my forte.

So I became a shop assistant. Instead of negotiating percentages, and doing a little juggling, I priced jam, sold wine and made no

1. Michel Fokine and Vera Fokina.

2. Impresario Serge Diaghilev with Serge Nouvel.

3. Impresario Julian Braunsweg with members of London's Festival Ballet.

4. Tamara Karsavina.

5.
Anna Pavlova.

6.

Teiko Kiwa.

Teiko Kiwa (seated centre) at a reception given for her by the Japanese Ambassador in Bucharest.

7.

Julian Braunsweg in Edinburgh
with Josef Cetner and Jadwiga
and Tadeusz Szymonowicz.

Julian Braunsweg on the continent with ENSA.

8.

Leonide Massine in *Gaite Parisienne*.

Irina Baronova in *Petrouchka*.

9.
Ram Gopal.

10.

Giselle

Alicia Markova and
Anton Dolin.

Yvette Chauvire and
Anton Dolin.

Natalie Krassovska and Anton Dolin in *Giselle*.

Le Beau Danube with Anita Landa, Sally Bradley, Louis Godfrey, Anna Cheselka, Pamela Hart.

12. Bullet in the Ballet – Leonide Massine in *Petrouchka*.

Alicia Markova and Anton Dolin in *Chopiniana*.

13. Alicia Markova.

14. Festival Ballet – Royal Gala Stoll Theatre, November 1950 (l to r) Herbert Wilcox, Anna Neagle, Prince Littler, HRH Princess Margaret, HM Queen Elizabeth, HRH Princess Marie Louise, Vera Braunsweg, Gwen Chenhalls.

Presentation to Alicia Markova, Anton Dolin and Julian Braunsweg of the Commemorative Gold Medal in Monte Carlo, April 1951.

15. *Scheherazade* – Marilyn Burr and Vassilie Trunoff.

The Pas de Quatre – Tatiana Riabouchinska, Alicia Markova, Alexandra Danilova, Natalie Krassovska.

16.

Benn Toff at the Royal Festival Hall with his fit-up stage.

Oleg Briansky, Belinda Wright and John Gilpin in *Vision of Marguerite*.

attempt whatsoever to learn the business. Alongside me worked a keen young apprentice, who came to me one day with a proposition. The Paris Municipality were building a block of flats on the Boulevard Mortier in the Porte de Lilas for working-class families. All the shops below the flats were empty. Why didn't we go into partnership and open a shop?

We did, but the opening was not as theatrical as I had hoped. All the artists I asked to do the honours refused. So I made sure that the store was advertised everywhere and leaflets were distributed. On opening day we gave so many free gifts away to customers that I was convinced we would be bankrupt in three months. I was wrong.

The customers in the upstairs flats flocked to buy our produce. There was nowhere else to go. Very soon my partner and I were working eighteen hours a day. Each morning at 1 a.m., I went to Les Halles to buy fruit and vegetables. Mixing in this very different world, I decided to play the part. I bought a beret, took less care with my appearance and became known as Julo. I sat drinking coffee and Armagnac with the wholesalers and porters until the lorry was loaded and carried our purchases to the shop at 6 a.m. During the first six months we made money, but then other shops opened and the competition became fierce. To combat being undercut selling wine, I installed three steel tanks each holding 500 litres and sold red, rosé and white at cost price.

During the second year of this diversion in the grocery business, we were employing twelve assistants and my time was fully occupied detecting their dishonesties. What with customers who did not pay their bills, and my desire to return to the theatre, I was only too willing to sell the shop. We received 300,000 francs for it and with my half share in the bank, I resumed my career as impresario. I opened an office and within twelve months had lost all my money.

The first disaster was the Salzburg Marionette Theatre – puppets who sang Mozart operas with the singers hiding behind the curtains. When I think about this venture, I wonder why the singers – who were quite presentable as singers go – hid their light under a bushel, or in this case a puppet, instead of singing opera. The audience did not come to see puppets mouthing Mozart and I lost a fortune.

I was penniless when I received a call from a doll-like Japanese singer called Teiko Kiwa. She was unknown everywhere, except Italy, where she had appeared as Madame Butterfly with great success. Could I go to Nice and discuss the possibility of arranging a European tour?

I could go to Nice, but I hadn't any money. I went to the café opposite the Comedie Francaise, the favourite haunt of impresarios and artists, and sought out Nicholas Koudriavetseff. He produced a souvenir album for the Ballets Russes de Monte Carlo. It carried advertising for the French Railways, who paid their bills partly in railway tickets.

'I'll get you a first-class ticket on the Blue Train. Go to Nice. If the deal works out you can pay me. If it doesn't, you owe me nothing,' he said.

Teiko Kiwa and her husband met me at Nice station and much to my relief, invited me to stay at their villa. After lunch, it was suggested we all retire for a siesta and begin our discussions in the evening. Far too excited to rest, I took a bus to Monte Carlo. With my last 300 francs I went to the Casino. After half an hour, I had won 22,000 francs and I took a taxi back to the villa.

To the singer and her husband, I proposed a minimum of sixty performances a year throughout Europe at a fixed rate of 2,000 francs a performance. When Mme Kiwa had signed the contract, I gave her and advance of 20,000 francs. The next day, in Monte Carlo, she confided in me that she was unusually lucky at the Casino tables. I expressed a mild interest, and she suggested we should play together. Between us we won 40,000 francs. With my share, I began organising the tour.

Performances were booked in Riga and Warsaw with opera companies with *Butterfly* in their repertoires. Then on to Berlin to negotiate contracts there. The Nazis had already embarked on a propaganda campaign identifying Jews with Communism and I found theatre managers, if not downright hostile, distinctly unfriendly. I had a feeling that I was being watched everywhere I went.

After booking into a hotel, I would return to my room to find my baggage had been gone through without any attempt at discretion.

As Teiko Kiwa had the support of the Japanese Government, the Japanese Ambassador in Paris had given me an introduction to Viscomte Mushakojt, their Ambassador in Berlin. He passed me on to Dr Goebbels, the Minister of Propaganda.

The name meant little to me when I presented myself at his Ministry in Wilhelmstrasse. I waited nearly three hours amid a host of heel-clicking, 'Heil Hitlering' officers. When I was eventually shown into Goebbels' office, I realised I knew him. In the early twenties, when the Russian Romantic Ballet had appeared in Munich's Deutsches Theater, he was a somewhat slimmer man, with a slight limp, who had been the theatre's very helpful press representative.

Party promotion had gone to his stomach and authority made him very pompous. There was little point in reminding him of our earlier association. After listening to my request, he instructed a subordinate in the theatrical department to arrange an appointment for me to see Wilhelm Rhode, the Director of the Deutsches Opernhaus.

Rhode was unfriendly.

'Since the Ministry of Propaganda has given you approval, I am compelled to give Mme Teiko Kiwa one performance. For that I will pay you 800 Deutschmarks.'

It was nowhere near enough. The singer, her husband and her wardrobe mistress had to be brought from Milan. Mme Kiwa's salary alone was 327 Deutschmarks.

'What is the seating capacity of the house?' I asked.

'If we had a full house, which is unlikely, the takings would be something in the region of 6,000 Deutschmarks. But she is unknown here, untried. You can take it or leave it.'

I knew that if Teiko appeared once, she would be a sensation, so I agreed to the paltry fee, fixed a date and asked Herr Rhode to advertise the performance. The following day, in one Berlin paper, appeared an advertisement so small, you needed a magnifying glass to read it. That afternoon Rhode called me to his office. The atmosphere was very different from that of our first meeting.

'Sit down, Dr Braunsweg, I have been thinking the matter over. Mme Kiwa does have the backing of the Japanese Government, something I hadn't realised when we discussed her engagement yesterday. In view of this, I might be able to give her a few extra performances.'

Knowing the sly old fox was up to something, I told him I hadn't the singer's diary with me, and I would have to return to the hotel. I promised to telephone him. On the way back, I called at the box office and asked if the booking had opened for *Butterfly*.

'Opened?' said the clerk. 'It opened this morning and finished half an hour later. Everything is sold. Many people in Berlin have heard of her success in Italy, and are keen to see her.'

Teiko Kiwa, who had been trained at Tokyo's Royal Theatre, was not only an outstanding soprano, but a talented actress. For *Butterfly* she wore genuine costumes which her mother had obtained from the Japanese Royal Household. She was capable of singing a wide range of lyrical soprano roles, and in Japan had specialised in Puccini and Verdi. But as she was Japanese, everyone in Italy wanted her to sing *Butterfly* and her success in this opera prevented her singing anything else. Her *Con onor muore* aria and the hara-kiri in the last act were so moving and dramatic that the La Scala management had come to regard her as the greatest exponent of the role.

On the evening of her debut in Berlin, I told the theatre manager to arrange for an ambulance to be on hand, as Teiko was so convincing that women in the audience became hysterical and often fainted. He thought I was exaggerating, but the singer was on top form and when it came to the death scene a number of overwrought ladies needed the services of ambulancemen. I was very pleased. It was excellent publicity.

At Herr Rhode's office the following morning, I told him that by cancelling some of Mme Kiwa's engagements some time ahead, I could arrange for her to give extra performances. The fee would be 1,500 Deutschmarks.

'1,500! But that's outrageous. You were quite happy with 800 two days ago.'

'That was two days ago, Herr Rhode. You drove a hard bargain. But as you can see from the newspapers, all Berlin is clamouring for Mme Kiwa. That is the fee I am asking. You can take it or leave it.'

Rhode took it. Eight performances were arranged, followed by another four for which I demanded, and got, 2,000 Deutschmarks each, an arrangement which left Rhode scarlet with rage.

'1,500 Deutschmarks is far too much,' said the theatre director in Breslau. 'With the theatre full we only take 5,000 Deutschmarks.'

'Very well, I agree to accept 40 per cent of the gross receipts.' He seemed quite happy about that, but when my share came to 500 Deutschmarks more than the fee I had originally asked, he warned directors and other opera houses not to do business with me.

Teiko was very pleased with her triumphs in the European capitals. When we were travelling to Bucharest by night train, the attendant told me that our party would have to wait a short time before alighting. King Carol was on board the train and he would be given an official welcome by various Government ministers when we arrived at the station.

I went along to Teiko's compartment and began my conversation by saying: 'There'll be a red carpet and brass band when we get to Bucharest.'

She did not let me finish, but jumped up clapping her hands. 'Oh, Julian, you are so clever. A welcome for me! I've never had one before! How marvellous.' Not wanting to spoil her excitement, I lit another cigar and hoped for the best.

When we got off the train, the red carpet ran the whole length of the platform and the brass band was playing loudly. Fortunately, King Carol, his entourage and welcoming ministers had already disappeared. As we followed in his footsteps the crowds went on cheering. From then on, Teiko had the idea that I could perform miracles.

In Stockholm there was a great argument about our fee, but eventually the theatre director, John Forsel, agreed to give me 40 per cent of the takings. After the opening performance, Forsel begged for more and Teiko sang twelve *Butterflys* in four weeks. Before each performance we would look out of the hotel windows, overlooking the theatre, to see if the two red lamps were lit. They signified that the house was sold out. Before the twelfth performance, the lights were shining as usual and I went to Teiko's room to tell her. She was very depressed. She was playing patience and all the black cards had turned up. I tried to cheer her up by saying that the management had asked her to give another seven performances. She said the cards boded ill for all of us and nothing could change it.

That evening, while she was singing, a union representative came to see me. He asked me not to allow any more performances of *Butterfly*.

'*Der Rosenkavalier*, which we presented last week, is playing to empty houses. The management will do nothing to help because *Butterfly* is sold out. If Mme Kiwa continues here, she will antagonise the entire opera company and the orchestra. Leave now and she can return next season.'

The cards had been correct. We left.

Meeting Lilian Baylis for the first time was not at all what I expected. I had come to London to try and arrange appearances for Teiko with the Sadler's Wells Opera. I had expected Miss Baylis to be the ideal refined, dignified, English lady. The person I saw was as forceful as Joan Littlewood. She made me very angry.

'Of course we've got *Butterfly* in the repertoire, dear boy. It's one of the favourites with my people,' she said, looming large behind her desk in a dingy office at the Old Vic. Her easy manner and vernacular speech made you forget her twisted mouth, but I thought she was rather vulgar.

'But a Japanese, singing Italian! No, I don't think so. My policy is opera in English. My people have got to know what's going on on stage and they wouldn't if she were yelling in Italian, would they, dear boy?'

Teiko flatly refused to sing in English. 'Listen to what it sounds like,' she said and then sang 'One Fine Day'. 'English is not a romantic language.'

I had to admit that it sounded rather funny, English with a Japanese accent. So London never heard her sing *Butterfly*.

During the final year of our three-and-a-half year association I could no longer accompany Teiko in Germany. The theatre as I had known it no longer existed. Theatre staffs wore brown shirts and swastika armbands. When I made an innocent inquiry about the staging of the opera in Essen, the theatre director leaned over his desk and laughing sarcastically said: 'Are you Japanese?'

I began juggling with a number of artists and small dance companies. I arranged for George Thill from the Paris Opera to sing in Warsaw. René Blum asked me to find dancers for his company appearing at the London Coliseum in 1937. The ballet had been invited to take part in the Coronation celebrations, and I came to London for the festivities.

I also became friendly with Colonel de Basil, the director of the Ballets Russes de Monte Carlo. On his office wall in Paris was a placard which read: 'The impossible we can do immediately. A miracle takes a little longer.'

In London, in 1939, I was with de Basil for one of the last performances his company gave at the Royal Opera House, Covent Garden. The house was packed and we were obliged to stand in the wings.

At the beginning of *Swan Lake*, Act two, he put his arm around my shoulder. 'Watch this Swan Queen. You'll never see such a moving interpretation as long as you live.' The Odette was Irina Baronova. I think de Basil was right.

Working with Eugene Iskoldoff, we organised tours for the Ballets de Paris. Leon Woizikowsky was the artistic director and one of the baby ballerinas in the company was Russian-born Natalie Krassovska, who became the star of London's Festival Ballet. Another dancer was Igor Youskevitch, a Russian who had hitchhiked from Yugoslavia to join us.

Vera Nemchinova was not a great beauty, but she was a marvellous dancer. The original Adagiotto in Bronislav Nijinska's *Les Biches* for the Diaghilev company in 1924, she headed a small group of dancers who toured the French spas with me. Appearing in short, classical pas de deux, the company included Nicolas Zwereff, his wife, a young talented dancer called Blinova, and a clairvoyant, Josef Marion. Marion read messages written by members of the audience on a piece of paper sealed in an envelope. This, he told me, was achieved by thought transference, but on one occasion he was utterly defeated and we had to flee the theatre.

We were playing casinos in the South of France, and Belgium. On this occasion Nemchinova and Zwereff had danced two pas de deux and Marion began his act. He asked members of the audience to write their messages, put them in an envelope, write their names on the envelope and place them in a hat taken round by an usher. Marion selected five envelopes and asked the people who had written the messages to come on stage. Five men sitting together presented themselves. He picked the first envelope and asked the writer to identify it. The five men all looked the same, solid and impassive. One said that it was his envelope and Marion looked long and hard into his eyes. He was always able to tell the writers what they had written. This time he failed.

'I'll try the next one. I'll come back to yours, sir,' he said, jocularly.

The same thing happened with the second man and the third. There was no rapport between the clairvoyant and the five, unresponsive, glum-faced men confronting him. I was getting rather agitated in the wings.

'Fraud! Trickster,' the audience began shouting. A plate was thrown on stage, the signal for a barrage of missiles. Hearing the breaking of glass, I rushed on stage and dragged Marion off. Quickly we collected the rest of the company and left the theatre. Marion told me that when he looked into the eyes of any of the five men, he could not get any reaction at all. He was certain that they had conducted a conspiracy against him.

A Brussels theatre asked me to find a small company to dance in a show they were producing. 'Something tasteful, something balletic,' was my commission. A teacher in Warsaw, Mme Tatiana Wysocka, ran a small ballet company. We put together a repertoire of pseudo-classical works and some national dances such as the Krakoviak and

Mazurka. After two weeks in Brussels the show went bankrupt and we were out of work.

While the show had been playing, I had invited several directors from various parts of Europe to come and see the girls. Among them was my old friend from the Casino de Paris, Marcel Varna. He was very enthusiastic about the company and offered me a very good contract. Mme Wysocka was sitting in on the discussions.

'There is just one thing, Dr Braunsweg,' Varna said to me as we were about to sign the agreement. 'The revue has to be slightly daring, you know. I think the girls will have to dance without brassieres.'

I was rather surprised by the request, but Mme Wysocka became a positive Carabosse of outraged decency. She began shrieking about depravity and insulting behaviour. At one point, I thought she was going to attack the Frenchman. I brought the discussion to an end, explaining that we could not provide the kind of entertainment Varna wanted.

To earn some money, I managed to arrange for the company to perform in Antwerp and told Mme Wysocka that I would go to Paris for a couple of days to try and find other engagements Arriving back in Antwerp, I was apprehended by the police.

Madame, convinced that I had absconded with what little money we had left, had reported the matter to the police. I explained the situation to the officer, showed him the money I had brought with me to pay the company's salaries and received an apology. Mme Wysocka assured me that it had all been an unfortunate mistake. She had mentioned my absence to one of the girls who had mis-understood her and gone to the police. I lost no time in telling Madame what I thought of her, paid the girls and gave them their return tickets to Warsaw.

In Paris, six months later, I received an invitation from Varna to the opening of his latest revue at the Casino. When the curtain rose I was amazed to see the sixteen girls I had sent back to Warsaw, their rosy breasts exposed for all to see. The company began with the slow Chopin ballet they had performed for me. The bosoms undulated, but were quite acceptable. Then came the mazurka and the girls had to move a little faster. In pirouettes, the unrestrained breasts bulged forward with a life of their own. When it came to the jumps, I laughed so much that Varna came to the box and ordered me out of the theatre.

I was asked by the Polish Ambassador in Paris to arrange performances for Poland's National Ballet Company in Warsaw – a commission I found rather extraordinary.

The Polish Government had invested a good deal of money in establishing the company. Practically the whole repertoire was choreographed by Bronislava Nijinska, the company's artistic director. She had used the music of some of Poland's foremost composers – Szymanowski, Krupinski and Kondratski. The works included *La Legende de Cracovie*, a ballet based on the Faust legend; *Le Chant de la Terre*, a folk ballet; and *Concerto de Chopin*, in which Nijinska had created some of her best, abstract choreography.

The forty dancers were led by Olga Slawska, Nina Juszkiewica, Czeslaw Konarski and Zbiegniew Kilinski. The company were rough-and-ready and could have done with a lot more rehearsal. They were happier in the national dances than the classical ballets.

For 50 per cent of the takings, I agreed to pay the theatre, orchestra and other overheads and to arrange publicity. There was a slight masculinity in Nijinska's manner, she was obstinate and accustomed to getting her own way. The Warsaw opening was successful, but despite my arguments, Nijinska insisted on taking the orchestra on tour. Many of the places we visited were no bigger than church halls, and consequently I lost a good deal of money. I complained bitterly to the Foreign Minister, Josef Beck, who promised that in some way I would be compensated.

To negotiate a contract for Berlin, I was again forced to visit Dr Goebbels at his Ministry of Propaganda. When we eventually appeared at the Deutschen Opernhaus, he attended the opening performance and gave a party for the company afterwards. It was an odd situation. The theatre directors disliked negotiating with me, but were always complimentary about the company.

After Brussels the company appeared at the Royal Opera House,

Covent Garden, but got panned by the critics. I was not with them as Nijinska's tantrums had become a scandal. The Polish Government asked me to find a new artistic director. I engaged Leon Wojcikowski and his wife, Nina Rajevska. He did not have many ideas, but his wife did. Under their joint direction, the company's standards improved. My brother Marian was looking for a job and when it was decided to send the company to New York to represent Poland at the World Fair, I suggested he went as manager. They were a great success, hailed by the press as 'The Million Dollar Ballet'.

Unter der Schirmherrschaft des Polnischen Botschafters
JÓZEF LIPSKI

und des Reichsministers für Volksaufklärung und Propaganda
DR. JOSEPH GOEBBELS

DAS POLNISCHE BALLETT

GENERALDIREKTOR: DR. ARNOLD SZYFMAN

DIREKTOR UND KÜNSTLERISCHER LEITER:

BRONISLAVA NIJINSKA

DAS DEUTSCHE OPERNHAUS-ORCHESTER unter Leitung von M. MIERZEJEWSKI

In the Spring of 1939, on one of my frequent journeys between Paris and Warsaw, I had to change trains in Berlin. As I was going from the Bahnhof Zoo to the Friedrichstrasse station, my taxi was stopped in the Unter den Linden by two brown-shirted, revolver-carrying hoodlums. They told the driver to stay where he was until the parade, which included Hitler and Mussolini, had passed by. Within minutes, martial music surrounded us and I stood with the brown-shirts watching the greatest show of military strength ever witnessed in Europe. Troops, tanks, armoured vehicles of every kind rolled by. The pauses in the music were filled with frenetic 'Heil-Hitlers'. I missed my connection as the parade took two-and-a-half hours to pass.

In Warsaw, I went immediately to see Minister Beck and told him what I had witnessed in Berlin. I predicted that the parade was a prelude to Poland's invasion by the Nazis. He asked me if I had experienced any anti-Polish feeling in my dealings with German theatres. I explained that it was difficult to know, as there was so much anti-Semitism in the country.

'I think you're exaggerating, Dr Braunsweg. There is nothing to worry about. They would not have allowed our ballet company to appear there and given them such a friendly reception if they were planning to invade us. Wait until you see our parade.'

I found myself on a seat at the saluting base near the Minister of War, Edward Rytz-Smigly. The parade was beautiful, with well-groomed horses, cantering along, ridden by cavalry officers who looked as if they had been costumed for a Hollywood musical. I was very depressed. I knew if the country was attacked by the Germans with their modern weapons of war, there would be no fight.

In May 1939, Foreign Minister Beck, implementing his promise, sent me to London to negotiate contracts with the BBC and the British Council for a Festival of Polish Music and Dancing. The Festival was planned for October and November. Vera had gone to visit her sister in Riga and we had arranged to meet in Paris.

Germany invaded Poland on 1 September 1939, just one day after the Polish Ballet returned from New York. It was incredible to think that the Polish Government allowed the dancers to return to Warsaw. I could only surmise that the Government leaders had no knowledge of the impending invasion. When Warsaw fell, my twin brother, with the help of some of the artists in the company, fled to Italy, where Beniamino Gigli helped him to return to America.

The Polish Embassy in London was in utter chaos. I went there regularly to collect my expenses. One day, I turned up as usual and was told by the first secretary that Mr Koreba, the cashier, wanted to see me. Koreba gave me an envelope containing £100 in one pound notes. The envelope had been sent by the Foreign Ministry in Warsaw by the last courier to leave the country. He had been obliged to travel via Sweden to get to London. I was very impressed. The German armies were sweeping through Poland and yet the Foreign Ministry had had time to think of a music festival in London.

At the Regent Palace, where I was staying, I met the singer, Herman Simberg. He mistook me for my brother Marian, whom he had seen in New York with the Polish Ballet a week before. I explained the situation. As he and his family were being evacuated to the country, he invited me to stay in his house.

For the next few months, I visited the Home Office every day to try to get permission for my wife to join me in London. The Home Office refused. I was very upset by this separation. It was one I had to endure for the next five years.

Early in 1940, I was informed by the Red Cross that my entire family, my mother, my eldest brother and his wife, my sister, her husband and their son, besides numerous relatives, had all been murdered by the Nazis in the Warsaw Ghetto.

CHAPTER 7

VARIETY IN THE BLITZ

———

For many months the loss of my family obsessed me. There was no one I could appeal to for comfort. Depressed and unhappy, I found sanctuary during the hot summer months in Kew Gardens. I would lie for hours on the grass, gazing up into the blue, clear sky. It was peaceful and quiet. Many years later, Vera and I bought a derelict house near the Gardens and have lived there ever since. I called it my second *Nutcracker*. We had just mounted *Nutcracker* for Festival Ballet without any money. The house too was renovated on promises.

Eventually, I adjusted to my new lonelier way of life and began doing the only thing I knew something about – artistic juggling. I arranged a number of recitals in provincial towns for Herman Simberg, Stefan Craig, the violinist, and Adela Kotowska the pianist. The performances were well attended, as all the towns we visited were overflowing with evacuees. Charities such as the Spitfire Fund, Polish Relief Fund and various other nationalistic causes benefited. I brought Witold Malcuzynski, the distinguished Polish pianist, to London to play Chopin and Rachmaninoff.

Jan Cobel, a friend of my eldest brother, was a Polish balletomane whom I met in London. I had already decided to form an Anglo-Polish Ballet company, but needed finance. Cobel agreed to contribute £500. Led by Alicia Halama and her husband, Czeslaw Konarski from the Polish company, the dancers included Alexis Rassine, Gordon Hamilton and later, Leo Kersley, Henry Danton and Sonia Arova. Besides *Les Sylphides*, *Spectre de la Rose*, the Blue Bird pas de deux and other classical divertissements, the repertoire included some excellent Polish dances.

Because of the bombing, rehearsals were chaotic. Incendiaries destroyed the costumes and musical scores for the opening season. Despite these difficulties, the company opened with great success at the Apollo Theatre in December 1940, and began touring the provinces.

My association with the Anglo-Polish Ballet was short lived. Cobel began to take an active interest in the artistic direction of the company. He was an engineer by profession, and I resented him teaching me the ballet business. Eventually I handed everything over to him and told him to get on with it.

He worked very hard for over four years, during which time the company toured continually. At the end of the war he brought the dancers to the Saville Theatre for a short season. It proved a financial disaster. British Actors' Equity had to pay the artists' salaries from funds deposited with them before the season opened. Although Cobel tried to persuade the dancers to undertake another provincial tour, they refused. For my part, I learnt a lesson. In all the years I ran Festival Ballet, despite the never-ending financial crises, the dancers were always paid.

Life in war-time London was one more gamble. My first-floor room at the Regent Palace cost 10s 6d a day for bed and breakfast. Breakfast was so good I did not eat anything again until evening. Then it was fish-and-chips for 1s 3d at a cafe opposite the Windmill Theatre.

In the early days of the bombing, I spent the nights in the air raid shelters with Jean de Kuharski, the film and theatre producer. One day we went to look at the lists of civilians killed and injured posted at the LCC offices, Charing Cross. There were only hundreds killed, but thousands injured.

'It's like a lottery,' said Kuharski. 'I would say the odds against us getting killed or injured are so great that they aren't worth considering. We're not going to spend any more nights in the shelters. We'll just hope that our names aren't on the bombs.' I thought about it for a time and came to the conclusion he was right.

One day I was travelling in a taxi when a raid began. The streets were deserted. Bombs were falling all around us. When we came to some traffic lights, the driver stopped.

'Keep going for goodness' sake,' I cried. 'Get a move on. We'll be killed.'

'We can't go yet,' replied the unflappable cabby, 'the lights are against us.'

On another occasion a young man was discovered on a roof signalling to enemy aircraft with a hand torch. He was brought down by some ARP wardens. I fully expected him to be lynched by the crowd who had gathered on the pavement. To my surprise they just jeered at him good-heartedly and let him go.

Every profession has its bores. In war-time London there were the bomb bores, who delighted in recounting their near misses or the cunning ways in which they had eluded death. Eventually I had a button made which I pinned underneath the lapel of my jacket. When one of these bores threatened me with a dissertation, I merely turned up the button: 'I am not interested in your bomb. Go away.' They did.

The Regent Palace was inhabited largely by refugees from Europe and each afternoon they would congregate in the restaurant. It was here I renewed my friendship with Josef Marion, the clairvoyant with whom I had worked in France and Belgium. There was also a General living in the hotel and he was joined by his newly married daughter and her husband on their honeymoon. The only room available was on the sixth floor, but as the daughter was rather nervous of heights, the General agreed to exchange rooms. He was living on the third. One morning, while I was dining in the restaurant, the hotel received a direct hit. The husband was killed, the daughter badly injured and the General escaped unhurt. I was called to attend the wounded and dying, but when I explained that my doctorate was of political economy and not medicine, my services were dispensed with. However, I was asked if I would vacate my room for the General's daughter for a few days prior to her admittance to hospital. I returned to my room about a week later and received a phenomenal bill for all the injured lady's room service.

Josef Marion and I came to the conclusion that there was a desperate need for live entertainment in London and the provinces. Apart from the Windmill, which never closed, there was very little theatre of any kind in the capital. Besides being able to read people's thoughts, Marion practised as a palm reader and he persuaded one of his clients to provide us with £5,000 for a revue. We intended to produce a varied programme of opera, ballet, comedy, drama, songs and modern dancing.

We began work. I engaged Enid Stamp-Taylor, Jerry Verno, Herman Simberg, Rubina Gilchrist (the first Mrs Donald Albery), and Nina Tarakanova, prima ballerina of the Ballets Russes de Monte Carlo. She danced a short work with libretto by the Dowager Marchioness of Townshend called *Midnight Romancing*, and the choreography was by a young, talented girl called Pauline Grant. The revue also featured Josef Marion – 'the brain wonder of the world'.

In addition to the corps de ballet there was a group of twenty-four high-kickers called the 'Julian d'lovelies'. Their numbers, arranged by Buddy Bradley, included boogie-woogie for the first time in England. The songs had lyrics by Val Guest and the music was by Stefan Craig and G. S. Mathis.

The dress rehearsal went so well that L. Nathan, who had costumed the show, extended our credit. 'The show will have a long run,' he predicted, 'you can't fail.' We did.

On the morning of the premiere, there was a rehearsal but I was unable to attend. The cast decided that their parts, which had been cut in some cases to make a tighter, fast-running show, were not big enough. Jerry Verno wanted more jokes; Simberg wanted more songs; Enid Stamp-Taylor wanted her cuts restored; Rubina Gilchrist wanted another song. Without consulting me, the producer, Jean de Kuharski, agreed.

Wednesday after the War opened at the New Theatre on 5 April 1941. It was too long and lacked speed and slickness. Although the artists and their material were good, the notices were universally bad.

Shortly afterwards, I was looking for another £5,000 to back a revue when I met a man who worked at the Foreign Office who, I was told, might be able to help me. He had the money but thought the venture too risky.

'Do you have any money of your own?' he asked me.

'About five shillings.'

'Is that all?'

'I'm not a rich man.'

He became terribly serious. 'Let me give you some advice. If you juggle with other people's money and you want to be a success make sure you have the best solicitor, the best accountant and the best doctor.'

I took his advice and engaged the best people in their respective professions. Their services have, throughout the years, proved invaluable.

In 1941, my old friend and collaborator, Eugene Iskoldoff, asked for help and advice on the production of Mussorgsky's comic opera *Sorotchinski Fair* backed by Jay Pomeroy. The cast included Oda Slobodskya, Daria Bayan, Kyra Vane, Nina Lenova, Zoe Valevska, Otakar Kraus, Marian Nowakowsky and Edward Boleslawski. The highlight of the opera was a ballet, *Night on a Bare Mountain*, danced by Diana Gould, who later married Yehudi Menuhin. The choreography was by Catherine Devillier, formerly character dancer with the Bolshoi Theatre.

The opera played with great success at the Savoy and Adelphi theatres in 1942. As a thank-you gesture for my help, Pomeroy hired the production to me for a nominal fee for a provincial tour. I engaged Walter Susskind as principal conductor and David Ellenberg as associate director. The pianist was Aubrey Bowman, who was later musical director of Festival Ballet. When we began the tour the production was excellent. As the war continued and the cast went off to the forces or to join ENSA, they were replaced by singers who couldn't sing and dancers who couldn't dance. Nevertheless, the public flocked to see the opera everywhere we played – the Howard and Wyndham circuit, then the London County Council's open-air theatres, and then back to Howard and Wyndhams. It was never ending. During this period, I travelled the length and breadth of Britain.

One evening, going from Birmingham to London, the train was rerouted, as was often the case, through Coventry. A short distance outside the city the train stopped and the dim lights were turned off. After about an hour, the German bombers appeared and the velvet blackness of the night was rent with the scream and explosion of bombs. Anti-aircraft fire and the spectacular illumination of incendiaries turned night into day. Thinking we were going to be blown up, we sheltered underneath the carriage seats. It was during this raid that Coventry cathedral was badly damaged.

In 1958, I was able to recall that night in the train. London's Festival Ballet had been playing at the Coventry Theatre when Anton Dolin had the brilliant idea of a Festival of Arts in the cathedral ruins. Sybil Thorndike, Markova, Christopher Hassall, John Gilpin and members of Festival Ballet agreed to give their services free to raise funds for the cathedral rebuilding fund. Everything was set for the performance when that august body, the Lord's Day Observance Society, stepped in. The possibility of raising funds and the idea of combining music, drama and the arts with a religious ceremony on a Sunday was, to them, sacrilegious. Their objection was binding. Would such a ruling be enforced today? I doubt it. The Lord's Day Observance Society is a Victorian relic out of touch with the present-day world.

The Society's opposition proved to be our salvation. ABC Television offered to transmit the programme from their studios. On 20 July 1958, we had an audience of two million viewers. Sybil Thorndike read the *Coventry Prologue* written for the occasion by Christopher Hassall. Markova danced *The Dying Swan*, followed by Festival Ballet in *Les Sylphides*. *The Psalm of David* was danced by John Gilpin. The City of Birmingham Symphony Orchestra conducted by Geoffrey Corbett played Beethoven's *The Consecration of the House*. The programme ended with a lone boy treble singing 'I Know That my Redeemer Liveth'. The rebuilding fund benefited by over £2,000.

Towards the end of 1943, *Sorotchinski Fair* was staggering along on its last legs, though still rapturously received by audiences everywhere. I realised that some other novelty was required, a production that included ballet. As always, I needed money.

Alexander Maximoe, a young Finnish film producer, offered to introduce me to a potential backer who had already lost a fortune financing Maximoe's films.

'I've squeezed him like a lemon. I don't know whether there is anything left, but there may be,' Maximoe told me.

The backer was a pleasant, quiet-spoken, cultured man called Henry Winwood Gossage who was keen to invest and work in the arts. Having tried films, he thought he might succeed in the live theatre. He came daily to my office, ostensibly to learn the impresario business. Perhaps that did not fill him with confidence. While waiting for him to make up his mind, I began looking around for someone else to provide the money.

An acquaintance of mine advised me to try Otto Kahn, a private banker who was interested in the theatre. The best means of contacting him, I was told, was through his clairvoyant who exerted a tremendous influence over him. She was a rather respectable middle-class woman who had her consulting room at the top of seven flights of stairs in Oxford Street. After puffing up them, I had to wait five minutes before I regained enough breath to explain my interests. The lady's crystal ball was not working at all well that day. She telephoned Kahn at his country house to be told that he had just suffered a heart attack and could not speak to anyone. Seeing my disappointment, she seized my hand and, despite my protestations, gazed at my upturned palm.

'By the end of the year you will receive a substantial cheque. It will enable you to finance your production,' she said. I was unimpressed by this information as I had already told her that I needed the money for a theatrical venture.

'It will be the beginning of a very successful period for you,' she continued, her eyes getting somewhat glazed. 'You will travel a great deal, your name will become a by-word in the theatrical profession. The dance, it will be the dance.'

Thinking she was getting quite beyond herself, I quickly crossed her palm with silver. I was convinced that she was only trying to alleviate my disappointment at not being introduced to Kahn.

I decided no time could be lost. I asked Gossage for enough capital to launch the new venture.

'I will have to ask my mother,' were his only words.

A week later he walked into the office.

'Mother is willing to help. But she doesn't have the ready cash. Her money is invested in Tate and Lyle and it wouldn't be a good time to sell shares at the moment.'

I told my potential backer that any bank would advance cash against the investments, then sent him back to his mother. Some time later he reappeared with a cheque for £2,500 – his first instalment. It was the beginning of a very happy association which, I'm sorry to say, lost him a good deal of money.

With Eugene Iskoldoff, I dreamed up an idea – which dated from 1926 – of a revue incorporating music, song and dance. The show would salute Anglo-Russian friendship, a sentiment very much in vogue at that time.

Under the management of our new company, United Ballet Foundations Limited, rehearsals began at the Stoll Theatre. A V1 spotter was stationed on the roof to give warning of approaching buzz bombs. They were frequent. We named the show *Anglo-Russian Merry-Go-Round* and the comperes were the comedian George Lacey and Iskoldoff, whose English was only slightly better than mine.

The show opened with a big production number in which the entire company sang and danced round a merry-go-round. It progressed with a short operetta set in Paris and included a brilliant display of Russian folk dancing. A young Australian choreographer, George Carden, was responsible for a romantic ballet called *A Gypsy Camp* featuring Nina Tarakanova. The finale was a light-hearted combination of Strauss songs and dances. During the fourteen weeks' run at the Adelphi Theatre, Harold Turner joined the company to choreograph and star in a ballet to music by Lord Berners called *Shore Leave*. One night, in the middle of the performance, a bomb fell at the back of the Savoy Hotel, just across the road from the Adelphi. The blast was so great that it dislodged all the dust from the flies in the theatre and quite suddenly the cast looked like the Black and White Minstrel show.

Europe had been liberated and Basil Dean, the director of ENSA, wanted shows for the troops in France and Germany. I was particularly keen the company should go, as the tours opened in Paris and I could rejoin my wife from whom I had been separated for five years. We all had to travel in uniform and I naturally wanted to look my best. Instead of accepting the badly-cut army issue, which did absolutely nothing for me, I asked my tailor to make me a uniform. It proved to be a costly business as the authorities insisted on having it returned to them when our short tour was over.

After an uncomfortable four-hour flight in a Dakota, I arrived in Paris to be re-united with Vera. She had not changed at all, except that she was slightly slimmer. She told me I hadn't changed either, but, in my newly tailored uniform, looked slightly fatter.

The company were given honorary membership of the British Officers' Club, housed in the Paris home of the Rothschild family. There was an acute food shortage in Paris, so Vera was invited to stay at the Club too.

Vera had suffered in the occupation. She had spent a good deal of her time in hiding at a maternity home in Paris. She decided she might be safer with her sister in Nice, as the Côte d'Azur was occupied by the Italians, who were not nearly so tyrannical as the Germans. With her sister-in-law, Vera left Paris and with the help of friends managed to reach Dijon. From there they were to walk, with a young boy on a bicycle reconnoitring the road ahead. He did not have enough time to warn them of the German patrol and they were arrested.

Vera's sister-in-law was so terrified she could not walk. The two women were separated and Vera was transported by bus back to Paris. There she was shut in a tiny room with fourteen people for eleven days, only being taken out for interrogation. Vera's salvation was that she pretended not to understand a word of German, and although her interrogators cross-questioned her over and over again, speaking in a mixture of French and German, she managed to convince them she was French. She was released and when she got out into the Paris street she could not stop vomiting. Although she escaped death, one of her brothers and a sister died in a concentration camp. Three other brothers who lived in Paris managed to avoid arrest.

Playing the Theatre de Marigny, the company were received with acclaim by the servicemen. This success was repeated in Belgium, where we shared a hotel with a concert party and the Old Vic, led by Laurence Olivier.

I was very impressed by a young army sergeant who dealt with all our accommodation problems and was responsible for the weekly ration of whisky and rum. We became friendly and some time later I was able to offer him a job. Duggie Abbot was Festival Ballet's company manager for twelve years before emigrating to Australia.

Immediately the tour ended, I successfully petitioned the Home Office to allow my wife to join me in London. She had managed to take care of various securities of mine throughout the occupation and we were able to lease a small flat in Talbot Square. I opened an office in Shaftesbury Avenue and started looking for a European ballet company to bring to England.

Shuttling between London and Paris to arrange Vera's residency in Britain, I met an old impresario friend of mine, Eugene Grunberg. He told me he was promoting 'the finest ballet company in Europe.'

The New Monte Carlo Ballet was led by Serge Lifar. He had been compelled to leave the Paris Opera in 1945, because of allegations of collaborating with the Nazis during the war. Although he was officially exonerated, the Opera stage staff went on strike when he tried to premiere a new ballet. He had worked as a dancer and, later, as director of the Opera since 1932. Still proclaiming his innocence, he left, taking many of the Opera's principal dancers with him, and formed a new company in Monte Carlo, where he acquired some of the scenery and costumes which had been stored there by the Diaghilev and Ballets Russes companies.

The New Monte Carlo Ballet was fantastic. I still regard them as the greatest company in talent and repertoire since the Diaghilev Ballet. The dancers included Olga Adabache, Janine Charrat, Yvette Chauvire, Renee Jeanmaire, Ludmilla Tcherina, Youly Algaroff, Edmond Audran, Alexandre Kalioujny, Gerard Mulys and Vladimir Skouratoff. The maitre de ballet was my old friend, Nicolas Zwereff.

I arranged for the company to play at the Cambridge Theatre. It was owned by Jay Pomeroy, who was promoting seasons of opera and ballet. The company were the first overseas troupe to visit London since the end of the war and they played for a six-week season. Among the classics and new ballets performed were *Prince Igor*, *Carnaval*, *Petrouchka*, *Swan Lake*, Act two, *Giselle*, *Coppelia*, and *Scheherazade*. The modern works choreographed by Lifar were *Mephisto Valse* (Liszt); *Aubade* (Poulenc); *La Peri* (Dukas); *Priere* (Beethoven); *Salome* (Richard Strauss); *Istar* (Vincent d'Indy); and a four-act work of dance and mime called *Chota Roustavel* (Honegger) based on a Georgian legend dear to Stalin, which had caught Lifar's imagination.

Janine Charrat, who was later to form her own company, had choreographed *Cressida* to music by Tony Aubin. The ballet had a libretto by Constaine Nepo, based on Shakespeare's *Troilus and Cressida*. The opening at the Cambridge on 17 June was a scandal. The theatre was picketed by balletomanes. They objected to Lifar being allowed to perform in London. Closeted in his dressing-room, Lifar again denied collaborating with the Germans. But he was very nervous about appearing. He need not have worried. The audience entered the theatre gazing at the demonstrators as if they were from some other planet. When Lifar danced in *L'Après-midi d'un Faune* the first-nighters gave him an ovation and went on to applaud the other members of this talented company.

The public have a very short memory. A year later, Lifar patched up his quarrels with the Paris Opera and returned to resume his career as Artistic Director.

CHAPTER 8

A BULLET IN THE BALLET

———

One of the funniest, and many people say most realistic, books ever written about backstage ballet life is by balletomane and author Caryl Brahms and her Bohemian, bridge-playing collaborator, S. J. Simon.

A Bullet in the Ballet tells the story of the Ballet Strogonoff whose Petrouchkas keep getting murdered. When an English detective inspector is called in to investigate the killings, and inevitably delves into the loves, hates, scandals and idiosyncrasies of the company, he finds that practically everyone has a motive for murder.

People in the ballet world say that the character of Strogonoff, the manager of the company, was based on me. That is untrue. I met Brahms and Simon long after *A Bullet in the Ballet* was published. While I may have some of Strogonoff's characteristics, Caryl Brahms told me that Strogonoff 'wrote himself'.

I thought the book would make a marvellous, dramatic whodunit on the stage. I asked Miss Brahms to dramatise the novel for me, but she was far too busy. She suggested Val Gielgud who had directed a radio adaptation of the book. I explained to Val exactly what I wanted – a murder mystery in which all the comedy of the original novel was retained. The plot would incorporate *Petrouchka* and two other ballets. The script he produced was an admirable whodunit, but not what I visualised. In the end Alec Coppel, a young Australian writer who had just had a success with a book called *I Killed the Count*, collaborated with Brahms and Simon on the play.

For *A Bullet in the Ballet* I needed two great stars who could dance and act. I remembered what de Basil had said of Baronova in 1939. An impresario friend of mine, David Libidins, a great practical joker, was living in New York. I sent him a telegram:

'Do you know Irina Baronova's address, regards, Braunsweg.' The following day I got his reply. 'Yes, regards, Libidins.' He did cable me the information later.

Leonide Massine's company, Ballets Russes Highlights, had just completed a tour which had been financially unsuccessful. The company had disbanded in Hollywood. My brother Marian, who was in Hollywood, was friendly with Massine. He undertook to persuade the dancer to appear in the play and produce the ballets. Massine, who thrives on endless negotiation and the small print in contracts, drove a hard bargain. One of his conditions was that I pay the travelling expenses for his wife and two children to accompany him to London and throughout the tour. Marian also persuaded Baronova, who had read the book and liked it, to dance and act the role of the ballerina, Irina Rubinskaya.

The producer was Marcel Varnel, who had successfully directed many of the Will Hay film comedies. I chose George Kirsta to design the sets and costumes. For *Petrouchka* he studied the original designs by Alexandre Benois, and faithfully reproduced them for the ballet. As maitre de ballet, I engaged Stanislav Idzikowsky who had been a member of the Diaghilev company. For Massine he had created the role of the Snob in *Boutique Fantasque* and the Dandy in *Tricorne*.

Rehearsal rooms in London were impossible to find. When Massine and Baronova arrived from America, the cast found themselves working in church and drill halls all over the capital, often until two or three in the morning. Viennese-born Charles Goldner was to play Strogonoff, and Ivy St Helier, a marvellous actress whose Anglo-Russian accent was a delight, was cast in the role of the aged ballet mistress, Arenskaya, who still tries to fascinate men. Barry Morse, the BBC's first Paul Temple and, more recently, the star of TV's *Fugitive*, played the troubled Scotland Yard detective. With the actors, corps de ballet, and orchestra, the cast numbered seventy-six.

On arrival, Massine told me that he was on an exclusive diet of steak and milk. 'I cannot perform unless I have two steaks a day and two pints of milk. I also need milk for my family.'

Stringent rationing was still in operation in Britain. Ginger beer was the only drink that could be bought in theatre bars. The meat ration scarcely amounted to a steak a week, even if steak could be obtained. By fair means and foul, usually the latter, I managed to provide the meat but at fantastic cost. At times Massine had to go and eat the steak at a restaurant, at other times it was brought to him on a plate from the kitchens of well-known hotels. These special feeding arrangements were to continue for three months.

Baronova was a delight, even-tempered, co-operative and liked by everyone. Massine too worked hard. With Idzikowsky, he revived *Petrouchka* and *Gaieté Parisienne* and created a new work, a ballet blanc, to Chopin music, called *Reverie Classique*.

I had used my own capital and investments from friends to finance the production, but shortly after starting rehearsals I realised that we did not have enough money. I asked Jay Pomeroy if he would make an investment.

'I'm not keen to go into partnership in a production like this,' he told me. 'The best thing I can do is to buy out you and your friends and take over full financial responsibility for the show.' We did a deal. Pomeroy repaid me nearly £10,000 – the show cost something in the region of £20,000 – and promised me the Cambridge Theatre for *A Bullet in the Ballet*, providing it did well on tour. I retained 50 per cent interest in the show.

The music for *Petrouchka* gave us some difficulty. Igor Stravinsky had scored the work for a full symphony orchestra. We could neither afford nor seat such an orchestra in the provincial theatres we were to visit. Boosey and Hawkes, Stravinsky's publishers, were sympathetic and willing to help, but only the composer could give permission for a reduced orchestration to be made of his score.

Massine was a great friend of Stravinsky. I asked him to write to the composer in Hollywood, and explain the circumstances in which the ballet was to be performed. The friendship did the trick. Stravinsky agreed to Massine's request but insisted on an extraordinary entry being made in all the programmes. 'In view of the limited sitting capacity in the orchestra pit the present reduced orchestration of *Petrouchka* is made with the permission of the composer but without his knowledge and without his actual participation in this arrangement:'

The next problem was finding a musician capable of making an orchestral reduction of the score. Boosey and Hawkes tried, but were unable to help. Eventually I persuaded James Turner, who had conducted the orchestra for *Anglo-Russian Merry-Go-Round*, to attempt the daunting task. The result was very satisfactory and years later the score, and indeed the costumes and decor, were all used for Festival Ballet's production of the ballet.

A Bullet in the Ballet opened at the King's Theatre, Edinburgh, on 1 October 1946. The first performance was a shambles. Varnel had had no time to polish the drama. Massine had used all the rehearsal time to perfect his ballets. Duncan Yarrow, the actor playing Puthyk, fell from Petrouchka's booth and broke his arm. His part had to be taken by an understudy who did not know the lines.

At one point, Charles Goldner, anticipating the entrance of another actor, turned to meet him. The audience roared when the actor made his entrance from the opposite side of the stage. The curtain came down unexpectedly and knocked Goldner out. Everyone thought these antics were all part of the play. The critics thought it hysterically funny but Jay Pomeroy, who also attended the first night, didn't.

As the tour progressed, the show improved. After Edinburgh, we toured Glasgow, Manchester, Leeds, Blackpool and Liverpool, spending ten weeks on the road. At the end of three weeks, Barry Morse and Goldner were ad-libbing their way through the comedy scenes with a slickness that brought gales of laughter from the audience. Caryl Brahms came to me and said, 'You've got to do something about it. They must stick to the script.'

'There's nothing I can do,' I replied. And indeed there was nothing anyone could do. The actors got the laughs and that justified the ad-libs.

Although the comedy was hilarious, it was the dancing that captivated the audience. In his early youth Massine had been an actor/dancer when he first appeared at Moscow's Maly Theatre in

1912. As Kasha, he was excellent. Despite the steaks and milk, he danced evening performances only. His role at matinees was taken by a talented Australian dancer called Henry Legerton. Later, when Massine was invited to stage *La Boutique Fantasque* for the Sadler's Wells Ballet at Covent Garden, Legerton went with him and remained with the company.

The role of Irina Rubinskaya might have been written for Irina Baronova. She was delightful in the part. She had been dancing since she was thirteen and suffered from heart strain. When she was overtired, her ankles swelled, but she never missed a performance.

When *A Bullet in the Ballet* ended its run, she rejoined the de Basil company in Cuba as guest artist and made her final appearance in Rio de Janeiro. She returned to London to star in the play *Dark Eyes*, made a film with Sir Michael Balcon called *The Train of Events*, and then remarried. She decided her children were more important than her dancing career. Baronova, one of the century's greatest ballerinas, retired at the age of twenty-seven.

The food on our travels was detestable. In Liverpool, at the hotel where the principals were staying, it was bad even by post-war standards. Of course rationing still existed, but steaks and milk for Massine was an unwritten contractual obligation. I asked the chef if he could do anything to help me and provide the rest of the company with reasonable meals.

'If you would care to eat with the staff it might suit you all much better than eating with the other hotel guests,' he said.

When we took our seats with the hotel personnel, we were surprised and delighted to find the table groaning with every delicacy imaginable – the sort of food we had not even seen, let alone tasted, since before the war. Massine ate his steaks and drank quantities of milk. The rest of us filled our bellies with food that was delicious and plentiful.

We played to packed houses everywhere and I thought we had a success on our hands. There was no word from Pomeroy and I could never get hold of him. He had promised the Cambridge Theatre, but there had been no definite agreement on the date for our London opening. Finally I contacted him and persuaded him to come to the final performance in Liverpool. I was confident that he would be impressed with the show and the improvements we had made on tour. He arrived in the middle of the matinee. I told him I had reserved an excellent seat for the evening show, which was sold out.

'But you can watch the remainder of the matinee as well. You'll see how much we've polished the show. It's good. Listen to the audience,' I said, as the gales of laughter filled the theatre.

'No, I'll see it tonight. Have you got £100, Julian? I've come up without enough money and I want to do some shopping.'

I gave him the cash and he disappeared. Throughout the evening performance his seat remained unoccupied. Although I searched the theatre hoping to find him standing somewhere in the packed house, he was not to be found. The final curtain came down amid cheers.

Backstage, Pomeroy appeared.

'Did you see the show?'

Looking very sheepish, he replied 'No'.

'Where were you then?' I asked.

'I'm afraid I was held up at the dog track.'

There seemed to be nothing left to say. The man had a sizeable investment in the show. He was reticent and uninterested and I assumed from his manner that he was not going to keep his promise and allow us to move into the Cambridge. I was very depressed. In a short speech I told the company that I still hoped to find a London theatre for the show. Although we were disbanding, I had every hope that we would re-assemble to prepare for our London debut in the New Year. There were many emotional partings and protestations of undying friendship.

Christmas passed without even a card from any of the dancers or actors. My search for a theatre proved futile. A number of shows were queueing up waiting for theatres to become vacant. So London never saw *A Bullet in the Ballet*. Subsequently, Pomeroy, in a fit of remorse over his addiction to dogs, gave me the entire production, which I put into store.

The theatre public want novelty. I have always believed that and tried to spice my programmes with something unusual. In 1947 there was a tremendous demand for ballet. The public had been starved of dancing during the war and wanted to see companies from abroad. When I saw a slim, lithe Spanish girl called Ana Esmeralda displaying her sinuous grace in cabaret in Belgium, I decided that she would be my Spanish novelty.

I knew absolutely nothing about her early life and I don't think anyone else did. She was fantastically beautiful and radiated an exciting sensuality in her dancing. She smouldered with suppressed emotion as she beat out complicated rhythms with her heels and castanets. I recruited more Spanish dancers and musicians and tried out the small company in the British provinces. Billed as 'Rhapsodie Espagnole', the company were a success. I imported more artists from Spain and Esmeralda made her London debut at the Savoy Theatre billed as 'The Daughter of The Devil'.

One of the young boys we had brought from Spain was a virile, hairy young gypsy, quite wild. He caused a minor scandal by urinating, in full view of the Savoy's elegant clientele, in the hotel forecourt. When I showed him the theatre lavatory, he had no idea what it was for. I dared not think what had been happening at his digs in Earls Court. He danced a solo in the second half of the programme. On the second night, as soon as he had finished dancing, he tore to this dressing room, stripped naked and returned to the wings wearing only a brief dressing gown. As the girls danced on stage, he flung his gown open, exposing himself, and shouting in Spanish: 'Take a look at that. That should make you dance.'

He did this night after night. At first our stage manager tried to prevent him. When he succeeded in doing so it was noticeable that the girls' dancing was rather lethargic. We all accepted the nightly display and the girls danced with vigour.

After the London season, Esmeralda and her company toured Switzerland and Italy and finally played Madrid. By this time the dancer had parted from her husband and my contract had ended. Although she caused a sensation in the Spanish capital, when the season ended she disappeared completely from the dance scene.

At Vichy, I watched a talented 13-year-old girl called Svetlana Beriosova dancing with the Grand Ballet du Marquis de Cuevas. I was introduced to her father, Nicholas Beriosoff, a Russian dancer, and her stepmother, Mme Lilyne, who made costumes. Some months later, in Paris, Beriosoff asked me if I could find work for them all in Britain.

The Metropolitan Ballet had been organised by Leon Hepner, formerly director of the Anglo-Polish Ballet. The company was led by Victor Gzovsky from Paris, with Letty Littlewood as artistic director. With such dancers as Colette Marchand and Serge Perrault from the Paris Opera, the company had a small repertoire of classics and new ballets such as *Masquerade* and *Episode* by Catherine Devillier and *Elegy* by Andree Howard. After a short time Gzovsky left, taking Perrault, Henry Danton and David Dulak with him. I asked Leon to engage Svetlana and to take on her father as ballet master.

For Metropolitan, Svetlana created the leading role in John Taras' *Design with Strings*, later taken into the Royal Ballet's repertoire, and *Fanciulla della Rosa* by Frank Staff. On the day Beriosoff received his first salary he came to see me.

'What percentage are you expecting for getting us the contract?'

I told him that I was not an agent. I was just happy to have been of some help. When Metropolitan disbanded, Svetlana joined the Sadler's Wells Ballet and became ballerina in 1955. Her father, who joined Festival Ballet as regisseur and ballet master, repaid my kindness a million times in getting the company going.

Boosey and Hawkes had bought Covent Garden Opera House. Ralph Hawkes introduced me to David Webster, the theatre's administrator.

'I don't know much about ballet,' he said when I first met him, 'opera yes, but ballet is something quite new to me.'

For some weeks we met every Thursday at the Bologna restaurant in Soho and Webster picked my brains about ballet companies and dancers. He was a genial businessman, quick to learn and determined to make Covent Garden the most famous opera house in the world.

When I received a telegram from Colonel de Basil asking me to arrange a European tour for his company, the Original Ballet Russe,

17. Gene Tierney and her mother back-stage at Festival Hall with Anton Dolin during Festival Ballet's appearance in the film 'Never Let Me Go'.

Symphony for Fun with Anita Landa, John Gilpin and Jeannette Minty.

18.

Members of Festival Ballet on board the SS Empress of Canada en route for the Canadian tour 1953.

Pamela Hart and members of the *Swan Lake* corps-de-ballet.

19.

Dianne Richards and John Gilpin in *Harlequinade*.

Belinda Wright and Wolfgang Brunner in *Alice in Wonderland*.

20.
Vilia (*The Merry Widow*)
(l to r) Vassilie Trunoff, Belinda Wright, Anton Dolin, Anita Landa.

Oleg Briansky with members of the corps-de-ballet.

21.

Nora Kovach and Istvan Rabovsky in *Esmeralda.*

Eros – and Festival Ballet.

22.

Moira Shearer and John Gilpin in
Le Spectre de la Rose.

Toni Lander and Oleg Briansky
in *Napoli.*

23. *Etudes* with Toni Lander, John Gilpin, Flemming Flindt.

24. Tamara Toumanova.

25. (l to r) Michael Somes, Julian Braunsweg, Margot Fonteyn with Princess Antoinette of Monaco in Monte Carlo, Christmas, 1955.

Vera and Julian Braunsweg with Toni Lander and Flemming Flindt after the premiere of *Coppelia* at the Royal Festival Hall, summer 1956.

26.

Festival Ballet in Israel 1956
Above: Sea of Galilee – Vera and Julian Braunsweg with Anton Dolin. *Left:* A kibbutz – Diane Westerman and Pamela Hart. *Below:* The company leaves the kibbutz for an open-air performance.

27. *Graduation Ball*

Alexander Benois with the company after the premiere at Theatre des Champs Elysees, Paris in 1957.

Peter White and Janet Overton.

28. *The Nutcracker*

Above left: Julian Braunsweg with children from the Arts Educational School. *Right:* David Lichine rehearsing. *Below:* Alicia Markova with four Sugar Plum Fairies (l to r) Belinda Wright, Olga Ferri, Dianne Richards, Marilyn Burr.

29. *The Nutcracker*
(seated) Vera Braunsweg and Alexander Benois (standing) Mlle Benois and Julian Braunsweg in the Benois' Paris flat, 1957.

Grace Cone and Julian and Vera Braunsweg auditioning girls from the Arts Educational School – in the background, Reg Cooper and Eve Pettinger.

30. *The Witch Boy* – Anton Dolin, John Gilpin, Anita Landa.

Variations for Four – And Prokovsky, Michael Hoga Louis Godfrey, John Gilpin.

31. Charlie Chaplin with Natalie Krassovska after the Gala Premiere, Theatre des Nations, Paris, 1958.

Leon Woizikowsky rehearsing Deirdre O'Conaire.

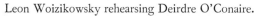

32. *London Morning*

Noël Coward plays his music for the ballet to Julian Braunsweg, Jack Car
and Anton Dolin.

Noël Coward inspecting the guards before the dress rehearsal.

I immediately thought of a Covent Garden season. Eight years had passed since the company had appeared at the Opera House and their tours of Australia, New Zealand, South Africa and South America had depleted de Basil's financial resources. He had married Olga Morosova, a good soubrette and reasonable soloist. Her promotion to ballerina had antagonised some of the principal artists who objected to her being given so many of the leading roles. A good number left. The original troupe of seventy dancers had dwindled to thirty-five.

I suggested to de Basil that I should pay to bring this nucleus from the U.S.A. and we would recruit more dancers in Paris to restore Ballet Russe to its former strength and glory.

At the Opera House, Webster told me he was thinking of engaging American Ballet Theatre, who had scored a great success at the Garden in 1946. The company's contract was on his desk waiting to be signed.

'You told me the de Basil company was in a terrible state. I couldn't offer them a contract on the information you have given me.'

'It's true, they are not as they were in 1939.' I told him. 'But they have the same repertoire and one or two new works, and I think with the dancers I could recruit in Paris, I can guarantee that the artistic standard will be very high.'

Like me, Webster had a certain nostalgia for the de Basil company. 'I'll take them on your assurance.'

De Basil and I went off to Paris where we engaged Helen Komorova, Vladimir Skouratoff and Renee Jeanmaire, who later changed her first name, took off her point shoes and won fame as Zizi. Joining the company for the London season was John Taras, Nicholas Orloff, who was to create a sensation as the Drummer in *Graduation Ball*, David Lichine and his wife, Tatiana Riabouchinska, the only ballerina of the 1939 season. Serge Grigorieff and Lubov Tchernicheva were to get the company into shape.

The company also included Genevieve Moulin, Moussia Larkina, Helen Constantine, Tatiana Dokoudovska, her husband, Vladimir Dokoudovsky and a 15-year-old 'baby ballerina' of English parentage born in Chile, called April Olrich. Among the strengthened corps de ballet were Barbara Vernon and John Gregory, who subsequently founded Harlequin Ballet.

There was a last-minute hitch. De Basil told me that Helen Constantine would not travel without her husband, Eddie, and their child. I was already paying out a fortune for travelling expenses and baulked at transporting the Constantine family.

'Eddie is a kind of stage manager,' said de Basil.

When he arrived, it was quite apparent that Eddie knew nothing about stage management. However, when the company went on to appear in Paris he was suddenly discovered and won fame and fortune playing toughie parts in French films.

The scenery from America needed repainting. So did the scenery from Paris which had been left to rot throughout the war. Michel Larionoff, the Russian painter who had worked with the Diaghilev company, was hastily summoned from Paris to restore the decor. We also needed new costumes.

'I'll get the material for them,' said de Basil, 'and you must come with me.' We were in Paris and the Colonel led me to one of the street markets. He sorted through piles of remnants and bought all the material he needed at about one-third of the price we would have had to pay elsewhere. There was no question about a designer approving the choice. De Basil bought what he thought, and the costumes were made. The repertoire included *Les Sylphides*, *Paganini*, *Graduation Ball*, *Carnaval*, *Beau Danube*, *Le Coq D'Or*, *Prince Igor*, *The Prodigal Son*, *Protee*, *Scheherazade*, *The Good Humoured Ladies*, *Presages*, *Symphonie Fantastique*, *Firebird*, *Aurora's Wedding* and two ballets by Boris Kniaseff – *Silver Birch* and *Piccoli*.

Covent Garden has an atmosphere all its own. On 27 July 1947, the Opera House, with its red plush and gold candelabra, was filled with an air of excitement and expectancy. The Original Ballet Russe was back, evoking memories of the pre-war company for the fashionably dressed audience.

De Basil knew his season would be compared with the 1939 visit. He was returning with a hastily collected ad hoc company. Many of the principals had not danced in any of the ballets before. For once, de Basil, usually so urbane and composed, had lost his sang-froid. He rushed about backstage muttering such things as: 'The repertoire is too large. There haven't been enough rehearsals. The decor is awful and the costumes, well, what can you do with them.' His nervousness was transmitted to the dancers and the tension backstage was almost unbearable.

The orchestra began the Overture for *Les Sylphides* and the corps de ballet, led by Riabouchinska, Larkina, Jeanmaire and Roman Jasinsky, took up their positions on stage. There was a whirring of the curtain as it drew backwards and upwards to reveal the sylphs in their moonlit glade. Riabouchinska was lightness and air in the Prelude and Jeanmaire flew through the Mazurka, more from nerves than artistry. There was, however, little romanticism. The spiritual feeling in Fokine's masterpiece had been replaced by neurotic technical competence. The curtain came down to a smattering of applause.

Paganini was Fokine in decline. The ballet was set to Rachmaninoff's *Rhapsody on a Theme of Paganini*. The principal roles were taken by Dokoudovsky as the demon-like violinist, Riabouchinska as the Florentine beauty, Moulin as the Divine Genius and Larkin as Guile. It was no great shakes as a ballet and the audience's response hardly filled the dancers with confidence.

Graduation Ball, the final ballet in the programme, was receiving its British premiere. De Basil told me that when the company had first staged the ballet in Australia in 1940, it had been somewhat of a failure.

'We took the ballet out of the repertoire and I made Lichine work on it until I thought it was right.'

Riabouchinska, Jeanmaire, Moulin and April Olrich were the breathless adolescents at their first ball. I have never seen their dancing equalled. The infectious Strauss music and the humour and pace of the ballet, found a warm response from the first-nighters. Sixteen-year-old Barbara Lloyd, dancing the 'pig-tail' variation, stopped the show. So did Orloff's brilliantly timed Drummer's variation. But it was Jeanmaire and Moulin turning like tops in the fouette competition, who got the biggest ovation. The clapping thundered on almost uninterrupted as the company took curtain call after curtain call.

De Basil breathed a sigh of relief. 'Thank God for *Graduation Ball*.'

Massine was in London keeping a close watch on the company's programmes, and I was afraid there might be trouble. He had never been on good terms with de Basil and when the Colonel included *Le Beau Danube* in the repertoire, and credited Serge Lifar with the choreography, I waited for the scandal. Lifar had reworked Massine's ballet in America, but it was undeniably the original choreographer's work. De Basil had hoped that, by using Lifar, he might avoid paying Massine royalties. After the first performance of *Danube*, Massine issued a writ restraining de Basil from performing the ballet. It remained out of the repertoire.

The season was extended for one week at Covent Garden and then I arranged for the company to play the Davis Theatre, Croydon, and the Palais de Chaillot in Paris. After a short holiday, de Basil re-formed the company on a smaller basis and toured throughout Europe until his death in Paris in 1951.

Olga Morsova tried to revive the company in London with a season at the Festival Hall in 1951-52. Moving immediately to the Adelphi, the company ran into financial difficulties and that was the end of the Original Ballet Russe, a great name in ballet history.

One man who pioneered Indian dancing in the Western world was Ram Gopal. He attained the peak of his popularity on both sides of the Atlantic in the late forties and early fifties. Gopal had had a great success with a brief season at the Aldwych Theatre in 1939. I had met him from time to time during the war. He was a handsome, exotic personality, flamboyant in dress, quick-thinking, quick-tempered and very talented.

Bertram Montague, the proprietor of the Prince's Theatre, asked me to find a pre-Christmas show to fill in before his pantomime opened on Boxing Day. The weeks preceding the Christmas festivities are dead for theatres unless you can produce one of those hastily thrown together children's shows which pass for entertainment around the festive season. I persuaded Gopal to give a three-week season of Indian dancing. It was a considerable challenge, and he, as well as I, knew the problem of attracting audiences just before Christmas.

He explained that the success of his programme depended as much on costumes and lighting as it did on dancing. A very close friend of his was Kay Ambrose, the artist and author of a number of books on the ballet. She was, to a large extent, responsible for the artistic presentation of Gopal's programme. It included examples of Bharata Natya, Kathakali, Kathak and Manipuri styles. Ram was the finest and, at that time, the sole exponent of these classical dances outside India. We engaged musicians and dancers and began rehearsals. To produce the show, Kay Ambrose recommended a friend of hers who had just been demobbed from the army, Benn Toff. Big, affable and with an agile, inventive mind, Benn Toff was a superb stage technician. He staged the Gopal season at the Prince's and after helping me with other presentations, worked for sixteen years as stage director of Festival Ballet.

With his musicians seated behind him on the stage, Gopal explained his dances before performing them. His costumes, based on classical and traditional models, were lavish, richly embroidered and covered with jewels. The show was a spectacular novelty and a great success. One item Gopal added to the repertoire later was *The Golden Eagle*. He appeared in a winged costume of burnished gold. The dance was a show stopper and attracted all the reviewers.

During the Prince's season I was also working with Charles B. Cochran. He had engaged Les Etoiles de la Danse for the Adelphi. It was not financially worthwhile for this small group of dancers to travel from Paris for one London engagement, so Cochran asked me to arrange a provincial tour.

The dancers included Renee Jeanmaire, Colette Marchand, Ana Nevada, Vladimir Skouratoff and Serge Perrault. The repertoire consisted of Lifar's *Namouna, La Peri, Romeo and Juliet*; Balachova's *La Fille Mal Gardee*, featuring Jeanmaire as a gorgeous, mischievous Lisa and Skouratoff as Colas; *Suite Espagnole* led by Ana Nevada; and classical pas de deux from *The Sleeping Beauty* and *Swan Lake*.

Les Etoiles de la Danse had backcloths and little scenery. I suggested a concert tour with performances in town halls in northern England and Scotland. Inevitably there was a problem of presentation. The flat platform stage you find in halls, often without wings, proscenium or adequate lighting, is not suitable for ballet.

Benn Toff, who had worked on Bailey bridges in the army, assured me that by using scaffolding, he could adapt the bridge principle to create a 'fit-up' stage. This would provide proscenium, curtains and supports for concealed lighting effects. It could also be toured easily. The other problem was the inability to 'fly' backcloths. Subsequently, scene changes were accomplished by tying the backcloths to bars. These were hoisted up to rest on supports run from the scaffolding holding the curtains. After one or two technical hitches, the 'fit-up' worked very well. Years later when Festival Ballet moved to the Festival Hall, Benn Toff used the same 'fit-up' to transform the 60-foot-wide concert stage into a theatre.

While the French dancers toured the provinces, Gopal and his company enjoyed a huge success at the Theatre des Champs-Elysees in Paris. Gopal came back to London for a short season at the Saville Theatre and then toured provincial theatres.

During the Saville season, Vaslav Nijinsky, the famous dancer who had lost his reason at the height of his career, came to see the company. I went down to the foyer to meet him and his wife, Romola, and accompanied them to their box. Nijinsky was nearing sixty, a thickset, balding figure with a shuffling gait. His eyes were blank, he did not seem to know where he was and behaved just like a child. He was passive and sad. Romola told him what to do and he obeyed.

When the dancing began, Nijinsky showed no interest, despite his wife's words of encouragement. Eventually his attention focused on Gopal and suddenly his eyes became alive. He followed the intricate Indian arm and hand movements with intense interest. He smiled shyly, almost naughtily, and then raised his hands above his head and imitated Gopal's expressive finger mime. He continued to imitate Gopal until finally his head and arm movements were reflecting the dancer's movements on stage. For a few moments he looked delighted. Then, as if a curtain had descended cutting him off from his surroundings, he dropped his arms and relapsed into apathy. The couple stayed for half the programme and when Nijinsky rose to leave, the audience stood up, turned to the box and applauded. But Nijinsky did not seem to hear and following Romola, shuffled down the stairs to a waiting car.

The splendour of Gopal's dancing and his sumptuous costumes assured his success everywhere. His rapturous receptions in provincial towns encouraged him to make curtain speeches, but Gopal managed to turn the applause into boos on occasions. He would forget where he was. The audience did not like to hear him say: 'How very happy I am to be dancing in Birmingham,' when he was in Manchester.

I took the company to Stockholm for a four-week season. Gopal and his dancers were invited to a splendid banquet by the Indian Ambassador. Anxious to do the right thing, Gopal felt it imperative to return the hospitality. On the last night of the company's appearance, he staged a lavish feast in the hotel with the Ambassador as guest of honour. It was a marvellous spread and everyone enjoyed themselves.

'I'm leaving by an early plane tomorrow, Julian,' Gopal told me as the party neared its end. 'I'll see you back in London.' Checking out of the hotel the following day, I was given a bill that took my breath away. It not only included my accommodation, but also the expenses of Gopal's party.

In the spring of 1948, I met Sol Hurok, one of the most important and influential impresarios in America. He was in London looking for theatrical attractions for an International Dance Festival he was arranging to commemorate the Golden Anniversary of the City of New York. Like all impresarios, Hurok is the puppet master pulling the strings, arranging theatrical presentations. Hurok has charm, but he is in business to make money, and where money is concerned, he's as hard as a nail.

The Sadler's Wells Ballet were presenting *The Sleeping Beauty* at

Covent Garden and I accompanied him on a number of occasions to see Fonteyn and the company. After these performances, we often walked across Waterloo Bridge discussing the performance and the merits or demerits of the dancers. I had suggested Hurok should engage the Wells for his festival. He was not very keen.

'Moira Shearer. Now there's a star. She's a big name in America, with *Red Shoes* to her credit. But who's ever heard of Margot Fonteyn?'

After seeing more of the Wells, and of Fonteyn, Hurok began to think that the company was not too bad. I knew very well what tempered his enthusiasm. He had always refused to pay travelling expenses for any artist or company, and the idea of the whole Sadler's Wells Ballet Company paying their own fares to appear in New York seemed unlikely.

'If you can persuade the company to pay their own transportation, I'll take them,' said Hurok. I introduced him to Webster and took part in the initial discussions.

'What do I get out of it if the deal comes off?' I asked Hurok.

'Twenty-five per cent of the profit,' he promised.

Webster went off to New York, looked at City Center where the company were to appear and decided the stage was quite unsuitable for the Wells' production of *The Sleeping Beauty*. He insisted that if the company travelled to America at their own expense, their debut must be made at the Metropolitan Opera House. Hurok agreed to take the Met the following year for the Wells' American debut.

Meanwhile, Gopal and his troupe had been touring the provinces and had visited Switzerland. Hurok, obviously in need of a novelty for his festival, sent me a cable inviting Gopal to appear at the City Center. The company would represent India at the New York International Dance Festival. It was not financially worthwhile for us to travel to New York for an engagement of only one week. I asked Hurok to arrange a tour for the company. The contract stated that I would finance the company's journey to America, but if the tour did not materialise, the festival committee would pay our return fares to England.

Clothing was still rationed and during our preparations for the New York visit it was necessary for me to get 5,000 clothing coupons to refurbish and recostume Gopal's ballets. Of these, only 3,000 were used and I returned the remainder to the Board of Trade.

The travelling arrangements were complicated and it was necessary for Gopal and me to travel by the *Queen Mary* and for my wife, Benn Toff and the rest of the company to follow a few days later aboard the *Queen Elizabeth*.

Gopal's costumes were truly magnificent. Gliding round the state rooms of the huge liner resplendent in full Indian regalia, glittering with jewellery, he was quickly taken for a wealthy Rajah and I for his personal physician. We were inundated with invitations from Americans. They were even more fascinated when the Rajah turned out to be Ram Gopal.

We steamed through The Narrows and up the Hudson to the incredible New York skyline. I felt that nothing could go wrong in this efficient, streamlined new world.

William O'Dwyer, the Mayor of New York, was in charge of the committee presenting the festival. He had cabled that accommodation had been booked for us at the Plaza Hotel. At the Plaza, I found only one room had been reserved – for Gopal. Because of the celebrations, no other rooms were available. I knew that if I produced the Mayor's cable everything would be put right.

The desk clerk viewed the crumpled piece of paper.

'Means nothing to me. Who is this guy O'Dwyer? I never heard of him,' he said, handing it back.

I telephoned Hurok to find, to my relief, that my wife and I had been invited to stay at the Waldorf Astoria at City Hall's expense. The remainder of the company were accommodated in a hotel close to the City Center.

Ram Gopal and his Hindu Ballet opened on 30 September with such success that Hurok immediately retained the company for a Broadway season. This impetuous decision proved to be the wrong one. Gopal's success was partly due to being featured in the International Dance Festival, and vice versa. Hurok knew that before the company opened on Broadway, publicity was needed. He explained to Gopal and his troupe that they would be paid rehearsal salaries for two weeks while the promotional campaign was launched.

Basking in the aura of Gopal's success, Vera and I were invited everywhere to be wined and dined by New York's upper crust. Overnight, Gopal was in vogue. Among the hospitable, well-heeled, dedicated followers of fashion was a millionaire president of one of the big American insurance companies who put his chauffeur-driven Cadillac at our disposal. It stood outside the Astoria and was at our beck and call day and night. One night the millionaire invited Benn Toff, Vera and me to an ostentatious dinner at the Riviera Cabaret. In a state of alcoholic euphoria he told us that he and his wife had arranged a dinner in our honour to coincide with Gopal's Broadway opening.

At the end of Gopal's engagement in the Festival, City Hall stopped paying our bills and we were obliged to move from the Waldorf to a cheaper hotel – the Park Central on Broadway. When I explained the change to our doting patron, I sensed that our gilt-edged appeal was losing its glitter.

Hurok had been advertising the Broadway season, but a few days before the opening the box office had taken only 100 dollars. Hurok postponed the opening and urged Gopal and his dancers to accept another four weeks' rehearsal pay during which time he would intensify the publicity campaign.

'Everything will be all right. We just need a little more time to build up interest,' he said.

Gopal was not happy about the situation. I explained to him that Hurok had already spent a vast amount of money and we had nothing to lose by sticking it out for another month.

Despite the postponements of the season, on the eve of our dinner with the insurance millionaire, the Cadillac appeared outside the hotel. Benn Toff, Vera and I were taken to an enormous mansion on the outskirts of the city. The only other guest was an Englishman.

I told our hosts and the family about the postponement, an explanation which met with uninterested stares. There were no drinks and the conversation was somewhat strained. Two butlers appeared with plates of hard-boiled eggs. I ate one, then a second, but refused a third, thinking that this binding hors d'œuvre would spoil my dinner. The glamorous lady of the house invited us into the dining room. Still standing, we were handed small plates of ice-cream and the party in our honour was quickly concluded. Not for us the luxury of a return drive in the Cadillac. We were taken in a tiny car driven by the Englishman to the nearest bus stop.

We boarded the bus in a state bordering on hysteria and laughed so much that we missed our stop. We ended up in the basement garage of the bus depot. With all speed we hastened to the nearest hot-dog stand. When I got back to the hotel, Gopal telephoned me.

'I will not accept rehearsal salary for another four weeks. It's quite impossible. I am a star. You can tell Hurok that unless he pays me full salary, I cannot give the season.'

I was depressed. I lit a cigar and went to see my friend David Libidins. He listened patiently while I moaned and groaned. He made no comment, but when I finished, he handed me a black-edged card which read: 'I have listened to your troubles. Please accept this card as a token of my sympathy – and jump in the river.'

Hurok said he could not finance the publicity campaign and pay Gopal and his company full salaries. I went to City Hall to collect our return tickets. It was a Jewish holiday. The only occupant was the door keeper. I explained what I wanted and he assured me that we would have the tickets. We did, five minutes before sailing.

Despite all our troubles, I had enjoyed New York. It is a concrete canyon of a city, but alive and stimulating. I had met dancers whom I had worked with in Europe, Oboukhoff and Romanoff of the Russian Romantic Ballet, and a friend who had sat next to me at my elementary art school in Warsaw, Stanislaw Walzcack, father of one of Balanchine's soloists.

I was touched by a visit from the doyen of the contemporary dance scene, Martha Graham. She came to talk about the development of the dance in Britain and Europe. She was tall and hawklike, charming and intelligent.

Shortly after getting back to London, I received a demand from the Ministry of Employment for an enormous sum of money to cover the engagement of dancers and musicians in Gopal's company. I pointed out that I had not employed these artists – they were Gopal's responsibility and therefore the demand for the health and welfare contributions should be referred to him.

For some time, I had been trying to obtain naturalisation papers for Vera and myself, but there seemed to be some obstacle to us becoming British citizens. After nearly two years of waiting, I appealed to my solicitor to find out why our applications were not acceptable. He made inquiries at the Home Office and came to see me.

'Listen Julian, just think, what have you done wrong? Think, man. There must be something.'

Now I have done millions of things wrong. All my life I've been devoted to doing things which, if not downright wrong, have at least been unconventional. However, knowing that my past would be thoroughly investigated, and my present too, I had become a paragon of virtue, even paying my income tax.

'Well, the Home Office are going to send someone to see you,' my solicitor warned me.

A few days later, three solid gentlemen appeared at my office. One was from the Home Office, the other two from Scotland Yard. They sat heavily and glumly on their chairs confronting me.

'Dr Braunsweg,' said their spokesman, 'we would like to know what you did with £10,000 you smuggled into England from Oslo in a brown leather suitcase in 1948. We would also like to know what became of 2,000 clothing coupons you obtained to costume a theatrical production, but did not use, during the same year.'

My secretary was with me and we realised simultaneously that their enquiries related to the costumes for the Ram Gopal season. I burst out laughing and just went on laughing as my interrogators looked more and more disconcerted.

'Gentlemen, I defy you to name any artist who can dance for a week in Oslo and make a profit of £10,000. The actual sum was £300. I have a statement transferring the money from Oslo to my bank here in London if you would care to see it. As for the clothing coupons, they were returned to the Board of Trade. Fortunately, I have a receipt.'

Shortly after this interview, Vera and I became naturalised British citizens. For both of us it was a momentous occasion. When we received our British passports, Vera got down on her knees and kissed hers. Anyone who has always passed through passport control without difficulty cannot really appreciate the indignities and humiliations foreigners are subjected to in England and elsewhere. We had been aliens for years. First we travelled on Russian, then Polish papers, and we were always questioned when we passed from one country to another. We were always made to feel second-class citizens and were invariably treated like bandits.

When I came to Britain, I remained an alien, having to report to the police from time to time. Our British passports gave us a feeling of belonging and aroused in me a great sense of patriotism. Years later I realised that it was because Vera and I had been accepted by the British that I wanted to do the best for Festival Ballet – a British company.

CHAPTER 9

FESTIVAL BALLET

———

The seeds of Festival Ballet were sown while I was in New York. Dolin had invited me to dinner at the Russian Tea Room. It was during this dinner that the idea of a major ballet company with Markova and Dolin entered my head. Fired with the idea, I asked Dolin if they would consider a tour of Britain using Benn Toff's 'fit-up' stage. Dolin promised to talk to Markova when he came to London to partner her at the first presentation of arena ballet at the Empress Hall. Both dancers had been working in America during the war and had made a triumphant return to London dancing with Sadler's Wells at Covent Garden in 1948, but neither of them had been outside the capital since the Markova–Dolin Ballet in 1938.

I was at their first performance at the Empress Hall, where they danced in an Italian garden before an audience of 6,000. While I disapproved of the arena setting for ballet, I was quite unprepared for the enthusiasm of the audience, who gave the dancers a great ovation. While the applause continued to echo around the cavernous stadium, I rushed backstage and asked Dolin to come and see me the following day.

I offered the two dancers the highest salaries ever paid to dancers at that time to make a ten-week tour of the provinces. Dolin was very excited about the offer. Markova wasn't. She did not particularly want to tour the provinces and thought it might be detrimental to her image to make such a tour with me – a foreigner she had never heard of.

Dolin exerted a tremendous influence over Markova and began his gentle art of persuasion. Hurok, who had been their impresario in America, also urged her to sign with me. But she continued to hesitate. Eventually, her indecision infuriated Dolin. While she was rereading the contract for the hundredth time, he yelled at her: 'For God's sake, sign the thing. If Braunsweg was good enough for Diaghilev, he's good enough for us.'

Their conception of a concert tour did not coincide with mine. They were used to dancing pas de deux to a piano accompaniment. I had more ambitious plans. They were to be the stars of the company, backed by a youthful corps de ballet and orchestra. The corps came from the Cone-Ripman School and included 18-year-old Anita Landa, a pretty girl who impressed Grace Cone, Markova, Dolin and myself with her Spanish dancing and castanet playing. The rest of the girls were chosen for their youth, beauty and personality, as well as their dancing ability. They were Sally Bradley, Daphne Dale, Shelagh Franklyn, Paula Gareya, June Greenhalgh, June Hamilton, Audrey Harman, Pamela Hart, Janet Overton, Eve Pettinger, Noel Rossana and Shirley South. The only two boys in the company were 19-year-old Malcolm Goddard and 18-year-old Louis Godfrey, who had come to London from South Africa to study dancing on Dolin's recommendation.

Markova thought the corps were too pretty and far too young.

'A diamond shines better in a good quality setting,' I told her.

While she and Dolin were dancing in South Africa, Grace Cone had choreographed some new ballets – *Chopin Nocturne*, a Tarantella to Rossini and the *Valse de Fleurs* from Tchaikovsky's *Nutcracker*. Markova was to dance *The Dying Swan* and Dolin a solo called *Vestris*. Both appeared in *Italian Suite*, choreographed by Dolin to Cimarosa's music. The repertoire was completed by the grand pas de deux from *Nutcracker*, and *Blue Mountain Ballads*, a rather dull ballet to my mind, choreographed by Don Saddler to music by Paul Bowles, in which Dolin spoke Tennessee Williams' verse.

The Markova-Dolin group played concert halls in Newcastle, Edinburgh, Dundee, Sheffield, Brighton, Harrogate, Leicester, Birmingham, Hull, Wolverhampton, Southampton and Manchester and then for a week in each of the large cinemas in Sutton, Kilburn and Bristol.

Victor Hochhauser, who presented Markova and Dolin at the Empress Hall, was rather annoyed that they had contracted to tour with me. He suggested that he should become my partner in the venture. The idea did not appeal to me, but Dolin was keen to involve Hochhauser, so I agreed to accept £4,000 to finance the tour. The contract stated that this capital sum would be repaid to the impresario, who would also receive 10 per cent of our gross takings.

The contracts for the Kilburn State and the Embassy Cinema, Bristol, were not included in this agreement, so I felt Hochhauser was not entitled to a percentage of these takings. He did not agree and took legal and religious advice. Hochhauser is an orthodox Jew – he would never do anything on a Saturday. I suppose – not that I have ever thought about it much – that I am an atheist. Hochhauser and his solicitor, a positive legal genius, suggested that we should take our disagreement to a Rabbinate – a Synagogue court of Rabbis who arbitrate on everything Jewish, from divorce to the type of pot you should cook in. It seemed a reasonable idea. Hochhauser said the Rabbinate would make a decision quickly and we would avoid a scandal. My solicitor at that time, who was not Jewish, agreed with me that this religious hierarchy could not fail to recognise who was right and the ruling would be in my favour.

The first shock came when the Rabbinate demanded, as a bond of my good faith, a deposit of £2,500 before they deliberated the case. Reluctantly I gave them the money. They promptly ruled against me. This arbitration took all the profit I had made on the tour. Altogether I had to pay Hochhauser £8,000 – the original loan of £4,000 and his interest on the takings. The Rabbinate have no legal authority but I kept the bargain, smoked another cigar and decided that I must never look to heaven for help.

When I signed the contract for the two big cinemas, I realised that the group would have to be expanded and we recruited another twelve dancers, who included Leslie Crowther, who later became the comic of the *Black and White Minstrel Show*. Dolin added to the repertoire *Swan Lake*, Act two, *Les Sylphides* and the Snowflakes scene from *Nutcracker*. As we had no Benno for *Swan Lake*, Ninette de Valois agreed that David Blair should play the role when we presented the ballet at Kilburn State. Leighton Lucas was the musical director and conductor of the enlarged orchestra.

Ballet companies can usually make enough money to cover operating costs. What puts you close to bankruptcy are the costs for new productions. At this time all the new additions to our repertoire were paid for by me.

I began discussions with Markova and Dolin about establishing a full-time company. Neither of them was very enthusiastic despite the phenomenal success of their tour, which clearly demonstrated that there was a big demand for popular ballet at popular prices. Before the war, Mrs Laura Henderson, who ran the Windmill Theatre for Vivian Van Damm, had financed the Markova-Dolin Ballet and lost over £80,000 in a short space of time. Neither Markova nor Dolin had lost any money, but they thought they might if they got involved with me.

'Have you any money?' asked Dolin.

'No, but with your names I can get money,' I told them. 'There is a need for a popular ballet company presenting good ballets at prices people can afford. I know that I can make the company successful, economically and artistically, but I cannot do it without you two.'

I also told Dolin that he wouldn't be able to go on dancing for ever. But as Artistic Director of the new company, he could be assured of work as long as he wanted. After endless discussions the two dancers signed a two-year contract and our prospects for future bookings looked very bright.

The company reassembled after the Christmas holiday to rehearse for a second twelve-week provincial tour, this time playing theatres. I instituted rigid economies to keep costs down to a minimum. I cajoled costumiers, scene painters and even the dancers to work for the lowest possible fee, explaining that this was necessary to get the company established. They all co-operated. Dolin worked hard rehearsing the enlarged corps de ballet and I was very proud of the high standard of dancing and the esprit de corps of the young boys and girls.

My insurance policy on Markova ended three weeks before the tour ended. Making what proved to be a very stupid economy, I did not renew it. At the Manchester Opera House our prima ballerina became ill and was whisked into hospital for the removal of her appendix. Noel Rossana deputised for Markova in Manchester and won a good deal of attention from the newspapers. Ninette de Valois came to our aid and loaned us the beautiful, Russian-trained ballerina, Violetta Elvin, for the remaining engagements in Southend and Brighton. She could not have been more co-operative. Realising our problem of being without the advertised star, she danced Markova's roles superbly, boosted the company's morale, and made us feel that what we regarded as a major catastrophe was not really the end of the world.

Hurok was in London during July. I went to congratulate him on the success of the Sadler's Wells Ballet in America, and reminded him in fun of our original deal – 25 per cent of the profits.

'Well, Julian, I let you have Markova and Dolin very cheaply and did a lot for you in persuading them to join you for the concert tours. I think we're about quits, aren't we?'

Despite Markova's illness, I had made a profit on the second tour. I decided to stake everything on launching a major ballet company. Disregarding Dolin's misgivings, and realising the danger of relying exclusively on two stars, I asked him to engage four soloists. I still had the costumes and scenery for *Petrouchka* from *A Bullet in the Ballet*. I invited Nicholas Beriosoff to join the company and reproduce Fokine's choreography. Massine, who was no longer addicted to steaks and milk, came to revive *Le Beau Danube*. He had filmed all his ballets, but the film of *Danube* was so bad that it was of little use in helping Massine with his original choreography. Beriosoff, who has a photographic memory for any ballet he has ever appeared in, tactfully reminded the maestro of the steps.

While Markova was recovering from her operation, Dolin went to Paris to look for dancers. Thirty-one-year-old Natalie Krassovska, who had been with the Ballets de Paris, was free and she was engaged as ballerina. Tata, as she was called, spoke English with a deep-throated, heavy Russian accent. She was a beautiful, children's story-book ballerina, always darning point shoes and talking incessantly about ballet. She was liked by everyone and she laughed all the time, usually when the joke was on her.

Later, when the company began touring, she always had to be guided on and off trains, aeroplanes and ships, and depended on someone telling her where she was. The spectacle of her going through customs was a sight to behold. When the customs officer asked her if she had any drink, she would look at him languorously and with a low-throated sexual ripple in her voice would say: 'Driiink?' – emphasising and extending the noun as if she didn't understand what he was talking about. When the officer asked her if she had any cigarettes, she would roll her enormous eyes and say: 'Cigarettes?' And he would let her through without question.

She revelled in going into hotel restaurants and insisting on making her own salad. The uncut lettuce and endive would have to be brought from the kitchen and the glamorous Tata, watched by a disapproving head waiter, would set about chopping up all the ingredients. She would then mix the dressing and toss the salad before serving it herself.

Charles Chaplin was one of her devoted admirers and came backstage to see her when the company appeared in Paris. After he had congratulated her on her performance there was one of those awkward pauses in conversation.

'Are you still doing something in films?' asked Tata.

One statement which always stopped conversation was Tata's declaration: 'I am the best Fokine dancer.' Her accent unintentionally made the statement obscene. It was noticeable that her fans quickly drifted away when she got round to talking about Fokine.

After touring many years the costumes became very dirty. We never had them cleaned. I was always struggling to find enough money to re-dress the ballets. In *Sylphides*, it was necessary for the lighting to get dimmer as the tutus got dirtier. The lighting was a constant source of argument between me and Benn Toff.

'The dancers can hardly see to get on stage. Talk about moonlit glen, it's more like a black-out,' he said.

It was unheard of for anyone to get a new costume, but when Tata's fell to bits, a new tutu had to be made. Just before going on in the ballet, I caught her in the wings with an enormous pair of scissors cutting away the stiff tarlatan of the underskirt. Horrified, I asked her what she was doing. She went on slicing the underskirt to pieces. 'I cannot dance with stiff things between my legs,' she said quite innocently.

John Gilpin was a 20-year-old dancer who had just finished an engagement with the Marquis de Cuevas company. He had been told to come and see me by his former teachers, Grace Cone and Olive Ripman. I had seen him dance and was impressed by his handsome appearance, speed, ballon and technical expertise. When he told me he had been offered a contract by the Sadler's Wells Ballet, I knew we must act quickly.

I telephoned Dolin in Paris and explained to him that a decision must be made on the spot. Gilpin was engaged. When the contract was signed he was packed off to Paris to learn the *Harlequinade* pas de deux from Volinine who had danced it with Pavlova.

Dolin returned with 21-year-old Anna Cheselka from the Marquis de Cuevas company and we further reinforced our strength with Anne Suren, Anthony Burke and Peter White, who were all engaged as soloists. We now had forty dancers.

Work began for a ten-week provincial tour which was to precede the company's London debut. Eileen Baker took regular classes, with Dolin coaching the boys and taking rehearsals. When guest artists danced with the company, I persuaded them to give classes. In this way, the dancers were able to experience the different styles of their art.

On our provincial tour we had the distinction of being the first British company ever to perform *Petrouchka* and *Beau Danube*. In the Fokine ballet, Dolin danced the title role superbly, with Krassovska as the Ballerina and Beriosoff as the Moor.

One night, Eileen Baker and Benn Toff were watching *Swan Lake* from the back of the stalls. When the Little Swans began their dance, Eileen thought the girls were ill. They were shaking, not in time, and finished the variation in a state of collapse. With Benn Toff, Eileen rushed backstage to find the four girls laughing hysterically in the wings. They quickly tried to control themselves when confronted by their infuriated ballet mistress, but it was impossible.

'What are you doing? Are you ill? I've never seen anyone, even students in a ballet school, dance the variation so badly. What is the matter with you all?' Eileen Baker was a stickler for time.

The girls had tears streaming down their cheeks and could not stop laughing.

'Now come along, control yourselves,' said Eileen, getting more and more angry.

'We had just crossed our hands, waiting for our entrance,' said Noel Rossana, 'when someone, er, well, well they passed wind. We all began laughing and we couldn't stop.'

Eileen was disgusted. 'I've never seen anything so, so, unprofessional,' she snapped.

'Oh, Miss Baker, it was on the beat,' said Pamela Hart.

We still had no name for the company. Although the matter had been discussed and suggestions made, no one could agree on one. Markova, looking pale and wan in her hospital bed, raised the matter when Dolin and Alfred Katz, who managed the two dancers, went to see her. Dolin told me the story afterwards. In her quiet, unassuming way Markova said: 'The papers are full of the Festival of Britain. It might be quite topical to call the company "Festival Ballet".' She waited to see Dolin's reaction and was somewhat startled by his enthusiasm for her suggestion. The new name coincided with her return to the company and on 9 October 1950 Festival Ballet made its debut at the Empire Theatre in Edinburgh.

CHAPTER 10

MARKOVA AND DOLIN

———

I got to know Markova and Dolin very well during the first year of Festival Ballet. Dolin was a showman and had a showman's panache. He was one of the most unselfish partners I have ever seen on stage and had been educated by Diaghilev, who took pains to see that his male dancers were not only taught dancing, but given an appreciation of music, painting, sculpture and literature.

He was an extrovert, happy at parties, witty, charming, conceited and a lively conversationalist. He was forty-six when he began working with me and although a superb partner, past his prime as a dancer. In his solos he had a frenetic nervousness, as if he were almost willing himself to get off the ground, but I don't think anyone fell so dramatically as he did in the second act of *Giselle*. His years of experience and expertise in handling an audience could – as when he danced a far from good solo to Ravel's *Bolero* – persuade them they were witnessing a great performance.

At forty Markova was still beautiful. She had the classical grace of a ballerina and was always immaculately groomed and gowned. When she was animated and happy she had a luminous attraction. She was unhappy frequently and then her high-pitched voice took on a nasal tone. Massine nicknamed her 'the Chinese Torture', a name that stuck. She was indecisive, temperamental, inclined to be lazy and one of the greatest Romantic ballerinas of the century, particularly in *Giselle*, a ballet she regarded as her very own. Artistically, her taste was exemplary and although she was often asked to dance choreography unsuited to her style, she knew exactly what she wanted in matters of costume and decor.

She toured with a Nutcracker pink carpet for her dressing room and a large box of 'Black Magic' chocolates. She had a voracious appetite and was addicted to them. She ate them by the box and ate them all herself. Benn Toff used to take great handfuls and give them to the stage staff.

'My chocolates seem to vanish,' Markova told him.

'It's because you have such an enormous appetite,' Benn replied.

To a large extent, Dolin was responsible for Markova's fame.

Dolin knew all Markova's virtues and faults. He presented her and displayed her to the best possible advantage. I doubt if she has ever had such a self-effacing and reliable partner. But their relationship was temperamental and tempestuous and eventually Markova could no longer endure it.

When dancing *Giselle*, both dancers were particularly irritable and difficult. There were always rows and temperamental outbursts and Benn Toff invariably got the worst of it. He always called *Giselle*, 'D Day'.

Before a performance at the Stoll Theatre, a diarist from *The Times* turned up unexpectedly to interview Markova and Dolin. Benn Toff was apprehensive about introducing the reporter to the two dancers at such a critical time, so he tried to answer the journalist's questions himself. He told *The Times* man how well the dancers worked together and he extolled the harmonious relationship that existed between them.

'They've been together for a long time. It's like a happy marriage,' he said.

The journalist, smelling an even better story, said: 'Would you say Markova loved Dolin?'

Somewhat stumped, Benn Toff replied, 'Well, yes, in a way.'

'Then why don't they get married?'

'Well, the relationship is more,' Benn searched desperately for a word, 'spiritual.' Thinking the interview was getting out of hand, he decided to risk introducing the reporter to the dancers. Backstage, he knocked at Markova's dressing-room door.

'She's in with Dolin,' said her dresser.

As they reached Dolin's dressing-room, sounds of a heated argument came through the door.

'Perhaps this isn't the ideal moment for an interview,' Benn said to the goggle-eyed reporter, leading him away. 'A lot of spiritual preparation is required for *Giselle*.'

Markova and Dolin had accumulated a great deal of money and both were extremely careful how they spent it. In London, Markova once invited Dolin, Vera and myself to tea. Dolin took her a present – an enormous box of 'Black Magic'. After tea, Markova began eating the chocolates.

'Aren't you going to give us any?' said Dolin.

Markova did not reply.

'You're so mean, you wouldn't even give us any of your chocolates when I brought them for you. I suppose you're going to sit there and eat them all yourself?'

Markova got quieter and whiter sitting in her chair. I knew she was irritated by Dolin's continual teasing. Suddenly she exploded.

'Yes, I am mean,' she said in a voice icy with rage. 'But I'll tell you why. When I was young we were always sent off to bed early in the evening because we didn't have enough money to have an evening meal. It is something I'll never forget, and something I'll make sure I never experience again.'

An oppressive silence descended on the room until Vera made a joke and relieved the tension.

Markova did have one formidable ally, her sister Doris Barry, who had once been a show girl at the Windmill. Doris was her publicist, confidante and defender in her many battles. Dolin had no time for Doris, who eventually usurped his position as Markova's adviser.

In a dancer's life, class is essential, yet in all the time Markova worked with me she never attended class and walked through every rehearsal usually in a fur coat and high-heeled shoes.

'I did class for thirty years. If my body is not good enough now it never will be,' she said. Before a performance she flexed her long, delicate feet, clenched and unclenched her hands, and then moved on to the stage as if blown by a gentle breeze.

The provincial tour was a preparation for our London debut, and I did everything possible to ensure the company's success. Nottingham-born Peter Williams, thirty-six years old, was a tall, thin balletomane who favoured flared jackets and a long cigarette holder. He was a great friend of ballet critic Richard Buckle, and was editor of a newly-launched magazine called *Dance and Dancers*. He had a nice sense of humour and was responsible for the story of Andree Howard's witty ballet, *Selina*. I thought he would be ideal as our press officer. As a dance critic, he had reservations about accepting the job, but I persuaded him to take it on. For a year he wrote articles and programme notes about Markova and Dolin, whom he admired tremendously, and handled our publicity. When he left us, he often toured the continent with the company, but by that time he had become our sternest critic.

With Markova as our ballerina it was inevitable that we revive *Giselle*. It was a triumph. Dolin's production was based on a version taught to him by Olga Spessivtseva, the delicate, beautiful ballerina who excelled in the role. Dolin worked out the ballet realistically, checking historic details with Cyril Beaumont, the ballet historian. The result was a *Giselle* that was full of dramatic pathos without being in the least 'ham'.

Hugh Stevenson designed the decor and costumes. There was a rural earthiness and warmth about the apricot-yellows, blues and browns of the peasant costumes in the first act, contrasting drama-tically with the steely coldness of the second act graveyard scene. A clever use of gauzes, flickering lights and Benn Toff's imaginative staging made the moonlit lake, fringed with twisted trees, a misty, enchanted setting for all 'unearthly things'.

Krassovska danced the implacable, evil, Queen of the Wilis. Later, dancing the title role, Paula Hinton gave a far more dramatic reading than Markova's but no other ballerina – and there were many who danced it with the company – surpassed Markova's not-of-this-world ethereality in the second act. Another recruit to the company was a virile young Australian, Vassilie Trunoff, who had danced with the Borovansky Ballet and Rambert on their Antipodean tour.

Ballet companies have to compete with one another. I knew that our very existence depended on our London debut and I planned the timing carefully. I chose the Stoll Theatre which had been built as an opera house. It had a deep, wide stage, large orchestra pit and excellent dressing and rehearsal accommodation. It was an ideal theatre for ballet.

We also needed new productions for the London season. David Lichine choreographed *Harlequinade* in which Colombine, Pantalon and Harlequin danced out their fates to Drigo's music. Beriosoff mounted a complete production of *Nutcracker* with a prologue and two acts. Our guest artists for the season included 33-year-old Yvette Chauvire who danced in *Les Sylphides*, *Nutcracker*, *Swan Lake*, and made her debut as the Ballerina in *Petrouchka*. Tatiana Riabouchinska also appeared in these ballets as well as *Spectre de la Rose*, with Gilpin soaring brilliantly in the Nijinsky role. Massine came to dance in *Le Beau Danube* and *Petrouchka*.

When Festival Ballet gave its opening performance at the Stoll on 24 October 1950, the only company we were competing with was the Rambert who were giving a season at the King's Theatre, Hammersmith. The Sadler's Wells Ballet were in America. Mona Inglesby's International Ballet, which disbanded in 1953, were on tour in the provinces. On our opening night everyone in the company knew that it was now or never. The London critics had already dubbed us the Braunsweg-Dolin follies, but I had no doubt at all that we would be successful. We were.

The following morning the critics praised the young, talented company, admired Markova and Dolin in *Nutcracker* and hailed Krassovska and Gilpin as new stars in *Le Beau Danube*. There were queues at the box office. I began negotiating our first overseas contract – for Monte Carlo.

Nothing succeeds like success. I was surprised at the speed with which the company was accepted. Dame Adeline Genée asked us to give a charity performance to raise money for the Royal Academy of Dancing's rebuilding fund. Queen Mary, as patron of the Royal Academy, attended and on 31 October, before an audience that would have out-dazzled any first night at Covent Garden, Festival Ballet danced *Capriccioso*, *Les Sylphides* and *Petrouchka*.

In the first interval, Dolin, soberly attired in evening dress, accompanied Markova, wearing her *Sylphide* costume to the Royal Box. Queen Mary, who was eighty-three, showed great interest in Markova's pink point shoes and talked of the days when Taglioni had taught her the mazurka. Queen Mary even went as far as to demonstrate a few steps she still remembered.

Dolin had many friends, among them Mrs Gwen Chenhalls, chairman of the Three Arts Club and an intimate companion of Princess Marie Louise. Dolin came to see me one day and breezily announced that we had been asked to give a second gala, this time in aid of the Club. It would be attended by Queen Elizabeth, now the Queen Mother, Princess Margaret and Princess Marie Louise. The Three Arts Club, housed in Great Cumberland Place, had been in existence since 1911. It was a centre where women artists – actresses, dancers, musicians, painters and designers – could meet socially. The Club was particularly successful in providing contacts for young people. It had a well-equipped theatre, music room, restaurant and provided overnight accommodation for its members.

To publicise the Royal occasion, I gave a back-stage party on 15 November. The scenery for *Petrouchka* was left standing on the stage and drinks and refreshments were served from three bars named 'Giselle', 'Petrouchka' and 'Fiesta'. Jack Buchanan, a friend of Markova's, made an impassioned speech from the top of Petrouchka's booth appealing for support for the fund-raising gala.

It was at this party that I met for the first time Lady Annally, a cousin of Queen Elizabeth's, who became a close friend of Vera and myself. She was an enthusiastic balletomane and kept asking me questions about the company.

'You've developed so quickly. One minute you're not there, and the next you're a fully fledged company, dancing all these famous Diaghilev ballets. You must have money. You must be very rich. Who finances all the productions?' she asked.

'I do.'

'You,' she said incredulously. 'But where do you get the money from?'

'Mostly from my own pocket.'

She looked at me disbelievingly.

'You must be crazy, quite off your head.'

From that moment on, Lady Annally bought tickets for all our London performances and distributed them to friends and her staff. We called them the Annally Supporters Club.

The gala programme on 27 November was *Le Beau Danube*, *Petrouchka* and the second act of *Nutcracker*. Massine was invited to dance his ballet, but the fee he demanded was too high for our budget. The guest artists were Chauvire and Tania Grantzeva, replacing Krassovska who had been given leave of absence to dance in America.

Vera and I were asked to take the royal party backstage after the performance to be introduced to the company. I could not tell whether the Queen was amused or amazed by my English, or whether she understood it at all. As she was moving out of her box, I told her she would need her fur stole.

'I'm sure I'll be all right,' she assured me.

Knowing the great draughts that swept across the Stoll stage, I replied: 'It is very cold backstage and you won't be warm enough. I am responsible for your health and wellbeing while you are in the theatre, and I insist on you wearing the stole.'

The Queen began to laugh. 'No one has ordered me about like that before,' she said, and continued to laugh until we reached the line of dancers waiting to be presented.

The takings at the Stoll totalled £5,000 a week. They were absorbed by our running costs. My own capital had completely disappeared in financing new productions and I appealed to Vera for help. She had the same enthusiasm for the company as I had. At first she sold jewellery and raised money on her assets. When they ran out, she visited her family in Paris, returning with gifts of anything between £500 and £1,000. The money disappeared immediately on the company's endless costs.

After the gala, Dolin persuaded Princess Marie Louise to become the patron of Festival Ballet. This proved to be a great morale booster. Her Highness not only encouraged the dancers during their frequent London seasons, but visited us whenever she could and showed an unflagging interest in the company's wellbeing. She knew we were always short of money, and in later years, she sent us all her old state gowns.

'The embroidery and jewellery can be cut off them,' she told me. 'It will do to decorate any costume that needs an added bit of glitter.'

Eugene Grunberg was an old friend of mine from pre-war days. Without seeing the company, he arranged for us to give a three-week season at the Monte Carlo Opera House. We were the first British company ever to appear there and the dancers were tremendously excited about performing in the theatre, with its historic associations with Diaghilev's Ballet Russes and the de Basil companies. To proclaim our birthright, it was decided to bill the company as London's Festival Ballet.

The team spirit prevalent during those early years was responsible for the artistic success of Festival Ballet to a large extent. There were frequent clashes of temperament – what ballet company doesn't have them? – but dancers, musicians and stage staff were united in giving of their best.

John Gilpin's twin brother Tony – as unlike John as chalk from cheese – had joined us and been trained as stage manager. He was a talented pianist, could read a muscial score and, under Benn Toff's supervision, became an excellent and efficient stage technician. With the ever-dependable Duggie Abbot taking care of the administrative side of company affairs, everything was running smoothly. Among a host of jobs, I had to arrange bookings and try to raise money to pay off our debts. There were quite a few hanging over our heads when we left London. They did not deter us from mounting two new productions for Monte Carlo. Dolin reproduced *Pas de Quatre* and Lichine created *Symphonic Impressions* to Bizet's *First Symphony*.

Our Monte Carlo debut coincided with the Battle of Flowers. The season provided as much pleasure as work for the dancers who where not nearly so sophisticated or blasé as they liked to appear. They were able to swim, sunbathe, and explore the spectacular Grande

Corniche. They were constantly being entertained. The performances were attended by glittering, gowned ladies, stiff with tiaras and jewels, ambassadors, millionaires, film stars and the playboys and playgirls who throng Monaco during the summer months. It was *de rigueur* to dress for the ballet. The only man who flouted tradition was Ali Khan. He appeared regularly with Rita Hayworth. He always wore an open-necked shirt. Ali Khan enjoyed the ballet but he enjoyed gambling at the Casino even more. On two occasions, when we had discussed particular ballets I wanted him to see, he was lured to the Casino during the interval. I followed him and insisted he return to see the ballet. He was always quite amiable about it – his 'cultural education', as he called it.

The success or failure of a ballet company in Monte Carlo is not decided by the audience, or the ballet critics, but by the stage staff. They are a sophisticated team of artisans who have seen it all. I waited impatiently for their verdict. It came about the third night, when one of the old stage-hands came over to me in the wings.

'The girls are really beautiful in this company. And they can dance. I think you are going to do very well here,' he said. I could have thrown my arms around him. I felt we were no longer the Braunsweg-Dolin follies.

To raise money, Vera invited her brothers to Monte Carlo to see the company. They were impressed and after long discussions agreed to advance Vera a considerable amount. Needless to say, these investments, which over fourteen years totalled something in excess of £90,000, never produced a penny profit for Vera.

Our Monte Carlo season ended with a Gala d'Adieu attended by Prince Rainier and his sister, Princess Antoinette. At the end of the performance Markova, Dolin and I were each presented with a gold medal, struck specially to commemorate the company's first appearance in the Principality. The following day, we discovered smaller versions of the medal were being presented to the winning entries at the dog show.

Returning to London for a nine weeks' season at the Stoll, Dolin and I agreed to engage a number of international ballerinas for the performances Markova was not dancing. The first was the dancer with the enormous reputation and the million dollar legs, Alexandra Danilova. Shura, as she was called, was a tonic for everyone. A marvellous dancer, a lively, humorous personality, she took class, rehearsed everyone who needed rehearsing and showed the girls a million and one things, from tips on make-up, to how to keep their hair from coming down in the most strenuous variation. She was a great friend of Markova's from the days of the Diaghilev company. Danilova had befriended the shy, somewhat reticent girl from London when she first joined the company. Markova was eternally grateful for her kindness. However, there were one or two problems. Danilova, who had created the role of the Street Dancer in the original production of *Le Beau Danube* in 1933, was cast in her old role, a decision that made Krassovska cry.

'But it is her part,' I said to Tata as she sat sobbing in my office. She made it famous and it is a role London audiences will want to see her dance. You dance the part magnificently, but the Street Dancer will always be associated with Danilova,' I explained. Tata listened to me, her eyes getting wider.

'I send old ballerina flowers,' she said.

Markova had given Dolin a lecture on why Danilova should not dance *Giselle*. 'It is my ballet and it is my repertoire,' she told him before casting was finalised. At first, Markova danced the leading role with Danilova as Queen of the Wilis. When Danilova did eventually dance the title role she took her curtain calls before a partisan, cheering audience and it was Markova's bouquet of flowers she was presented with.

Perhaps one of the most memorable evenings was the premiere of *Pas de Quatre*, a romantic divertissement in which Markova, Krassovska, Danilova and Riabouchinska were the reincarnation of their illustrious forebears, Marie Taglioni, Carlotta Grisi, Fanny Cerrito and Lucile Grahn. Never was the quartet so exquisitely and stylishly danced.

Our next guests were the two Yugoslav-born dancers, Mia Slavenska and her 24-year old partner, Milorad Miskovitch. They danced *Giselle*, *Sylphides*, *Swan Lake*, and *Nutcracker*, with Slavenska giving a formidable display of fireworks in the flashy *Don Quixote* pas de deux.

Beriosoff reproduced Fokine's *Prince Igor*, in which Trunoff spun with barbaric authority and wooed his two leading ladies, Krassovska and Hinton, with verve and passion.

Dolin wanted Markova to dance *Nutcracker* and *Giselle* with Gilpin.

'He's too young and inexperienced. I will not dance with him. He makes me look very old.'

The partnership was announced, but there was no rehearsal.

'If you do not rehearse with John,' Dolin threatened her, 'I will announce that you are indisposed. Your part will be taken by Krassovska '

Markova danced, without rehearsal, and gave an excellent performance. A few days later she did the same with *Giselle*. For a few days at least, all was light and harmony between Markova and Dolin. Gilpin was reduced to a nervous wreck.

Princess Marie Louise wanted to see a dress rehearsal of *Giselle*, in which Chauvire was due to make her debut. I arranged for Her Highness to come to the theatre one Saturday morning. Benn Toff and I brought down a high chair to the circle at the Stoll and made the Princess comfortable.

The orchestra were ready. Dolin, Chauvire and the corps de ballet, all wearing practice costume, began the rehearsal. From the wings, Markova appeared. She was wearing a sable fur coat and high-heeled shoes. Without any word to Dolin or Chauvire, she began to walk through the ballet, calling on the perplexed conductor to change the tempo. I watched anxiously while Chauvire regarded Markova in utter astonishment. Then the French ballerina went over to Dolin and said something.

Replying, Markova called out in French: 'This is my rehearsal.'

'It is not, it's mine, isn't it, Pat?' replied Chauvire.

Princess Marie Louise did not quite grasp the significance of what was going on. Eventually the argument hotted up. She leaned over to Benn Toff: 'What is the matter? What is going on?'

'Nothing, your Highness. They're just having a friendly discussion about artistic interpretation,' he replied diplomatically.

By this time, Dolin was sitting down at the back of the stage with his head in his hands. That's exactly how I felt when I had to pay the orchestra an extra £100 for a full-scale rehearsal with Chauvire on the following Monday. I never knew whether Markova or Dolin realised that their squabble had been witnessed by the company's royal patron. When she danced Giselle with Dolin, Chauvire, at thirty-five, was hailed as one of the ballet's greatest interpreters.

From the Stoll, the company went to the Golder's Green Hippodrome where we were joined by 23-year-old Belinda Wright and her contemporary Oleg Briansky, from the Ballets de Paris.

With her delicate, oval features, beautiful legs and excellent ballon, Belinda Wright could have become a great ballerina. Dolin created an enormous amount of publicity for her when she joined the company, but later in her career she felt she could exist without the backing and organisation of a ballet troupe. Markova, Beryl Grey and Nadia Nerina all hoped to shine as guest artists, but without the discipline of a company and the backing of a corps de ballet, it is a difficult thing to do. Margot Fonteyn and Rudolf Nureyev make repeated and highly rewarding forays, dancing as guest artists all over the world. But they realise the importance of retaining their contacts with the Royal Ballet. Without them, they would not have endured so long. The Royal provides the stability and a consistent artistic environment for the special talents of the two artists to be seen at their best.

In Glasgow, Markova slipped on stage. She injured her foot but insisted on performing both acts of *Nutcracker* that evening. Afterwards she returned to London for treatment while the company took a brief holiday. We were to open in Monte Carlo on Christmas Day, 1951. On Christmas Eve, Markova, Doris, Benn Toff, Vera and I spent a very happy evening together discussing the forthcoming season. Markova seemed to have forgotten her foot injury and I was surprised to find her so happy. She laughed and joked so much that I said to Benn Toff as we were leaving, 'We'l suffer for this tomorrow.'

Dolin had arrived late from New York. He told Markova that he was so exhausted he could not dance *Nutcracker* with her on opening night. She would be partnered by Gilpin. Markova was convinced that the only reason for his late arrival was that he had been living it up in America. She was furious. She complained that her foot was troubling her again, but decided she would dance.

She walked through *Nutcracker* as if it were a rehearsal. Even Gilpin's excellent dancing could not save the performance from catastrophe. The only excitement came at the end of the coda when she jumped into Gilpin's arms and appeared to collapse. The applause was for Gilpin, but as Markova took her bows, floral tributes were carried on stage until she was hemmed in by twenty-three giant baskets of every kind of blossom.

The company redeemed itself in the eyes of the aristocratic Monte Carlo audience with a dazzling performance of *Beau Danube* danced with gusto by Krassovska and Briansky.

The following morning Madame Robin, the florist who ran the shop just outside the theatre, came into the Opera House demanding her flowers. They had not been returned and Madame had absolutely no stock. The extravagant bouquets presented to Markova were hired each night by Doris from Madame Robin and returned to her every morning. We discovered the flowers at L'Hermitage, where Markova was staying. They were restored to the flower shop lady, but Markova's dressing-room was completely empty.

'My sister is leaving the company. She has a bad foot and cannot dance,' Doris told me as she swept past carrying the Nutcracker pink carpet and the box of 'Black Magic'.

Dolin tried to argue with Markova, but she and Doris were adamant about leaving. Markova's contract still had six months to run, but her foot injury gave her the right to go. And she went. I smoked a good many cigars. What would the Opera House think of our prima ballerina's departure? Casts were quickly changed. Colette Marchand happened to be in Monte Carlo and agreed to give several performances. The season went ahead.

A doctor's certificate duly arrived from Markova. Then I heard that she was in New York contemplating dancing for Hurok. I wrote to him pointing out that Markova was still under contract to London's Festival Ballet and, if she danced at any time during the following six months, I would sue her for breach of contract. In the event, she did not dance anywhere during the period, so the situation never arose.

With Markova gone, everyone in the company seemed more relaxed. But others were convinced that without her, we could not continue. I was equally determined that we would.

CHAPTER 11

FESTIVAL 'FIT-UP'

Three days after this calamity, we had another one. Dolin fell badly during *Symphonic Impressions* and injured his knee. He was unable to dance for three months. He was wheeled to the rehearsal room every day where he taught the majority of his roles to Oleg Briansky. Oleg realised that this was the chance to make his mark. He grasped the opportunity and very soon established himself as a premier danseur. He did particularly well in the *Don Quixote* pas de deux which suited his dark looks to perfection. He also added *Swan Lake*, *Nutcracker*, *Giselle* and *Les Sylphides* to his repertoire.

The Opera House made no comment on the loss of our star, but showed their appreciation of our short season by presenting us, at Prince Rainier's suggestion, with the costumes and scenery of the original Diaghilev production of *Scheherazade*. They were in a terrible condition. The costumes were so worn that they were nearly transparent and had to be held together by numerous safety pins. The original dancers' names were tabbed inside. This gift did, however, enable us to recreate the exotic Bakst designs for the ballet. Trunoff was the Golden Slave when it was first re-produced by Beriosoff on 19 January 1952, two days after David Lichine's new ballet, *Concerto Grosso*.

On our return to England, Sonia Arova joined us and proved to be an excellent partner for Briansky. But our guest artist was the beautiful, glamorous and extravagant Tamara Toumanova, the 'black pearl' of the Russian Ballet. Tamara danced all Markova's roles during a short provincial tour and stayed with us for the first three weeks of our Stoll season. She was accompanied by her no less beautiful Mama, the prototype of every ballet mother. Both were larger than life, outrageous, delightful, pursuing a way of life that could only exist in the ballet world. There was a romantic story that Tamara had had to scrub floors to finance her ballet studies when she was a young girl in Paris, but Mama was very vague about those years !

The Toumanovas hit Festival Ballet like a whirlwind, launched a hundred and one fascinating intrigues, interfered with everyone's lives and proved to be an enormous stimulus for us all. Tamara, with her classical beauty, her phenomenal technique and her remarkable ability to balance in arabesque or developpe a la seconde – a feat which made the conductor furious – was reasonably restrained on this, her first engagement with the company. Later, on the American tour, her dancing became more and more exaggerated. Yet no one could remain indifferent to her charms. If they did, they had Mama to contend with.

For Mama, no other dancer in the company, or in the world for that matter, could be compared with Tamarotchka.

'Such elegance, such beauty. Name anyone with the talent of Tamarotchka,' she would say, and woe betide anyone who dared to.

Mama was a shrewd, intelligent woman and an admirable poker player. She employed every subterfuge to ensure her daughter's happiness. She prayed a lot, particularly during crises not of her making. She could conjure up spirits from the other world in seances and had quite a reputation for being a healer.

'With a wave of my hands I cure any physical injury,' she said. Often when a dancer had a bad knee or ankle, she waved her hands with surprising results.

'Have you been to church lately?' one of the dancers asked her after she had made the sign of the cross in the wings, a ritual she practised every time her daughter went on stage.

'Why?' she answered, looking surprised. 'We dance our *Giselle* tomorrow, what more you want?'

Frederick Ashton, one of the world's greatest choreographers, is a close friend of Markova's. They had been partly responsible for launching British ballet in the thirties. Ashton never forgot his debt

to Markova, one of the first English dancers to interpret his imaginative choreography. During those early days, Ashton created a
short ballet to Liszt's *Mephisto Valse*. With decor by the talented
Sophie Fedorovitch, the extended pas de trois was danced by
Markova, Ashton and Walter Gore. Ashton had promised Markova
that he would create another ballet for her on the same theme and
using the same music.

With Markova gone, the choreographer went ahead and created
the ballet for Belinda Wright. Called *Vision of Marguerite*, the ballet
had ravishing costumes and decor by James Bailey. It told the story
of Marguerite's temptation by Faust. Gilpin danced the lover and
Briansky, Mephisto. It was an essay in pure romanticism, evocative
beautiful and, I think, one of the best short ballets we ever had in our
repertoire. It was the success of the Stoll season. As a choreographer
Ashton could have commanded any fee he liked. I knew he had
turned down dozens of offers from companies far richer than ours
For the ballet he charged us £50, and I don't think he was ever
paid.

Markova's disappearance and Dolin's injury had an adverse effec
on our box-office takings at the Stoll, so I had to start juggling
Vera's investments were completely exhausted and I began asking
friends for loans. I knew quite a number of financiers in London
rich men who played the stock exchange, or ran lucrative businesses
I appealed to them for help. I got loans because they liked me and
knew I was using the money to finance the company.

Isadore Winton had an office in Pall Mall, ran a club and dabbled
in various other money-making concerns. Initially I asked him for
£200. He gave me a cheque and a little later I was able to repay the
loan. The second time I borrowed £200, and then a few days later
I had to go to him again.

'I owe you £200. Lend me another £300 and that will be £500,
I said to him.

He wrote me a cheque, but I had more bills than I expected.
decided to ask Winton to help me again and went to his office.

'I owe you £500. Lend me another £300 . . .' He interrupted me
'I can see I'm not going to get any of it back. You owe m

nothing at all.' I was delighted, but I had to leave his office empty-handed.

Dimitri Schpount was a businessman who loved playing poker at Crockfords. I used to sit at his elbow, urging him to win. When he did he always gave me a loan of a few hundred pounds. When he lost, I got nothing. One day when I was in financial difficulties, I went to see him and met the theatre impresario, Peter Daubeny.

'I need £500. I've got to pay the dancers' salaries,' I told them.

Schpount had no money, but Daubeny said he would help me.

'When can you pay it back?' he asked.

'Say, three weeks?'

Daubeny gave me a cheque without charging me any interest on the loan.

The takings at the theatres we played were never enough. My debts were running into thousands of pounds. I began to think I would never be able to repay them. Schpount introduced me to the professional money-lenders, or Shylocks as I called them. They lent me money to cover expenses at rates of interest which ranged from 12 to 20 per cent.

But by this time I had a promise of a regular income. During the Stoll season an acquaintance I had worked with in the Jay Pomeroy days came to see me. Owen Mase was Concerts' Adviser at the London County Council's Royal Festival Hall. He was looking for an attraction to compete with the BBC's annual Promenade Concerts at the Albert Hall. The prospect of a regular summer season for the company at the South Bank concert hall was very appealing. A number of meetings were held with the hall's deputy manager, Leonard Mathews, Benn Toff and myself.

Mathews thought that it would be possible for Festival Ballet to dance on a flat platform, without proscenium arch, wings or indeed any scenery of any kind. This idea did not appeal to me. I quoted Diaghilev: 'Ballet is a fusion of three art forms, dancing, music and painting.'

I went on with the argument. 'Take away one of these elements and what remains might, in certain circumstances, be reasonably attractive, but it definitely would not be ballet,' I told him.

Benn Toff explained how we could turn the concert hall into a theatre, but Matthews, and indeed the entire engineering staff of the LCC said it was impossible. Benn persuaded them to allow us to erect the same kind of 'fit-up' stage we had used for our first concert tours. The only problem was the stage area at the Festival Hall. It was about three times the size of the stages where we had used our original 'fit-up'. Neither Benn nor I was absolutely certain whether his Bailey bridge principle would work spanning such a large area. However, we were so keen to get this important regular booking, we were willing to try anything.

Tons and tons of heavy steel scaffolding were used to transform the hall into a theatre. It took five days and nights to build the stage and erect the 'fit-up'. The scaffolding had to be screened from the audience. Thousands of yards of velvet had to be bought to cover the false proscenium and the areas on either side between the stage and the wall. The tabs had to be opened and closed by hand-operated winch. All this was installed at Festival Ballet's expense.

When the whole thing had been clamped together there remained one central support holding the proscenium. Benn Toff and I looked at each other and crossed our fingers as the scaffolders gingerly began removing the support. Would the 'fit-up' hold? The last piece of central scaffolding was removed. The entire structure remained in position. Benn Toff spent the whole night before our Festival Hall opening stitching yards of white tasselling on the bottom of the red curtains with nylon thread, just to make them look more acceptable. Years later, the LCC staff, working with our own stage staff, could transform the orchestra pit into a stage quite quickly using light tubular alloys.

We could not fly scenery so we had to lower all the backcloths to stage level, roll them up and return them to their storage bars high above the stage. The set pieces of scenery had to be lifted by the stage hands on to the rostrums at the rear of the stage. In our first two seasons at the Festival Hall these time-consuming operations resulted in lengthy intervals and we had to engage more staff – we had three only – to accomplish the changes. Later, with lots of practice, they were made much quicker and more efficiently.

Our problems were still not resolved. The Festival Hall had been built for concerts. It had no fire curtain. Consequently, the LCC insisted that the company's costumes and decor must be fire-proofed. Treating the costumes and remaking much of the scenery proved to be a very costly business.

The Festival Hall provides a shallow stage with no wings to speak of and no trap-doors for dramatic or magical effects. The dressing-room accommodation was sparse. Festival Ballet made the hall their London home and for many years entertained thousands of people during the summer and winter seasons and earned money which kept the company going. Without these regular bookings, and the support the LCC gave us, we would not have been able to continue.

Dolin had heard Don Gillis's *Symphony for Fun* and thought it might make a modern ballet for our eight-week Festival Hall season. It was Peter Williams who suggested a choreographer – 25-year-old Michael Charnley. Charnley had just created a work for Ballet Workshop, a showcase for new choreographers at Marie Rambert's Mercury Theatre. I went to see the ballet, thought it had promise, and asked Charnley to create a work for us. The choreographer heard the music, liked it and set to work. He was young and comparatively inexperienced. As rehearsals progressed, he became more and more uncertain of his talent. He wanted to give it all up. He had lost his self-confidence. Dolin encouraged him and things began to go better.

With a repertoire of fifteen ballets, we opened our first season at the Festival Hall on 30 July 1952. Charnley's *Symphony for Fun*, with decor by Tom Lingwood, was presented on 1 September. It was a gay, inconsequential modern work in four movements, danced with *joie de vivre* by Noel Rossana, John Gilpin and Anita Landa. It was Festival's first contemporary ballet. The audience and critics gave it their full approval. Some weeks later, at the Empire, Sunderland, of all places, the audience would not stop applauding until the last movement was repeated. Of all the ballets we ever presented, *Symphony for Fun* summed up Festival Ballet. It had gaiety, enthusiasm and happiness and it was a balletic expression of the young company's spirit.

During the London season the company appeared in a film starring Gene Tierney and Clark Gable called *Never Let Me Go*. In the film, Miss Tierney played the part of a ballerina who, inexplicably, had to swim to freedom in her *Swan Lake* costume.

Daphne Dale was the same height as Miss Tierney, so she doubled for the actress in the long shots of the ballet sequences. Both artists were partnered by Dolin. Excerpts from *Scheherazade*, *Nutcracker* and, of course, *Swan Lake*, were shot in three hectic days at the Scala Theatre.

Clark Gable was liked by everyone in the company and became very friendly with the girls in the corps de ballet. During breaks in filming he would sit and drink coffee with them, talking about anything and everything.

'They're all such professionals, and so good-mannered,' he said to me when we were saying goodbye at the end of the shooting.

With the box office receipts from the Festival Hall and the money we received from MGM, I was able to repay my Shylocks. But nothing remained with which the company could continue. I was introduced to another financier, Boris Kilaczycki, who issued a debenture financing the company to the tune of £15,000. Repayments were to be made after twelve months.

I had opened five bank accounts in London. In order to make an appearance of financial affluence I frequently transferred what little money I had from account to account. This enabled me to get overdrafts at all the banks. While playing at the Festival Hall, I was often compelled to sign cheques for ballet shoes, costumes and royalties in the middle of the week, knowing that there was not enough money in any account to meet them. However, I depended on three days' clearance and just hoped that by the time the cheques were presented, the takings from the Festival Hall box-office would have been paid in to meet them. One morning, after some complex financial juggling, I arrived at one of the banks to be set upon by the infuriated manager. After criticising me for my overdraft which had climbed from £500 to £6,000, he threw up his hands in despair and shouted, 'I don't want your account. I don't ever want to hear anything more about you. You're a madman. For goodness' sake, take your overdraft somewhere else.'

For a nominal rent the LCC had provided the company with spacious offices in the Festival Hall. Among the many visitors was one of the Council's clerks, a young man who always dressed in drab browns, called Clive Barnes. A balletomane, he helped Peter Williams and never stopped asking questions about dancers, the repertoire and future plans for Festival Ballet.

I had negotiated a contract for Festival to visit Italy, where the standard of ballet was appallingly low and visiting ballet companies something of a rarity. The Italians have always preferred opera to ballet. As the tour progressed, they heard a good deal of singing from our conductor, Geoffrey Corbett, but more about that later.

When we arrived in Naples, we were met by a representative from the San Carlo Opera House. He asked Benn Toff if he was the principal tenor.

'No,' Toff replied, 'I'm a baritone actually.'

Throughout the tour, which included Venice, Florence, Turin, Modena, Bologna, Parma, Biella and Vicenza, we experienced difficulties with orchestras.

Corbett, our musical director, a slim man with a goatee beard, was called *Professore* by the Italians. He accomplished marvels in beating the locally recruited musicians into shape. But even his baton could not combat their prejudice. To the 120-strong orchestra at San Carlo, Tchaikovsky had some slight merit as a composer, but Johann Strauss was completely unacceptable. At the first performance of *Le Beau Danube*, two-thirds of them downed their instruments. Corbett waved his baton and glared angrily while they stood in the pit trying to catch a glimpse of what was going on on stage. In desperation, Corbett leapt to the piano and continued playing the score himself. The audience were overjoyed with his ability to keep the ballet going. When the curtain came down, 'Bis, Bis' re-echoed through the gilded opera house. Anita Landa was sobbing in the wings. She was convinced the audience were hissing.

'Don't cry,' I told her. 'That means they love you. Go and take your bows.'

At the beautiful Teatro La Fenice in Venice the elegantly gowned ladies and their escorts arrived by private gondolas, decorated in Renaissance splendour, and made their entrance to the theatre up a sweeping staircase lined with liveried flunkies. Before the performances, the dancers used to peep out from behind the curtains to see the red, blue and gold decorated interior and the glittering audience. They always thought that the spectacle in the auditorium outdazzled anything to be seen on stage.

The Roman amphitheatre in Vicenza was the ideal setting for ballets such as *Swan Lake* and *Les Sylphides*. But the dancers were crippled. The stage was solid rock.

In Rome we performed at the Teatro Quattro Fontane, a cinema which had been acquired by a new management who wanted a prestige entertainment for their opening. 'What better than Festival Ballet,' I told the director as I signed the contract. The cinema was quite unsuitable for ballet. The group of musicians the management had recruited for the season were hopeless. Faced with the scores of *Scheherazade*, *Nutcracker*, *Sylphides* and *Beau Danube*, they could not play them. By this time, our conductor could cope with any emergency. On more than one occasion when the orchestra petered out, he sang at the top of his voice. It happened in *Le Beau Danube*. Corbett sang louder and louder. The audience began clapping in time and the dancers went on dancing. An attendant appeared at Corbett's elbow with a cup of coffee. He peered down at him and sang: 'Go away.'

Roman audiences are incapable of arriving punctually. They usually get to their seats during the second interval, in time for the curtain to go up on the final ballet.

We were all short of money in Rome, so I was somewhat surprised to hear that Dolin had given his dresser a bundle of lire notes to buy falsies for all the corps de ballet in *Nutcracker*.

'Ex-King Farouk is in the audience tonight. You know how he likes well-developed women. It might do us a lot of good,' he said.

The ex-King, with his bodyguards and a positive harem of busty beauties, occupied an entire row. Like the rest of the audience, Farouk did not appear until the second interval. He agreed that he would come again another night to see the ballets he had missed. But, possibly on the strength of the falsies, we never saw him again. Someone may have told him the truth.

At the end of the tour I got a letter of commendation from the British Council. It became customary for me to receive letters of this kind after every foreign tour the company made. They came from ambassadors, cultural attaches, British Council representatives, even the managers of the theatres we played. The letters praised the company, praised British dancing, were adulatory about the great contribution Festival Ballet had made to Anglo-Italian, Anglo-Spanish, Anglo-Portuguese, Anglo-everything relations. These letters gave the company great joy.

What I thought was extraordinary was that here we were, making so many friends for Britain, and yet there seemed to be no communication between our admirers and the British cultural organisations who doled out the money for the arts. Often I received congratulatory letters with a dozen bills. They cannot be paid with compliments, however genuine.

Peter Darrell, one of our soloists, had on several occasions asked me if he could create a ballet for the company. He was enthusiastic and full of ideas. I thought he should be given a chance to mount a work for our 1952–53 Christmas season at the Festival Hall. He produced *Harlequinade*, not a great ballet, but imaginative and inventive. It was designed by Kenneth Adams – a pseudonym used by Kenneth MacMillan. One evening the curtain went up too soon to reveal Paula Gareya, a very tall girl who danced in *Harlequinade*, sitting in a very unballetic position putting her point shoes on. The audience rocked with laughter, as she stumbled about trying to get off stage. After that the story of Harlequin, Colombine, and the other Commedia dell'arte characters could not be taken seriously.

Darrell later left Festival and joined Elizabeth West to form Western Theatre Ballet. In the early fifties, this experimental group, based on Bristol, produced some fine ballets and excellent dancers. They too experienced financial difficulties and at one time, Miss West set members of the company dancing in the street for pennies.

It was a constant problem to keep Festival working. I had been unable to find any provincial theatres immediately after our Festival Hall season. They were all occupied with pantomimes. I had no alternative but to accept the only engagement offered, a contract for the Theatre de l'Empire in Paris. For such a company as ours, lurching from one financial crisis to the next, Paris was a great risk. There was no question of receiving a guaranteed fee, or even a fixed percentage of the takings. The cost of the theatre, orchestra and publicity, as well as the artists' salaries, all had to be paid by me.

Our four-week season opened with *Nutcracker*. It received notices that would have made Tchaikovsky turn in his grave. Subsequent performances of *Giselle*, *Petrouchka*, *Prince Igor* and *Sylphides* brought better notices and by the third week we were playing to 100 per cent capacity.

I returned to London several times to try and raise money to cover our losses of £18,000. Eventually Vera's brother sold a house in Paris and we were able to pay off some of our debts and transport the company back to London. Despite the financial failure of the season, I felt the company had been well received and we had laid the foundation for future acceptance. This proved to be the case. On our second Paris engagement the company only lost £7,000, on the third only £2,000, and for our last visit we received a guarantee to cover expenses.

In the Paris season, Krassovska had danced a remarkable performance of *Giselle*. In the first act mad scene, she had accidentally bitten her lip, and the blood pouring from her mouth gave her death scene a touching realism. The Marquis de Cuevas had been in the audience, and immediately the ballet was over, offered her a contract with his company.

I agreed to release Tata from her contract and amid tears, she left us. A week or so later, she was back again. I asked her what had happened.

'I dance *Giselle* for them. Rosella Hightower see me and tell de Cuevas either I go, or she go. I come back.' Tata, as usual, had brought a gift for every member of the company. They were tiny, insignificant presents, but it was a gesture she made every time she was away.

On another occasion, when she had been dancing as guest artist in America, she arrived at London airport and was refused entry. I had forgotten to get her visa.

'Ballerina detained at London airport', ran the headlines in the evening papers. When Benn Toff went to get her, Tata had stopped darning her point shoes and was eating an enormous steak. She was quite unconcerned about being delayed.

'When they tell me I can't go, I sit down. Then I realise I dance *Giselle* tonight. I demand steak, big one, and got it,' she told him. 'They wouldn't allow me to do salad.'

The title 'Director General' sounds very grand and conjures up a vision of a luxurious, gleaming office, staffed by a legion of secretaries. Everything runs smoothly, nothing goes wrong. As Director General of Festival Ballet I had a staff of two. After many years, I had three. What they lacked in numbers, they made up for in loyalty and devotion. As for running smoothly, I had to use every conceivable trick combined with know-how and guile to keep the company running at all.

I worked fifteen hours a day. In seven years, Vera and I never had a holiday. Working as an impresario before the war I was constantly on the move, so we decided to postpone having a family. Then we were unexpectedly separated during the war. When we were reunited in 1945, both of us thought that it was too late to start raising children. Festival Ballet became our family. Vera listened to everyone's troubles, comforted the girls in affairs of the heart and gave sympathetic advice to anyone who needed it. She firmly believed in keeping people happy by feeding them. She was always making sandwiches for the office staff and at one time or another, cooked for practically everyone in the company.

Festival Ballet worked forty-eight to fifty weeks of very year.

The two engagements at the Festival Hall were always successful. Apart from the Marquis de Cuevas troupe, we were the only company continually touring the world. Our dancers were cultural ambassadors for Britain. Their continental engagements were entirely the result of the fact that I went abroad and dealt with managements personally. I have always favoured personal negotiation. You can write a hundred letters without getting results. Ultimately the company gained such a reputation that the managements came to me, but that was many years later. In all dealings I preferred a gentleman's agreement, but some of the gentlemen were far shrewder than I was and I paid the price.

One of the main reasons for Festival Ballet's popularity was that it was a happy company. The dancers danced with their hearts. The Royal Ballet – a mass-produced band of talented civil servants – is for the snobs; Festival was for the masses. Perhaps our dancers did not have perfect turn-out or impeccable line. Perhaps they didn't finish their pirouettes in exactly the correct position. But they enjoyed dancing and that enjoyment is what the dancer must never forget. On stage, a dancer might give a technically perfect performance that will delight her ballet master, but if there is no heart, no feeling, no spirit, she might as well stop dancing. The audience have paid to see a performance. They won't even know whether the dancer has done two or three pirouettes and they won't even care. Who's counting? But they have the right to be entertained and the dancers of Festival Ballet knew they had to entertain. They had no subsidy. They knew the future of the company depended on their ability to bring in the audiences.

When we appeared in Monte Carlo, the American choreographer Ruth Page came backstage to see me. She had danced with Pavlova and Diaghilev's company in the twenties and had choreographed ballets for the Ballets Russes and Champs-Elysee companies. She had her own troupe in Chicago.

'I'd like to do a ballet for your company, Dr Braunsweg. I have in mind a choreographic version of *The Merry Widow*.'

I was flattered and the idea appealed to me.

'It sounds ideal, but we haven't any money at the moment. However, there may come a time in the future . . .'

'I'll finance the whole thing. I would retain the right to re-produce the ballet for my own company and I expect the usual royalties.'

Miss Page began work. Georges Wakhevitch was engaged to design the sets and costumes, which were beautiful. They were made by Karinska, cost a bomb, and after ten performances began to disintegrate.

The English copyright owners of the operetta refused to allow the name 'The Merry Widow' to be used. So the ballet was entitled *Vilia*. The cast featured Daphne Dale as the Widow, Dolin as Baron Popof, Oleg Briansky as Danilo and Keith Beckett as Nish. The ballet opened at the Palace Theatre, Manchester, on 30 April 1953. The music was familiar, the sets and costumes colourful and romantic. It was a welcome addition to our expanding repertoire.

In negotiating contracts for the continent, I was constantly being asked to include a typically English ballet in our repertoire. 'Something by Dickens,' one impresario said. 'Something by Shakespeare,' another demanded. Choreographers are rare birds and we could never find anyone to transform any of the English classics into a balletic spectacle.

We commissioned Michael Charnley to make a ballet of Lewis Carroll's *Alice in Wonderland*. The music was specially written by Joseph Horovitz and scenery and costumes designed by a young Australian, Kenneth Rowell. He used gauzes to achieve fantastic effects, but these caused trouble from the beginning. None of the materials we found complied with the fire regulations laid down by the LCC. Benn Toff was sent to Paris to find a suitable material. He found one – a by-product of coal.

Alice in Wonderland was given its world premiere on 2 July 1953, at the Pavilion Theatre, Bournemouth. Belinda Wright looked just right as Alice, John Gilpin was the White Rabbit, but the ballet belonged to Keith Beckett, the zaniest Mad Hatter imaginable. The animal masks for Carroll's characters made the ballet very popular with children and adults. As the story line could not be interpreted balletically, we used a narrator for parts of the book such as the Lobster Quadrille and Father William.

Charnley had rehearsed the company during our Canadian tour. We had one drama. In the ballet Charnley had choreographed a Tiger Lily pas de deux for Sonia Arova and Oleg Briansky. They danced it so well that Dolin thought it might overshadow John Gilpin's performance as the White Rabbit. It was cut. Arova, always keen on publicity, gave a news conference where she threatened to sue the company for 25,000 dollars. I didn't have 25,000 dollars. The trouble blew over after Sonia and Oleg got all the press they needed.

Krassovska was prima ballerina on the Canadian tour. In Niagara she was the guest, together with Dolin and Gilpin, of a wealthy, handsome businessman. The following morning, when we went to collect her, she appeared wearing the most enormous, extravagant picture hat.

'I no want to leave,' she said standing in the driveway. 'They all so nice to me.'

She tried to get into the car, but the breadth of the hat prevented her. She reluctantly agreed that it should be put in the boot. 'Be careful, it very precious that hat,' she said as she supervised its storage.

'You know, twenty handsome young men stay there. I love them all, but one specially. I want to stay,' she said, breaking into tears. 'They all so nice.'

The car sped on to Toronto.

'Did they give you the hat?' Vera asked.

'They had wardrobes everywhere, full of women's dresses. They ask me to dress up, but they just stand there waiting for me to choose. I could not, so I choose hat. They have hats, feathers, tiaras – even women's shoes. Don't know who clothes belong to. No women there.'

Krassovska kept the hat for months and always ran into difficulty when trying to get through doorways. Her favourite colour was green, not a colour that suited her. Benn Toff began to chastise her for not taking more care with her appearance. We were making a long train journey when Benn first broached the subject.

'Now listen, Tata, you're the prima ballerina. But you must look the part. Now you can look ravishing, without all that green tat you insist on wearing. When we get to our next stop there will be masses of photographers waiting to take pictures of you. I want you to get into your most glamorous outfit and be ready for them. I'm coming to see you before we get there, just to make sure you look right.'

Five minutes before we were due to arrive, Benn went to see Tata. She looked beautiful in a tight-fitting black costume and black picture hat – not the one that caused problems in doorways. He eyed her from all angles.

'You look fantastic,' he told her and she smiled radiantly. 'Now wait until all the company get off the train and then you get out. The photographers will be waiting for you, so pose in the carriage doorway.'

The train entered the station. The company filed out and then Tata appeared in the doorway looking extremely exotic in her smart black outfit. She was carrying a huge string bag full of onions. The photographers clicked away madly.

Benn Toff fumed. 'Why the bloody hell have you got that hideous bag of onions with you,' he yelled at her.

'I like onions,' was Tata's husky reply.

CHAPTER 12

BATTLING MAMAS

———

Besides *Vilia* and *Alice*, two other new ballets were presented during the ten-week Festival Hall season in the Coronation year. They were short works by a young Greek, Vassili Lambrinos, who had caught Krassovska's eye. Lambrinos choreographed *Concerto* to Grieg's Piano Concerto, using six dancers.

For his second ballet, *The Laurel Crown*, he used the music of a young English composer, Michael Hobson. *Concerto* was very successful and remained in the repertoire for some time. But both ballets had tragedies connected with them. In *Concerto*, the piano was played by a young New Zealander, Richard Farrell. He was later killed in a car crash. Michael Hobson died a tragic and somewhat bizarre death a few years later.

However, it was not our new productions that caught the public imagination in 1953, but two remarkable Hungarian dancers, 22-year-old Nora Kovach and 21-year-old Istvan Rabovsky. A husband and wife team who had been trained at the Budapest Opera and danced in Russia, they were one of the few cases where the effect of politics in the East proved beneficial to the arts in the West. They had been dancing in Berlin when they defected to the West. Gerry Sevastianov, Baronova's husband, was at that time serving in Austria with the United States Air Force Intelligence Service. He was awakened at his Vienna hotel at three o'clock in the morning by a phone call from Military Intelligence in Berlin.

'What's the name of that ballet dancer you're married to?' asked the officer.

'Irina Baronova.'

'Name a few other famous dancers from behind the Iron Curtain.'

Gerry named a number.

'What's the matter? Have you fallen in love with one or something?' he asked.

'No, this is strictly business, and it's serious. I've got two here. Say they're married and they're dancers. They've defected. They might be spies. What do I do?'

'Fly them to Munich tomorrow. I'll soon tell you whether they're dancers.'

Gerry met Kovach and Rabovsky the following day, bought them practice clothes and shoes, hired a studio at the local theatre and gave them an audition. They danced the most fantastic pas de deux he had ever seen.

He was on the telephone to me straight away. 'I've got the most marvellous dancers, Julian. They have an extraordinary technique, fantastic leaps, endless pirouettes and that wonderful strong, flowing Russian style. You must engage them. I've already talked to Hurok in America and he suggests they come and dance with Festival.'

Kovach and Rabovsky had not only danced their way to freedom. With Gerry's help they had danced themselves into a job. And Gerry helped them with all their problems. They were being interrogated up to six and seven hours a day by the U.S. Intelligence Service. They were also being exploited for propaganda purposes by Radio Free Europe and the Voice of America. Gerry secured their release and got them to London.

At that time, Western audiences had never seen dancers from behind the Iron Curtain. Kovach and Rabovsky's performances were a revelation. She was beautiful and technically superb. He had all the virility and strength for which Russian-trained dancers are renowned.

They were an immense stimulus to the company. It became a case of 'anything you can do I can do better'. A perfect example was the gala performance celebrating the company's fourth anniversary. Kovach and Rabovsky danced the *Moskowsky Waltz*, a flamboyant spectacular pas de deux full of breathtaking lifts, speedy pirouettes and gigantic leaps for the man. It was greeted by cheers. Krassovska and Gilpin followed in the *Black Swan* pas de deux. Knowing they would be compared with their Hungarian colleagues, they threw caution to the winds, pulled all the tricks out of the bag and danced as they had never danced before. The audience were jubilant.

I always paid the Hungarians in cash. Later, when they got to New York, Gerry took them to the Chase Manhattan Bank in the Rockefeller Plaza and opened a joint account.

Sol Hurok phoned Gerry two days later: 'Why are your gypsies borrowing money from everyone on my staff? They've got money.'

Gerry went to see the dancers. Yes, they had borrowed money.

'We've got to eat,' said Nora.

'But you've got lots of money in your bank.'

Nora and Istvan thought the money was paid into their joint account in accordance with a practice in Communist countries – as a compulsory subscription to a Government fund. The money could not be spent. Gerry told them to get their cheque books and, after endless practice, taught them how to make out a cheque. Then he took the husband and wife down to the hotel cashier, who, much to their surprise, exchanged the cheque for cash.

'It's the best thing I've ever seen in the West,' said Nora, jumping about waving the dollar bills in her hand.

A few days later the bank manager called Gerry. 'Miss Kovach is spending money like mad. Her account is overdrawn by hundreds of dollars. You must do something.'

At the Hotel Windsor, the dancers' room was packed from floor to ceiling with boxes. They contained dresses, shoes and every kind of commodity imaginable. Gerry gave Istvan and Nora a stern lecture on the banking system.

'I thought you could just go on writing cheques. Life in the West is not as good as I thought,' said Nora.

In Las Vegas, the Hollywood Hungarians became friendly with Nora and Istvan. King Vidor, the film producer, Romola Nijinksy and other expatriates were their constant companions. There was also a young Hungarian engineer who was Nora's admirer.

Nora wanted to learn to drive. The admiring engineer offered to teach her in his open white Cadillac.

'But you must have a driving licence,' Gerry told Nora. She was seated at the driving wheel with her engineer beside her. Romola and Istvan were in the back.

'You've got to have a licence and you've got to be insured. If you have an accident, there'll be trouble.'

'Oh well, it does not matter,' said Nora, starting the engine and lurching down the road. Her destination was Boulder Dam, sixty miles away.

That afternoon, Istvan telephoned. They had had an accident. Could a car be sent to collect them? The party arrived back in a pitiful state. Nora's legs were bleeding badly. Istvan was cut about the head. Romola could not walk and the engineer was black and blue. There was only one tree in the desert through which Nora was driving. It had attracted her like a magnet. The Cadillac turned out to be secondhand, being bought by the engineer on the instalment plan. It was a complete write-off.

Ever since our successful tour of Canada, I had been having pro-tracted discussions with Sol Hurok about the possibility of a coast-to-coast tour of the United States. As usual, he resolutely refused to pay transportation costs, but I thought there would be every chance of making money if the tour were long enough. Hurok invited me to New York where I signed a contract for a twenty-week tour to start on 12 October 1954. Hurok stipulated that besides Kovach and Rabovsky, we would engage Toumanova and Violetta Verdy as guest artists. He agreed to pay the company's operating costs and salaries, estimated around £12,000 a week. The remainder of the box-office takings would be split fifty-fifty. I had faith in the company. So had Hurok. I returned happily to Britain to finalise arrangements for our first visit to the New World.

Negotiations were in progress with Moira Shearer to dance with the company during our Christmas season at the Festival Hall, but a foot injury made it impossible. Knowing she had narrated Proko-fiev's *Peter and the Wolf* at a symphony concert, I suggested she might like to narrate *Alice in Wonderland*. She proved to be an excellent draw at the box-office.

Shearer had agreed to dance with us when her foot was better and my contract with the Monte Carlo Opera House depended on her appearance. Always helpful and co-operative, Shearer had agreed to dance for a minimal fee, but two weeks before we were due to leave for the South of France, she wrote to me to say her doctor had forbidden her to perform. I was horrified and went to see her.

'If you don't come, it will be a catastrophe,' I told her. 'Without you we'll have to cancel the season.'

She was very upset and sat for a long time thinking about the problem. 'I have awful pains in my legs,' she said at one point. A little later, looking very determined, she said: 'I'd hate you to lose the engagement. I'll come, even though the doctor will be furious. But I can't dance things like *Nutcracker*. Perhaps I could do something less strenuous.'

Moira Shearer accompanied us and scored a personal success dancing the girl in *Spectre de la Rose*. One morning she invited Vera and me to go with her to San Remo to buy presents for her family. On the way she talked about *Red Shoes*, the film that made her internationally famous. It had been shot on location in Monte Carlo and she pointed out some of the backgrounds used. She was charming, good-humoured and unassuming.

'I want you and Vera to be my guests for lunch,' she said after finishing her shopping. I was very touched. In all my years as impresario she is the only ballerina who has ever invited me to lunch.

On our return to Monte Carlo, Vera, who is far more perceptive than I am, noticed that Moira appeared to be very sad. She did not talk much but pointed out the final scene where *Red Shoes* had been shot. The scene ended with her death on the railway line in the red shoes that would not stop dancing. She must have had a premonition that she was ending her dancing career. A few nights later, she danced for the last time. It was an odd coincidence that her fictional role in *Red Shoes* and her career as a ballerina should both end in Monte Carlo.

Originally we were to play Monte Carlo for two weeks, but I asked the management for an extension. They said that business was falling off near the end of January and there was no point in the company playing any longer. I asked them to check their takings at the Casino. They discovered that on the nights we performed, the takings at the gaming tables were considerably higher than when the Opera House was dark. They promptly extended our season for ten days. And undoubtedly the company's dancers contributed considerably to the Casino's takings.

Pamela Hart, Noel Rossana and Graham Smith had worked out an infallible doubling system which, they thought, couldn't fail. They pooled their salaries and bought so many chips of small denominations, they could hardly move. They went off to the tables to put their system to the test and lost everything.

Feeling very hungry they went to a restaurant patronised by the company called The Snack, managed by a friendly extrovert called Pierre Bollier.

Pamela Hart explained they had no money.

'Never mind, my dear. I'll see you get some food.'

Pierre approached a prosperous-looking gentleman on the next table. As he cleared away the dishes, he asked the diner if he had seen the ballet.

'Yes.'

'They're very good, don't you think, sir?'

'Very, they're young and charming.'

'I'm amazed at their dedication. They work so hard and you know, they get no money at all. Some of them come in here and all they can ever afford is a cup of coffee. As a matter of fact,' he said, bending over the man with an air of confidence, 'the two girls and the boy at the next table are from the company. They're starving.'

The man looked hard at the trio.

'They don't eat. How can they dance?'

Pierre shrugged his shoulders.

'Feed them, do feed them. I'll pay the bill.'

Pierre took orders from the gambling dancers who gave a shy smile of acknowledgement to their benefactor as they consumed a three-course meal with wine. In those days the girls were so innocent they could go happily through the same routine every night until the next pay day without giving anything more away than a smile. They ate, and I got the reputation of never paying my dancers.

After Monte Carlo, the company toured Italy and paid its first visit to Spain and Portugal. We also began rehearsals for Beriosoff's new ballet *La Esmeralda*, based on Victor Hugo's *Notre Dame de Paris*.

Esmeralda is the only ballet that began as a three-act spectacle and finished, twelve months later, as a ten-minute pas de deux. The music was by Pugni and could only be obtained from the archives of the Paris Opera. Charles Mackerras and our own musical director, Geoffrey Corbett, rescored it for the ballet. When Beriosoff had finished work, I thought we had an entertaining, lavish, colourful and dramatic ballet. The dancers thought the choreography was uninspired and unmusical.

Beriosoff had decided that Esmeralda would be accompanied by a goat on her first entrance. Benn Toff got on to the London Zoo.

'We need a goat,' he told the very snooty gentleman who dealt with such matters.

'What kind of goat, male or female?'

'It doesn't really matter. It's got to look good,' said Benn.

'What nationality? Russian, Greek, Spanish, Irish, or,' and here the voice became quite scornful, 'a plain Billy?'

'It's a non-speaking part.'

'In that case, we'll send you an English goat.'

The goat was sent in a taxi. By the time it reached Festival Hall it had eaten most of the back seat and was starting on the carpet. The voracious animal was handed over to our prop-master. In the prop room, it ate everything in sight, papier-mâché goblets, shields, helmets and even wooden swords.

Initially Krassovska and Marilyn Burr, a young Australian promoted to ballerina status from the corps de ballet, alternated in the title role with Gilpin dancing the poet, Gringoire. Every time Tata went on with the goat, it peed all over her. She stood centre stage, looking beautiful, while the goat wet her legs and point shoes and the pool of water grew larger and larger.

After this had happened to her, and her alone, four times – and we had no props left at all – Tata came to see me.

'I no like that goat,' she said.

'I don't think it likes you.'

We agreed that for point work, wet shoes were no good. The goat was banished. But we had other problems with *Esmeralda*.

After the first performance, Dolin asked Beriosoff to make changes to speed up the action, but he would listen to no one. Dolin then asked Ninette de Valois to come and see the ballet and suggest ways of improving it. Secreted in a box, Ninette watched three performances, made copious notes, had them typed out and delivered to the choreographer. Changes were made, but the action, if anything, became more and more confused. In a fit of pique, Dolin refused to have anything more to do with *Esmeralda*.

The ballet was designed by Nicolas Benois, the son of the famous Alexandre, and cost £14,000. Benois used yards and yards of red velvet curtains painted with fleurs-de-lys. When the ballet was shelved, I thought I should salvage something from what proved to be a costly disaster. I got Barkers to wash out all the fleurs-de-lys and had the material made into curtains and coverings for my house.

The Danish dancer and choreographer, Harold Lander, arrived to produce his one-act Bournonville classic, *Napoli*. The dancers were led by Harold's wife, Toni. *Napoli* is an exuberant festival of dancing that precedes a young fisherman's marriage. The soft, rounded Bournonville style, with its springy ballon and soft pliés, has been perfected by the Danes and is very difficult for any company to imitate. Festival were the first British company ever to tackle a Bournonville ballet, and Lander, a hard task-master, worked the company mercilessly to achieve as near perfection as he could.

We commemorated the twenty-fifth anniversary of Diaghilev's death with a special performance on 19 August 1954 instead of our customary gala. All the dancers who had been associated with the master were invited. They included Ninette de Valois, Alicia Markova, Lubov Tchernicheva, Lydia Sokolova, Stanislas Idzikowsky and Serge Grigorieff.

The most moving tribute was that paid by Tamara Karsavina, who had created the role of the young girl in *Spectre de la Rose* with Nijinsky in Monte Carlo in 1911. It was the highlight of the evening. Karsavina had rehearsed Belinda Wright in her role, and when she came to rehearsals, she looked just like the young girl. She wore a similar bonnet to the one the girl wears in the ballet and when she sat in the chair showing Belinda how the ballet was staged originally, she looked seventeen.

At the gala, the curtain rose to reveal 69-year-old Karsavina gazing out of the window in the Bakst setting she knew so well. The lighting made her look even younger than she had looked at rehearsals. The silence in the house was absolute. As she turned to the audience, her arms in the fifth en avant position, it was as if she were going to dance. For a brief moment, this beautiful old lady held the audience in a state of breathless expectation. Then she moved down centre stage. Without appearing to project, her quiet voice could be heard all over the theatre as she brought vividly to life the days of Diaghilev's Ballets Russes. No one else in the ballet world has her eloquence, or her ability to people a stage in the imagination. She talked of the first night of the ballet and of Nijinsky's famous leap through the window. Then, she gave the conductor a gentle nod. The first bars of Weber's music began. As Karsavina walked slowly off the stage, her place was taken by Belinda Wright and a few moments later, John Gilpin soared through the window as the spirit of the rose.

Our American tour opened in Canada. Our visit to Toronto coincided with Hurricane Hazel. Despite the whirlwind, we grossed over 31,000 dollars in three performances and everywhere notices and business were excellent. Our company now included Nicholas Polajenko, Toni Lander, Tamara Toumanova and Violette Verdy. And two Mamas.

Mama Toumanova and Mama Verdy lost no time in becoming enemies. Mama Verdy was not loved. She made the fatal mistake of asking members of the company to draw, on a piece of paper, the house they would like to live in. From this she read their character

and predicted their future. Her comments were invariably uncharitable.

On the other hand, Mama Toumanova's comments were good-
humoured even when she was being endearingly malicious. She was
always bustling about, carrying her daughter's baggage, making the
sign of the cross, and giving advice from the spirit world – a world
with which she was able to achieve instantaneous communication.
When she took over an entire restaurant, bustled the chef out of the
kitchen and cooked a meal for practically the whole company
single-handed, she became top of the popularity poll. She nicknamed her adversary Madame Merde. The whole company followed
suit.

When Tamara and her mother weren't holding seances, they were
playing poker. Mama was a great friend of mine and often helped
me at cards when I was being bamboozled by members of the
orchestra. But eventually I was compelled to take her to task about
the constant quarrelling between her and Mama Verdy.

'If there was a little more goodwill on both sides, it might be to
everyone's advantage,' I told her.

Mama Toumanova beamed. 'There will be no trouble. After all,
she is only the amateur Mama. I'm a professional.'

In Chicago, Mama Toumanova stood in the wings, making the
sign of the cross when Tamarotchka went on, and spitting when it
was the turn of Violette Verdy. We received the only bad notices of
the whole tour. Advance business at the Civic Opera House was
good. Sixty per cent of the houses were sold before our arrival.
Unfortunately the anti-British sentiments for which the *Chicago
Tribune* was well known at the time seemed to be reflected in the
notices of their ballet critic, Claudia Cassidy.

'It's rather a withered plum, this London's Festival Ballet,'
she wrote. 'I was trapped in the shambles of the three-act *La
Esmeralda*.' Of Toumanova: 'She is no longer really a dancer, but
there is just one thing to do if she hopes to hold her own in ballet.
Get to work.'

Reviewing *Scheherazade*, with Kovach and Rabovsky, Miss
Cassidy's comments began: 'Shoddy on the production side (this

was a small time Shah with a pint sized harem), slip-shod on the dance side, and as a whole, a kind of ludicrous hash of the Fokine original.' She described the production as 'unauthentic' and Kovach and Rabovsky's dancing as 'of the purest, most succulent ham.'

These notices did nothing for the box office. However, one of them at least united, albeit only temporarily, our two Mamas. Clutching a ragged copy of the Chicago paper, Mama Toumanova, accompanied by Mama Verdy, bore down on me backstage. Mama Toumanova was weeping, Mama Verdy furious.

'How dare she write such a notice, Julian. Who does she think she is? Listen, *mon cher*, listen to what she writes about your company.' Tears still streaming down her face, Mama Toumanova began to read: 'This London's Festival Ballet gets sillier by the minute. One night you have *Swan Lake* with Toumanova who can't dance it any more and the next night with Violette Verdy who undoubtedly never could.'

She glared at me defiantly. 'My daughter is the greatest Odette in the business.'

I looked at Mama Verdy to see if she would allow this claim to go unchallenged. She just looked outraged.

'We demand a public apology. Tamarotchka will not dance unless she gets a public apology. You must demand it, Julian.'

I asked the theatre director to arrange an interview for me with Miss Cassidy. She turned out not to be the virago I had imagined but a thin, plain woman who looked rather like a hard-working English schoolmarm. I could hardly argue with her about her opinion of our dancers, but what had annoyed me was her claim that *Scheherazade* was unauthentic.

'The production can hardly be unauthentic. Did you ever see the original?' I asked. 'No, well these costumes and decor are the originals, designed by Leon Bakst for the Diaghilev company. They were presented to us by Prince Rainier in Monte Carlo. The safety pins and the names of the original dancers are still in them.'

'I am sorry,' she replied airily. 'You see, I had had a very trying day when I saw *Scheherazade*. My husband is a writer and he suffers from bad eyesight. I'd been helping him and I wasn't in my most receptive mood that evening.'

'I sympathise with your domestic problems,' I said. 'If they interfere with your ability to view a performance objectively, my advice is – stay away.'

I left Miss Cassidy sitting with the theatre director. Her subsequent notices were more polite, but by then the damage had been done. Business did not improve.

Problems never come singly. The next thing I heard was that Ruth Page of the Chicago Opera Ballet, and her husband, Thomas Hart Fisher, a solicitor, were suing the company for 2,000 dollars. Even more frightening was their threat to take out an injunction to stop our performances altogether. Under the terms of the *Vilia* contract I had with Miss Page, I was obliged to submit a statement of performances of the ballet and pay her the royalties she was entitled to every six months. As Miss Page planned to produce *Vilia* for her company, we were denied permission to perform it in America or Canada. My last statement had been made some months before our arrival in the States when I had written a letter confirming that the ballet was not being performed and no future performances were planned. I assumed no further statements were necessary. Mr Fisher's interpretation of the contract was that we still had to make six-monthly reports, regardless of whether the ballet had been performed or not. As I had not fulfilled this obligation, he demanded 2,000 dollars damages. A legal wrangle began. As I hadn't any money at all, Dolin gallantly came to the rescue and paid the money out of his own pocket.

Igor Stravinsky was invited to conduct *Petrouchka* in Chicago. In the normal course of events we would have taken two conductors with us. But the American Musicians Union ruled that if we had two English conductors, we would be taking employment away from an American musician. Therefore, we had to employ one American conductor. Robert Zeller was engaged for the tour and was paid a salary accordingly. Extra payments had to be made to Zeller even when our own musical director, Geoffrey Corbett, conducted rehearsals.

I was therefore delighted when Stravinsky agreed to conduct his own ballet and three rehearsals. He was an American citizen. I would not have to pay Zeller. To my surprise, Zeller demanded payment for the Stravinsky rehearsals. When I refused to pay, he threatened to bring the musicians out on strike. I was compelled to peel off the dollar bills and look happy.

And Stravinsky conducting Stravinsky brought other problems. He conducted all three performances with his eyes glued to the score, not once looking at the dancers or what was going on on stage. The principals found his tempi disconcertingly different to those they were used to. Anita Landa, who danced the ballerina, had the courage to raise the matter with the composer.

'Please, Mr Stravinsky,' she said rather timidly, 'I cannot dance to that tempo. It is very different to the one I usually have.'

He looked at her dolefully. 'The artist must learn to dance to my timing. I wrote the score,' he said.

After more complaints from the dancers, Benn Toff talked to the composer.

'Your speeds are too fast. They cannot keep up with you, they'll most probably break their legs,' he said.

'You're paying me by the minute, aren't you?'

Benn nodded.

Stravinsky beamed at him. 'What are you worried about then?'

We played fifty-two towns in America. A number were one-night stands. A special train was reserved exclusively for the dancers, musicians and staff. It consisted of three wagons for the scenery, and a dining car, club car and sleeping accommodation for over 100 people.

Festival Ballet's stage staff were accustomed to doing any job that needed doing, but they found their American colleagues – it was necessary to have a number on the tour – worked in quite a different way. You did your own job. There was no question of helping anyone else. Electricians could not touch a spotlight. Tony Gilpin, our stage manager, nearly caused a strike when he was caught replacing a bulb in one of the arc lights.

In the smaller towns, a visit by a ballet company was an unusual event. The local managers explained that their audiences would enjoy the performance, but because of their lack of knowledge about ballet, they were nervous about applauding in the wrong place. At these towns, Vera, Benn Toff, Duggie Abbot or myself positioned ourselves at strategic points in the auditorium. We found that it was quite easy to begin the applause, but almost impossible to stop it. Once started, the audiences' enthusiasm ran wild.

With the exception of Chicago, Festival Ballet conquered America and enjoyed one of the greatest triumphs of its history. Everywhere we had wonderful audiences and excellent reviews and were feted by the local celebrities. In San Francisco, where we spent Christmas, Stravinsky was again conducting *Petrouchka*. At a champagne and turkey party which followed, the hospitality was lavish. Our middle-aged, blue-rinsed hostess constantly made the rounds, seeing that we had enough to eat and drink and making a suitable balletic comment to each one. Her *bon mot* of the evening was reserved for me.

'I just adore Tchaikovsky's music for *Petrouchka*, don't you, doctor?'

Our two Mamas continued their battle. Everyone searched their point shoes for needles before they put them on. Mama Toumanova stood in the wings making the sign of the cross on one side, while Mama Verdy stood on the other casting malevolent spells.

Toumanova was to make a tour of South America after concluding her engagement with us. She had been trying to persuade Oleg Briansky to partner her, but he wasn't interested. Mama arranged a seance. With Tamara, Vera, Oleg, Dianne Richards, Ronald Emblen, Benn Toff and one or two others, we sat around a table. Mama told everyone to put their hands on the table, palm downwards and touching, while she began calling on the spirits of the other world. One knock for no, two for yes. Everyone had to behave as if they took these spiritual excursions absolutely seriously. Oleg certainly did.

After numerous knocks, Mama managed to make contact with the spirit of Nijinsky.

'This is the voice of Nijinsky,' mumbled Mama, deep in concentration with her eyes gazing unseeing straight in front of her.

'I have a message for Tamarotchka. She is not to worry about Chicago notices. They were all Pat's (Dolin) doing. It does not matter. You are still the greatest dancer in the world.'

Other messages were received for one or two members of the group. Then came a warning to everyone to beware of Mata Hari. Mata Hari was Mama's nickname for Nora Kovach. Nijinsky had already adopted it.

'Those acrobatics she dances is not art,' Nijinsky went on. We waited for a similar caution on the subject of Madame Merde, but Nijinsky had something more pressing on his mind.

'I have message for handsome, dark-haired boy.' Oleg was the only one who fitted the description. 'He will find great success, success such as he has never imagined, in South America. He should take opportunity presented to him and seize it while he can.'

Oleg looked suitably surprised, then the seance broke up. Nijinsky's spirit had done his stuff. Mama Toumanova was quite exhausted – so were we all, and I never found out who did the knocking.

At the Shrine Auditorium in Los Angeles, John Moss, the manager, told me that he was very relieved to see that the auditorium was full and remained full.

'That's because you don't speak,' he said.

'What do you mean?'

'Recently we had Moira Shearer and Robert Helpman playing in *A Midsummer Night's Dream*. The audience dwindled every night. People just walked out until by the end of the play, there was no one here at all.'

'Why?'

'Well, although it looked lovely, the people didn't understand the language.'

'They didn't understand English?' I queried.

'No, no. They didn't understand Shakespearian English.'

We had two weddings in Los Angeles. Nicolai Polajenko married Daphne Dale at the Russian Orthodox Church. It was like a three-

act spectacular, colourful and impressive. I gave Marilyn Burr, away
at her wedding to Louis Godfrey at a simpler ceremony at the
Episcopalian Church in Beverly Hills. The sun was shining brightly
and it was a very hot day. When we left the church an enormous fir
tree had been covered with artificial snow, just to remind us that it
was Christmas.

Toumanova invited members of the company and the two newly
wedded couples to her palatial home where she lived with her film
producer husband, Casey Robinson. Flinging open the door of a
wall safe, she revealed a pile of uncut precious and semi-precious
stones. She invited Marilyn and Daphne to take their pick. Marilyn
chose a topaz and Daphne an aquamarine.

I asked Tamarotchka if she were paid her salary in jewels, but
she just laughed. 'I like them, they come in handy at times,'
she said.

In Cleveland we played in one half of an enormous circular
auditorium, divided down the centre by an iron curtain. The other
half was occupied by a three-ring circus. The clowns were having
difficulty in obtaining wet-white make up, so they popped through
the communicating door in the iron curtain and borrowed it from
the corps de ballet. The circus shot a lady out of a cannon. The
tremendous report came at exactly the moment when Anita Landa
jumped on to Nicolai Polajenko's shoulder in *Le Beau Danube*.
The two dancers timed it so perfectly that the audience thought the
bang was all part of the performance, and always applauded.

Our final dates were Brooklyn and Boston and both were sold
out. Writing in the *New York Times*, John Martin, the distinguished
American critic, said of Festival Ballet: 'It is undeniably a handsome,
young, talented group.' After praising the individual abilities of
Anita Landa, Marilyn Burr, Toni Lander, Jeannette Minty, John
Gilpin and Oleg Briansky, he continued: 'So far, everything fine,
but there is no dodging the dark side of the picture – those guest
artists! Tamara Toumanova made two appearances which were
hard to take seriously. The things Istvan Rabovsky did, assisted by
Nora Kovach in *Scheherazade*, and without her help in *Prince Igor*,
were similarly appalling vulgarisations. Rabovsky can also out-bow

even Toumanova. But night club specialities are, after all, night club specialities.'

Fortunately Kovach and Rabovsky couldn't read English. When I asked Mama Toumanova what she thought of Martin's review, she winked at me and said: 'You know, Julian, I never pay any attention to the critics, only to the spirit of Nijinsky.'

On the tour I estimated we made about 42,000 dollars a week, but I had no money. Hurok had paid the company's salaries and expenses, but he had not given me any accounts of the 50 per cent of the profits stipulated in the contract. We had left England confident that we would make money in America. I had spent a good deal preparing for our visit and had persuaded the bank to advance me a substantial loan to cover the cost of transporting the company three thousand miles. Other money had been raised by selling the LCC the 'fit-up' curtain which transformed the Festival Hall into a theatre.

Hurok could not be reached. I repeatedly telephoned his office asking for the accounts to be made available, and was eventually told that it might take six months or more.

I consulted an American attorney, David Holtzman. He read the contract I had with Hurok.

'Well,' he said, 'while this might stand up in English law, it is doubtful if the wording of the clause about him submitting accounts every four weeks would be binding in an American court.

'Over here, it's best if you have a band of solicitors, attorneys and everyone else in the legal business when you make a contract. I don't think there is a thing you can do about it.'

'But I haven't any money. We've made a fortune on tour and I haven't had a penny of it, apart from selling the souvenir programmes. How are we going to get back home?'

'I'll tell you a story,' he said. 'Quite recently, a world famous German soprano signed a contract with a manager here for fifty-two weeks commencing on January 1st, at a weekly salary of 1,000 dollars. At the end of the first week she received the money, but the concert had had bad notices. She was told that there were no other engagements for the present time. She protested. Under the terms of her contract, she claimed, she was entitled to a guaranteed salary every week for a year.

"Ah yes!" said the manager, "the contract states fifty-two weeks, but these weeks depend entirely on my discretion. Nowhere does it mention that those weeks would be consecutive. They might be spread over several years.'"

Holtzman and his sister, Fanny, also an attorney, helped me in every way they could and spent hours trying to solve our difficulties. They refused to accept any payment for their work. Finally they advised me to go to the American Guild of Musical Artistes, one of the American trade unions that is the equivalent of British Actors' Equity.

AGMA, after considering the contract, said the only way to combat Hurok was to cancel our week in Boston, despite the fact that all the performances had been sold out. Hurok was informed and immediately offered to pay the fares of the company back to Britain providing I would repay half this amount from our future box-office takings at the Festival Hall. This may sound outrageous, but we were stranded in America. I had absolutely no bargaining power. I reluctantly agreed to Hurok's terms. All of us were depressed to think that we had been so successful in America, but were returning to Britain to face bankruptcy.

Just before we sailed Hurok threw a party for us in the Russian Tea Room in New York. He made a complimentary speech about our success. It was received in silence.

'What's the matter with them, don't they appreciate what I've done for them,' he raged at me. 'I've made their names well known all over America and they show no gratitude at all.'

He pushed a bill into my hand showing the company's running expenses for the week in Boston. Among the large amounts for theatre hiring, publicity, etc., it listed a rather odd item – a sizeable sum for toilet paper.

We had already said goodbye to our guest artists and our two fighting Mamas.

Shortly after our return, Oleg Briansky left to partner Toumanova in South America, called by the spirit of Nijinsky. More than a year later, he returned to Festival and told me the sequel to this spiritually motivated partnership. With Mama Toumanova giving class, he rehearsed all the dances for the tour in the basement of Tamarotchka's Los Angeles home. Mama was constantly in touch with the other world about repertoire and future plans, but after the tour there were no other bookings.

Oleg found himself sitting around with nothing to do. He had had offers from Maria Tallchief, Alicia Alonso and the Marquis de Cuevas company, but turned them all down on Mama's advice. None of the engagements had supernatural approval. With no salary, Oleg told Tamarotchka that he would have to start dancing again, whatever the spirits said. Then one day. Mama arrived with excellent news, fresh from a new contact in the spirit world.

'Darryl Zanuck of 20th Century Fox, is casting *War and Peace*. He wants Tamarotchka to play Natasha and you will play Andre Wolkonsky,' she told him.

'But Zanuck doesn't even know of my existence,' replied Oleg.

Mama made the sign of the cross. 'The spirit world will make him know.'

Oleg's wife, Mireille, gave ballet classes which kept the couple going for some time and Oleg went on 'resting'. Then one day he said to Mama: 'The spirits have had a long time, if they haven't given Darryl Zanuck the message by now, they're never going to.'

When an offer came from Ruth Page to partner Markova in *The Merry Widow* in Chicago, he signed the contract. It was something that neither Mama, Tamarotchka nor the spirit world had expected. He ended his association with some very unpleasant messages coming in.

CHAPTER 13

ENTER THE GARNISHEE MAN

Festival Ballet had debts amounting to £58,000 including £11,000 still outstanding to the debenture holder who had advanced us the initial £15,000. The collapse of the company seemed inevitable. I did make an effort to raise money, but it proved to be nowhere near enough.

Vera had a very beautiful diamond ring and various other exquisite pieces of jewellery, some of which were heirlooms. Back in London, I rushed to the flat, got them all together and pawned them. The sum I raised was less than a fifth of the amount I needed.

'Julian, we've been robbed,' cried Vera when I returned home. 'Someone's been in, they've taken all my jewels and the diamond ring.'

I began laughing out of nervousness. She immediately knew who the burglar was.

'What have you done?'

'I've pawned them all.'

'How could you! You know the ring has sentimental value. How could you, Julian!' She began to cry.

'Never mind, I'll get them back sooner or later, you'll see,' I reassured her. But it was nearly a year before Vera could wear her jewellery again. By that time she had got used to the idea of the gems being in hock. They were pawned at regular intervals for years after that.

The company's creditors called a meeting with the idea of putting Festival Ballet into liquidation.

Since the company's inception in September 1949, we had earned enough money to keep our head above water, but a company cannot exist without new ballets. They are the life blood of any ballet troupe, but they need enormous amounts of cash. No other company in the world had such an extensive repertoire as ours, but the total cost of producing twenty-six ballets and innumerable pas de deux and of remaking costumes had amounted to something over £150,000. As I have already stated, well over £90,000 of this came from myself, my wife and her brothers. The balance of £58,000 was owed to our creditors.

Although I was paid a salary, there were often times when the rent of our flat was months overdue. In all my time guiding Festival Ballet's fortunes, I used whatever money I had to pay the dancers – they always got their salaries. I regularly borrowed from Shylocks and these debts, plus interest, were always repaid, usually from our Festival Hall takings. My staff got so used to this procedure they used to joke about it.

'Julian has gone to get another transfusion,' they would tell callers when I was out borrowing money. But that was the only way we could exist.

There is an extravagant waste in producing new works. The odd thing about artistic directors is that they never dare say what's wrong with a new ballet when it is in the rehearsal stage, or what can be done to put things right before it is presented to the public. Diaghilev did, and so did de Basil, but they were exceptions. Once in a theatre in Paris, I sat in the stalls near Diaghilev, watching a rehearsal of a new work by Fokine. To me it looked marvellous. When the curtain came down, Diaghilev called Fokine over and said the ballet was terrible.

'Merde,' was the word he used. 'It cannot be performed as it is,' he added, and then began discussing ways of putting it right. I never knew what became of the ballet or whether it ever appeared in another form. But today, no one has the courage to tell choreographers that their ballets are unsatisfactory. Many people may have their doubts about a new production, but what usually happens is that everyone keeps their fingers crossed and prays everything will be all right on the night. When it isn't, as with *Esmeralda* and quite a few other productions mounted for Festival Ballet, the money just goes down the drain.

I explained all this to the creditors. I met with little sympathy. Then suddenly I found myself with a persuasive and eloquent advocate. Cork Gully and Company are a firm of chartered accountants in the city and Norman Cork was at the meeting to represent one of the creditors.

'Gentlemen,' he said, 'the only assets the company have are their costumes and decor. Without the dancers, those have little value. Dr Braunsweg has explained that all the debts incurred have been for the company. He has a three-year contract with the Festival Hall and an engagement in Spain which he assures us will make money. I think we should allow Festival Ballet to continue – in that way there is some chance of us being paid.'

'But who will look after our interests?' cried one man at the table.

'My firm will,' said Cork. 'I'm prepared to provide the services of a financial adviser to try and get things straightened out. Are we all agreed?' They were.

The LCC advanced us £5,000 on our contract for the summer season and I promised to try and reduce our debts. In two years we had cut them down considerably. With Gerry Weiss as our financial adviser, prospects looked much better.

Danilova and her young South African partner, Michael Maule, joined us for our second Spanish tour. It opened at the Liceo in Barcelona. Shura had not danced in Spain for many years and had not been doing any classical work for some time. She was naturally nervous. On the Liceo stage, which has a terrifying rake, she practised and practised. At the end of her first performance, the public, nostalgic and generous, pelted her with flowers.

Krassovska could never make her entrances on time. In the second act of *Swan Lake*, when Odette flutters in to protect the swans from the bows of the huntsman, her late entrance was particularly noticeable. In realistic terms, by the time she got to the lake, there wouldn't have been a swan left alive.

Everyone told Tata, but she blamed the conductor, her partner, the corps de ballet – anyone but herself.

'You must count. Do you count?' asked Benn Toff one night.

'Yes, I count,' Tata assured him.

'Then there's no reason for you to be late. I'm coming to stand by you to listen to you counting.'

At the relevant moment in the ballet, Benn went and stood by the beautiful Swan Queen waiting in the wings to make her entrance.

'One, four, seven, nine, three two,' said Tata in her deep Russian voice, gazing around her as if she had all the time in the world. She was still late.

Danilova was very annoyed with Tata's inability to get on the stage on time. 'It isn't the maestro, Tata, it isn't your partner, it isn't the corps de ballet. You know whose fault it is? Tchaikovsky.'

Tata looked at Shura for a while and thought about it.

'I never think about him. You must be right,' she said as she went off to her dressing-room.

Returning to London, I received another adulatory letter from the Foreign Office on our great contribution to Anglo-Spanish relations – but no money.

Before our Festival Hall season, Zachary Solov choreographed a witty little ballet for Danilova to music by T. la Jarte called *Mlle Fifi*. It was a gay divertissement featuring Danilova in a delicious soubrette role with Maule and Dolin competing for her favours. Later, Russell Kerr danced Dolin's part to perfection, giving a foretaste of his success as Dr Coppelius the following year. Danilova's greatest triumph of the season was in the role she had originally created in *Le Beau Danube*. As the Street Dancer, no one could look so ravishing or shake her red skirt with so much allure.

Harald Lander had returned to the company to teach them his one-act ballet to Czerny studies, *Etudes*. This masterpiece exploits every progression in classical ballet from the first simple classroom steps to dazzling virtuoso displays of artistry. It was one of the most successful and the cheapest ballet ever produced for the company.

Among our guest artists was the ice-skating star, Belita. She had been taught by Dolin and could turn with such ferocity that the hairpins flew out of her hair like machine-gun bullets. Our other guests were the French dancers, Ludmilla Tcherina and her husband, Edmond Audran. At the gala performance, they appeared in a pas de deux to Sibelius's *Swan of Tuonela*. At the morning rehearsal, Tcherina hurt her toe and was in great pain. Before the evening performance I accompanied her to the Festival Hall restaurant.

'I need a piece of veal,' she told the chef.

'Cooked or raw, Madam?' replied the chef without blinking an eye.

'Raw, and not too much.'

She stuffed this into her point shoe and danced the pas de deux as if there was nothing wrong with her.

Margot Fonteyn and Michael Somes were our guest artists for the Monte Carlo season. Although my relationship with Fonteyn has never been easy, on this occasion everything was fine. She danced *Les Sylphides* with Gilpin and the *Sylvia* pas de deux with Somes.

I had planned to give a supper party for our Royal Ballet stars after the first performance, but I was forestalled by Fonteyn's host, Aristotle Onassis. Fonteyn was staying aboard his yacht, *Christina*, and Vera and I were invited aboard for dinner on a number of occasions. Onassis's wife, Tina, who later married the Marquis of Blandford, became a fan of the company and joined the Board of Governors in 1962.

With our regular visits to Monte Carlo, I had long cherished the ambition for the company to have two homes, one at the Festival Hall and the other at the Monte Carlo Opera House. I talked of this plan to Fonteyn, pointing out that it would cut down our travelling expenses considerably. She agreed to mention it to Onassis and see if he would be willing to help financially.

The day before our season ended, Onassis invited me to dine with him on board *Christina* to discuss the matter. I arrived at nine in the evening. The secretary showed me into one of the sumptuous state rooms and said her employer was absent but would not be long. I admired the Goya on the wall, wandered around and marvelled at the other objets d'art, and eventually fell fast asleep. I was awakened hours later by the secretary.

'Mr Onassis has been trying to telephone from Cannes and has only just got through. He asks me to explain that there has been a heavy fall of snow, and he's stranded there. He can't get back tonight and wonders whether you could come back and see him tomorrow at his office in Monte Carlo.'

In life there are moments when you have a premonition that the time is right. As I sped back to the town on the launch, I knew my moment had passed and nothing would come of my plan.

Next day, when I arrived for the meeting, Onassis had Maurice Besnard with him. He was Artistic Director of the Monte Carlo Opera House. Naturally he had little sympathy for a British ballet company using his theatre as their base. I explained my plan.

'I think it would be better if you put these proposals in writing,' said Onassis. 'I always prefer things in writing.'

I never bothered.

Years later, I met the Greek shipping millionaire in Nice when he was having strikes and staffing problems with his tanker fleets.

'I really admire the way you manage to keep your company going without a subsidy,' he said, patting me on the back. 'However, you're lucky. You've only got one enterprise to worry about. I have so many.'

Our two new productions for the Monte Carlo season were *The Gift of the Magi*, choreographed by Simon Semenoff to music by Lucas Foss, and *Les Deux Errants*, a modern work by Wolfgang Brunner to music by Bill Russo of the Stan Kenton orchestra.

I had been approached by Semenoff some months before. He reminded me that we had worked together in Paris in the twenties, when he had choreographed and danced in a Max Reinhardt production of *Die Fledermaus* at the Theatre Pigalle.

'I was called Shapiro then,' he said, 'but when I went to America, I changed my name.'

I recalled the time quite vividly. With Hoyedien Dvorski, Reinhardt had staged the most lavish production of the Strauss operetta with Lotte Lehmann, Lotte Schone and Jarville Navotna. The Theatre Pigalle was built and patronised by the Rothchilds. It had a revolve and lifts and various other modern innovations which were all put to use by Reinhardt. On the gala opening, a spectacular waltz scene was in progress with the dancers circling a revolving staircase lined with the chorus who sang beneath enormous chandeliers. At the climax of the scene a horse and carriage drove on stage to carry off the leading lady. Immediately the horse stopped centre stage, it relieved itself, spraying the orchestra and fusing the footlights. Having done more than a Reinhardt performance, the horse refused to move. The leading lady sat immobilised in the carriage, not daring to descend to the flooded stage. Amid gales of laughter the singers had to repeat their chorus again and again until the horse was lured off with lumps of sugar.

Besides being a choreographer, Semenoff was the director of a ballet school in Stamford, Connecticut. He owned the entire production of *Gift of the Magi*. He said the father of one of his 12-year-old pupils, Melinda Plank, would bring the ballet to Monte Carlo providing his daughter could dance the principal role. For old time's sake, I agreed. The premiere took place on 19 January 1956. The ballet was never seen or heard of again.

Les Deux Errants survived a little longer. It had beautiful costumes by Dan Snyder, a young American artist, but it was one of those works known within the profession as a 'dancer's ballet.' That means that only dancers are likely to appreciate it. As dancers have to entertain the public and earn their living, I think it is far better for such 'in' productions to be confined to the dance studio.

Two weeks after our return to England the marriage of Grace Kelly and Prince Rainier was announced. I returned immediately to Monte Carlo to see if Festival Ballet could take part in the wedding celebrations. The Prince was in America, so I saw his sister, Princess Antoinette. Shortly afterwards, we received an invitation to give seven performances to celebrate the occasion. The contract called for one new production which would be presented on the eve of the wedding.

The new ballet had to have an American flavour, as a compliment to the future Princess of Monaco. Dolin thought a ballet to Gershwin's *Rhapsody in Blue* might fill the bill. Remembering how many ballets had been produced to the music, I was not enthusiastic. Fortunately, Dolin could not obtain permission to use the score – the publishers, too, thought it had been done to death. Stan Kenton's orchestra was scheduled to start a tour of Britain and Benn Toff suggested Kenton would be an ideal composer. Michael Charnley was commissioned to do the choreography. The ballet was called *Homage to a Princess* and had decor and costumes by the brilliant young Frenchman, Andre Levasseur, formerly of the House of Dior. As an added attraction, Fonteyn and Somes agreed to appear with the company. I thought everything was fixed.

Suddenly the Paris Opera realised that they had been left out of what promised to be the most spectacular wedding of the decade. They brought pressure to bear on the Monegasque Government. Despite the fact that I had a contract signed and sealed, I was called again to Monte Carlo to discuss ways of including the French company in the wedding celebrations.

I suggested Yvette Chauvire should be invited to dance with us. This was regarded as too small a concession to a wedding which, after all, was a French occasion. Eventually I had to allow the Paris Opera Ballet to take part in two of the performances – the official gala at the Opera House on 18 April, and an open-air performance in the sports stadium the following day.

When Festival Ballet arrived in Monte Carlo, the French company were already in residence. On the principle that occupation is nine points of the law, they considered themselves fully in charge. Serge Lifar and Constantine Nepo had created a new ballet for the wedding, *Divertissement à la Cour*, set to music by Handel. They had already arranged the running order of the programme and in our discussions everyone became very nationalistic and tempers were lost. Knowing that Dolin was a life-long friend of Lifar, I left them to sort out the programme planning. It emerged as *Divertissement à la Cour* (Paris Opera), *Etudes* (Festival Ballet), *Homage to the Sun King* (Chauvire/Lifar), Grand pas de deux from *The Sleeping Beauty* (Fonteyn/Somes), *Homage to a Princess* (Festival Ballet).

Lifar was very much against our dancing *Etudes*. Lander had mounted it for the Paris Opera in 1952, and Lifar would have preferred the Paris Opera to dance the ballet. With Toni Lander, John Gilpin and Flemming Flindt leading our dancers, I was equally determined it would be our showpiece. We won the day.

Festival were also to dance the engagement scene from *Esmeralda* in the courtyard of the Grimaldi Palace on the evening of the wedding. This performance was to be viewed from the balcony and windows of the palace by Prince Rainier, Miss Kelly and the royal guests. We shared the stage with groups of singers and dancers from nearby villages who were paying their homage to the Prince.

For two days before the wedding it rained nonstop and was unusually cold. In the Grimaldi Palace dressing-room accommodation was non-existent. The dancers had to change in the cells of the police station and make a run for the stage. Rehearsals were chaotic. A strong wind blew away the orchestra's music, carpenters were still trying to fix up the temporary stage. It was damp and freezing. When the time came for the performance to begin, the square was so crowded you couldn't move. With Eugene Grunberg, I got stuck behind the orchestra drummer and had to stay there throughout the performance. Everyone said we looked like two Mafia leaders.

The Principality was *en fête*. Practically every building was decorated with flowers and American and Monegasque flags. All the hotels were crowded with guests and the world's press, who had descended on Monte Carlo to cover the wedding of the century. They also wanted to see the gala performance, so it was decided to give a press preview of the programme at ten o'clock in the morning.

They packed the Opera House and sat there opening and closing their briefcases, rustling through piles of itineraries and biographies of the wedding guests. The Paris Opera opened the programme with *Divertissement à la Cour*. At the end of the ballet the silence was deafening. We were to follow with *Etudes*, but the reception the journalists had given the French dancers made Festival very nervous.

'We know they're a hard-boiled lot, but this is ridiculous,' said Toni Lander.

Etudes began. I was standing at the back of the auditorium with Serge Lifar, and the company's teachers, Lubov Tchernicheva and Serge Grigorieff. As the ballet gathered momentum and the steps became faster and more difficult, I could feel the excitement in the auditorium. In the final coda, with its exhilarating jetes, fouettes, pirouettes and tours en l'air, the press did not wait for the music to end. They began to applaud and went on applauding. The company had danced the ballet marvellously, so well that Tchernicheva and Grigorieff burst into tears. I looked at Lifar. He was not only applauding but bravoing. His eye caught mine and he immediately stopped clapping.

'What am I doing?' he said, throwing his arms in the air. 'They're not my company.'

The journalists had seen enough. The publicity that resulted from the preview went round the world. London's Festival Ballet got all the praise and Prince Rainier decided *Etudes* must be screened for television. As part of the gala programme, it was seen on the Eurovision network by 20,000,000 people.

The gala was a glittering occasion. The ladies vied with each other in creations from all the Paris fashion houses. The auditorium was a blaze of jewellery and gold braided uniforms. Guests included ex-King Farouk, the Dockers, Somerset Maugham, Jean Cocteau, Hedda Hopper and Gloria Swanson. The wedding lunch the following day was attended by ladies dressed in garden party splendour and gentlemen in full dress uniform or white tie and tails.

Princess Antoinette presented me to the newly married couple.

'It was a very good performance,' said Princess Grace. 'You must have had a lot of difficulty in the courtyard. Weren't the dancers cold?' she asked. I did not tell her that they had practically frozen to death and were so cold that they could hardly move their limbs. Prince Rainier asked me to thank the company for their gift of a model stage, built by Benn Toff. Later we watched the bridal pair depart for their honeymoon on their royal yacht. Fireworks, dancing and drinking ended the evening, but most of the guests, like the bride and groom, had already left. Festival Ballet stayed on to give another eight performances at the Opera House and a peoples' performance with the French Opera Ballet in the open-air stadium below the Rock of Monaco.

Shortly after leaving Monte Carlo, Dolin and Gilpin came to see me.

'Julian, there's a young dancer who wants to join the company. He's quite good, he's been working with Joos and one or two other companies,' said Dolin.

'We don't need any dancers at the moment.'

'Yes, but he will pay you a substantial sum to have a contract,' said Dolin. From past experience, I knew that this was not a satisfactory arrangement.

'I think you should take him,' Dolin went on. 'Otherwise John and I might consider the possibility of leaving the company and starting another one, based in Monte Carlo, with the money he has to offer.' In retrospect, I realise that Dolin and Gilpin could never have established a company by themselves. But at that time, the idea of Festival without them was unthinkable. I knew I would be in great difficulty without them.

The dancer was Jean-Pierre Alban. He had been following the company around for some time. I inquired about his dancing and was assured that he was very capable. I duly gave him a contract. He gave me a cheque for £5,000. This was money provided by his sponsor who, from time to time, helped me financially in subsequent years. I refused to accept the £5,000 as a gift, and drew up an agreement for this sum to be repaid at weekly instalments of £50. He was also paid a salary.

Jean-Pierre was by no means a principal dancer. He had worked with a young French girl, Josette Clavier, and she too joined the company. With tuition his dancing improved. He spoke seven languages and had a vivid imagination, so much so that it was difficult to separate fact from fiction in the numerous stories he told about his birth and how he became a dancer. At one point he claimed to be related to Prince Bernhardt of the Netherlands and there were other royal families mentioned. After Frederick Ashton presented *Ondine*, Jean-Pierre threw a lavish party. Among those invited were principals from both Festival and the Royal Ballets as well as Ashton and other artists. As he had titled himself 'financier of Festival Ballet', everyone came. At other times he was 'manager' of the company; he had bought all the costumes and decors for the ballets. His world of make-believe knew no bounds.

It is true that with the money he loaned, I financed a new production of *Coppelia*, mounted by Harald Lander for our summer season at the Festival Hall.

For some months I had been receiving requests from Israel to present a season there. No full-scale ballet company had ever appeared in the Holy Land and I was very keen we should be the first. In Israel, no single impresario could be found to guarantee the trip financially. I took the risk and decided we should go.

In Tel Aviv, I was welcomed and given every assistance in arranging a month's season. The Director of Tel Aviv's Habimah Theatre agreed to suspend the resident company's repertoire for ten days. Bookings were made in Haifa, at two Kibbutzim near the Sea of Galilee, in Jerusalem and the Ramat-Gan stadium just outside Tel Aviv. El Al, the Israeli airline, offered to charter us two aircraft and transport the company and scenery. They generously agreed to defer payment until our box office takings began to come in.

When we touched down at Tel Aviv airport on 2 June 1956, we could not have had a more magnificent reception. Customs and immigration formalities were dispensed with, and even before we began performances everyone was thanking us for coming.

The Habimah Theatre had been decorated with garlands and British and Israeli flags. The Government were present for the opening performance as well as the British Ambassador, Sir John Nicholls. Our programme included *Napoli*, *Swan Lake* act two, the pas de deux from *Esmeralda* and *Prince Igor*.

Because so many of the youngsters were seeing ballet for the first time, we were asked to extend our season. The auditorium was packed every night with people sitting in the aisles. One day, a young man carrying a double-bass came through the stage door. He paused and looked around. This proved to be his undoing.

'What do you want?' said the door keeper.

'I'm a member of the orchestra. I've just lost my bearings.'

The door keeper, who knew most of the orchestra by sight, was suspicious.

'I don't know you.'

The man insisted he was playing for the company.

'Open your case.'

He wouldn't, so the door keeper opened it himself. It was empty. The impostor had hoped to watch the performance by posing as one of the musicians. He had tried to buy a ticket, but none were available, even on the black market.

Our farewell performance took place at the Ramat-Gan sports stadium some miles outside Tel Aviv. The arena, accommodating 18,000, was completely sold out. Under Benn Toff's direction, and in sweltering heat, the Israeli army erected a temporary stage in the centre of the stadium, but there was no possibility of using scenery.

'What we need are some cypress trees,' Benn said to the army officer in charge. In a day, towering cypresses were erected behind the stadium. The army had also provided us with an orchestra and the searchlights to light the ballets. Benn was worried. He had had no time for a lighting rehearsal.

'I've got just the man for you,' said the army officer. 'He can read music, so if you tell him what lighting you want and give him scores for the ballets, you'll find everything will be fine.'

The Jewish boy marked the scores and took his seat behind a small control console. He had never seen any of the ballets we were performing. He was only eighteen.

Just before the performance began, I noticed a large block of seats empty. I couldn't understand this. That morning hundreds of people wanting seats had been turned away.

'They were bought by the Government for officers and men of the armed forces,' explained one official. 'Earlier this evening there were reports of troop movements on the Jordanian border. The soldiers had to forgo the ballet in favour of defending their country.'

It was dusk as *Swan Lake* began. Right on cue, a full moon arose above the cypress trees. The lighting was magical. It was a perfect setting for one of the most memorable performances the company gave in Israel.

The highlight of our summer season at the Festival Hall was Lander's *Coppelia*. The French artist Jean-Denis Maillart was commissioned to provide sets and costumes. The sets were cleverly contrived to enlarge the dancing area of the Festival Hall stage, and with the ingenious use of lighting, Maillart achieved a marvellous perspective in the first and final acts of the ballet. The production was danced at the first performance by Toni Lander and Flemming Flindt. The critics missed the variation for Dawn and Prayer in the last act, but despite this, the ballet was very popular. The fundamental difference between Lander's version and productions familiar to British audiences was the predominance of character dancing and the logical development of Franz's wooing of Swanilda.

I had been popping out for lots of 'transfusions' during the season, but there was never enough money to meet all our bills. I often fell behind with my payments of royalties. This happened with Michael Charnley, although it only amounted to a few hundred pounds.

In the ballet world everyone takes a delight in telling you everything before it happens. I had been warned that Charnley was pressing for payment and that the garnishee man would be visiting me. I didn't know what a garnishee man was. It turned out to be a small, black-suited, bowler-hatted man whose full-time occupation was serving me writs. He became the terror of my life.

One day at the Festival Hall there was a knock on my office door. I opened it and there was the little man.

'Dr Braunsweg?' he inquired.

'Yes.'

'I have a garnishee for you,' he said, holding out a piece of paper.

Thinking it was a gift, I invited him in. He looked around the office and then sat down. When I looked at the paper, I saw that it was a summons for the non-payment of royalties. I quickly showed him out. Having found out what a garnishee was, I made some inquiries as to how they could be avoided. I was told that the writs had to be served personally, after their deliverer had established identity. I posted look-outs. When the cry 'The garnishee man is here' rang round the foyers of the Festival Hall, I immediately went to ground. It was not always easy.

He usually sat outside the office trying to catch me, and one night I had to sit with the lights off for nearly three hours. I daren't even smoke a cigar in case the smell of tobacco revealed my presence.

A few days later, coming into the foyer, I saw the garnishee man, paper in hand, bearing down on me. I also recognised Ivor Smith, a tall executive of the Rank Organisation, walking in another direction. I rushed up to him, propelled him into the lift and stood talking to him incomprehensibly, waiting for the doors to close. I hoped his presence would stop the garnishee man serving the writ. Fortunately, the doors closed before my pursuer reached us. The lift shot up to the fifth floor with me giving a somewhat garbled explanation of what was happening. I got out, leaving my flabber-gasted friend, tore across the top foyer to the lifts on the other side of the hall, and descended to my office.

The staff advised me to go home. When I got there, Vera said the only way for me to avoid the writ was to go to Paris for a few days. The car taking me to the airport had hardly left the house when the garnishee man rang the doorbell.

Vera answered. 'What a pity, you've just missed him,' she told the caller. 'He's gone to the Festival Hall.'

Two or three years later, I bumped into Charnley on King's Cross station. By that time, with the help of a 'transfusion', the royalties had been paid. He told me he was travelling home to Manchester to see his dying father.

'He's been declared bankrupt and the shock has ruined his health. I think it's awful when people make an old man like him bankrupt. It seems so unnecessary and humiliating,' he said.

I sympathised and wished him well.

CHAPTER 14

LANDER, LICHINE AND BENOIS

In 1957, Toni Lander was the company's prima ballerina. She and her husband, Harald had been associated with Festival for some time and had done much to improve the dancers' technical abilities and to school them in the Bournonville style of dancing. Harald Lander had been ballet master and director of the Royal Danish Ballet for nearly twenty years until a disagreement with the management ended the association. There was a good deal of ill feeling and he left Denmark to work in France and other countries. Since leaving Copenhagen, he had never worked professionally in his own country. Toni, who was twenty-six, was his second wife. She too had been trained at the Royal Danish school.

Following a short provincial tour, Festival Ballet embarked on a sixteen-week visit to Europe. At the Tivoli Garden's Concert Hall I talked to everyone who knew anything at all about backstage politics in the Danish Ballet to find out what the reaction to the Landers' return would be. I went to Aarhus to see Dame Adeline Génee, the famous Danish ballerina who became the toast of London's Empire Theatre in the early ninteen-hundreds. She still took an active interest in the ballet and presided over Britain's Royal Academy of Dancing. She was seventy-nine.

'I don't think you should worry about it,' she told me. 'A long time has passed since Harald left the country and he's achieved a fine reputation abroad. Don't worry,' she said, patting my arm. Later, I heard that she had done a great deal of mediation work in preparation for our visit and had, to a large extent, paved the way for Harald's return.

Copenhagen's Royal Theatre is the home of the Royal Danish Ballet and the home of the Bournonville tradition. The Danes might not do as many pirouettes as dancers trained in other schools, but the turns will be perfectly executed, always on the beat and finished correctly. The soft jumps and beats and the flowing, bouncy style of the dancing is achieved by constantly exploiting the plie. The virtuosity of the male dancers is renowned.

In Festival, neurosis was rife. It was inevitable that our dancers would be compared to the home team. Lander's *Etudes* was in the programme. Would it be greeted with cheers or boos? Everyone, from the principals to the corps de ballet, rehearsed continually in preparation for our opening performance. Nerves were screwed up to screaming pitch and everyone was ready to shriek, or cry hysterically if the slightest thing went wrong.

Dame Adeline, and the Danish Prime Minister, H. C. Hansen, and all the Danish dancers were at the opening performance. It began quietly, with the second act of *Nutcracker*. *Symphony for Fun* with Gilpin and Landa got a friendly reception. Then came the moment everyone was waiting for.

The curtain rose on *Etudes*, the ballet Harald Lander had created for the Danes in 1948, when it had been danced by his first wife, Margot, and Hans Brenaa, now the Royal Danish company's ballet master. Festival knew they had to be on their mettle and, as always on such occasions, gave a remarkable performance. Flemming Flindt, Toni Lander and Gilpin gave a phenomenal display of virtuoso dancing.

One of the rarest compliments that can be paid to a visiting ballet or opera company in Denmark is for the orchestra to play a C major chord fortissimo, indicating approval of the performance. As the curtain went up and down and bouquets of flowers were thrown on the stage, the orchestra played the chord three times. The cheers continued. Hans Brenaa appeared from the wings and placed a garland of flowers around Toni's neck. She promptly burst into a flood of tears. Dolin made a speech. Then Harald Lander walked hesitantly on stage. The audience rose to its feet and cheered him. He was unable to speak for a few moments and then he said how happy he was to be back home.

Lisa Boeck, Director of the Tivoli Theatre, threw a lavish supper party for the company. There were lots of speeches and lots of laughter. Then, quite unheralded, the Danish Prime Minister arrived. Giving his official approval of the Landers' return, he made a speech welcoming them back and congratulated Festival Ballet on an excellent performance.

King Frederik and Queen Ingrid came to subsequent performances and Toni was decorated with the country's highest award, the Order of Dannebrog. Later, when we were performing in Dame Adeline's home town, the university presented Toni with an Honorary Arts Degree.

The Danish visit was one of the happiest in the company's history. With Dame Adeline's help we had re-established the Landers in their own country. In doing so, Festival Ballet had won the public's affection.

After playing Germany and Holland we began our second season at the Champs-Elysees Theatre in Paris. During the course of the season, David Lichine reproduced his gay, light-hearted, bubbling ballet about cadets attending a ball at a girls' school – *Graduation Ball.*

Etudes was also scheduled for performance, but it was in the repertoire of the Paris Opera. The director refused permission for it to be danced. A last-minute intervention by the British Ambassador in Paris, Sir Gladwyn Jebb, saved the day. The critics declared our version better than the Opera House production.

In *A Bullet in the Ballet*, the company's director, Strogonoff, has one hope in life. He feels one thing would give his troupe enormous prestige – the attendance of Alexandre Benois at one of the performances. 'If Benois come' is one of the standing jokes of the book. As Benois had agreed to re-create his designs for *Graduation Ball*, it became the catch phrase of the company.

Benois' knowledge and experience date from the great days of St Petersburg's Maryinsky Theatre. It was his childhood memories that gave life to *Petrouchka* and it was he, with other talented artists and musicians, who influenced Diaghilev and were largely responsible for the Ballets Russes' artistic success. He was eighty-seven.

Although we all kept saying 'If Benois come', no one really thought he would.

Then, at the final dress rehearsal, the grand old man, wearing a little woollen hat, was there. He was interested in everything, giving advice, pointing out a slight imperfection in a costume and missing nothing. Anita Landa, Keith Beckett and a Hungarian refugee, Margit Muller, danced *Graduation Ball*. Its success with the chic Parisienne audience was tremendous. Financially we made a loss on the engagement, but this season, more than any other, established Festival as one the leading international dance companies in the world.

Krassovska, who had been guesting in America, returned for our summer season at the Festival Hall and other guests included Liane Dayde from the Paris Opera. At the annual gala on 5 September, Majorie Tallchief and George Skibine danced *Annabel Lee* and Dolin presented *Variations for Four*. Set to music by Marguerite Keogh, the ballet was a companion piece to *Pas de Quatre*, but instead of featuring ballerinas, it was danced by four male principals, Gilpin, Flindt, Godfrey and Andre Prokovsky, a talented eighteen-year-old. Prokovsky had started his training late, but had an extraordinary ability to execute the most advanced and difficult steps without any preparation. He had been trained in Paris and had won the coveted Silver Medal at the International Competition in Moscow. Dolin had taught him pas de deux which achieved perfection years later in his partnering of Galina Samtsova.

Variations for Four was choreographed to show the particular qualities of each male dancer. It was so popular that a year later, Ed Sullivan asked Dolin to allow it to be performed on his nation-wide television show. It was a rare distinction. The ballet was seen by thirty million American viewers.

When Festival celebrated its twenty-first birthday at the London Coliseum in 1971, Gilpin was unwisely persuaded by Dolin to dance his solo from the ballet. He had trouble with his leg and, having fallen out with Beryl Grey, was no longer with the company. Although his solo was somewhat of an embarrassment, he was cheered by an audience who remembered all his great performances when he was Festival's principal star.

Ever since Gerry Weiss had been appointed to watch over our finances the profits from the company had been carefully conserved. By the end of the summer season, with the help of a gift from a friend, I was able to clear our debts and wind up the United Ballet Foundation Limited, the name under which the company operated. A new company, London Festival Ballet Limited, was formed. I still found it necessary to borrow from my Shylocks and I often had to avoid the garnishee man, but this had become a way of life.

Norman McDowell, affectionately nicknamed Ruby in the dance world, was a slight, wispy dancer who, in the early days of Festival Ballet, had been in the corps de ballet. Together with Jack Carter, a talented pianist and choreographer, they had created a ballet called *Witch Boy* for a company in Holland. To music by Leonard Salzedo, the ballet was designed by McDowell, who had also danced the principal role when the work was first presented. Carter's work was unknown in Britain and he was keen to see *Witch Boy* in the repertoire of a British company. He thought it would provide an excellent dramatic role for Gilpin, but initially I was not very enthusiastic. I agreed when I found that we could get the production for as little as £1,500, which is cheap for a ballet.

The Witch Boy had its first performance at Manchester's Palace Theatre on the 27 November 1957, and was an immediate success. John Gilpin in the title role and Anita Landa as Barbara Allen were ideally suited for this dark story of lynching and mysticism.

Although *Nutcracker* had been in our repertoire since the company's inception, I had long cherished the idea of mounting a new production. When David Lichine told me he was ready to choreograph his version of the ballet, I gave him the go-ahead. I had no money at all, but convinced of the ballet's popularity, I smoked a cigar and decided to worry about the bills later.

As Benois had helped Lichine with *Graduation Ball*, we decided to ask him to design *Nutcracker*. Benois had seen the ballet at the Maryinsky Theatre when he was a child. He had also designed and produced it for three companies including La Scala, Milan. Lichine, Benn Toff and myself travelled to Paris to seek Benois' co-operation. He received us in his large studio flat in Passy and gave us tea. His companion was an enormous black cat which he carried about everywhere. The walls of his studio were hung with examples of his work, including sketches of costumes and decor and pictures of dancers in Diaghilev's company. The studio was dominated by a large concert grand. During tea our mission was hardly mentioned, but immediately the cups and plates were cleared away the old man picked up the cat, sat it on top of the piano and motioned to Lichine to stand behind him. He began to play Tchaikovsky's score.

'What's happening in your production now?' he said, speaking in Russian.

Lichine told him, and demonstrated a few steps, watched beadily by the cat.

Benois played a little more and stopped.

'What's happening now?'

Again Lichine answered.

This question-and-answer session continued throughout the entire score which Benois played beautifully from memory. Occasionally when Lichine answered, Benois shook his head and the cat waved its tail angrily. As the music continued, the head began to shake more and more. Realising that Benois was not happy with his answers, Lichine became more and more nervous about replying. When the final chord was played, Benois got up slowly and closed the piano lid. He picked up the cat and cradling it in his arms, moved to his chair.

'I cannot collaborate with you, young man. You don't know anything at all. What you envisage is not *Casse Noisette* as I know it. You have no feeling for time, or period and your conception hasn't anything to do with the magical fairy story of my childhood. I'm a very old man, but I have no time to waste. I do not wish to be associated with a production which promises to be inaccurate,' he said, his watery eyes fixed on Lichine.

The younger man could hardly hide his embarrassment.

'I've had to create the ballet from my imagination and the books

I've read. I don't know the story as well as you do and perhaps I've been influenced by some of the productions I've seen.'

Benois nodded. 'I'm afraid I cannot work with you.'

Feeling Lichine needed some help, I tried to persuade Benois to change his mind. He was adamant. This stalemate continued for nearly half an hour until Lichine said: 'Why don't you give us your idea of the story?'

Benois seemed interested.

'As well as designing the ballet, could you help us with the whole production?' said Lichine.

'I'll think it over. Give me a few days. If I decide to do it, you must promise to follow my instructions. But give me time, give me time.'

None of us were sure what his answer would be, but we left his flat relieved to think that he would at least consider the possibility of helping us.

We returned a few days later. He presented Lichine with a bar-by-bar synopsis of the story, written in his own meticulous hand.

'If you are prepared to follow my directions as I have given them here, I will design the production for you. It needs lots of magic.'

A contract was signed and Benois told us he would post the designs as soon as he had finished them. When they arrived, they were perfect in every detail, even to the most insignificant prop. Benn Toff worked out how he could transform von Stahlbaum's living room into the Land of Snow in full view of the audience. 'If Benois come' again became the catch phrase in the company. We sought his advice by telephone, sometimes as many as seven times a day, and every time he answered the queries patiently and succinctly.

We were so elated with Benois' collaboration that in the throw-away leaflet announcing the new production, we inadvertently omitted Tchaikovsky's name. This was particularly unfortunate as, for the first time since the original production in Russia, the whole score was to be used, including an extra three-bar-coda at the end of the Dance of the Sugar Plum Fairy.

Lichine had a talent for working with children. He could get them to do anything and they loved him. For *Nutcracker*, the youngsters were recruited from the Arts Educational Schools. They were rehearsed separately from the company, but two weeks before the first performance, they joined us for a dress rehearsal. It was as if they had never worked by themselves. They knew the ballet entirely, Lichine had explained it all to them. As mice, I don't think any children scampered so superbly.

I decided to give a special preview performance for the children of Dr Barnardo's Homes. On 23 December 1957, with ice-creams and chocolates on the house, the Festival Hall was packed from floor to ceiling with children. From the moment the curtains drew back to reveal the exterior of von Stahlbaum's house, I knew I had a success. Everything looked so beautiful. The only problem with the first performance was that the Christmas tree refused to grow in the transformation scene and I could hear the mechanics failing and Benn Toff's curses as he willed it to climb to the proscenium as a full-grown fir tree for the icy, sparkling splendour of the Land of Snow. When it finally did, there was a great 'aaahh' from our appreciative audience.

Benois had answered my invitation to the opening performance: 'I am too old to travel, I cannot come, I'm afraid. My cat won't let me.' Immediately backstage the catch phrase changed from 'If Benois come' to 'Benois he not come'. It was a pity. *Nutcracker*, created by Benois and Lichine, was one of the greatest successes Festival Ballet ever had. The fairy-tale ballet played to capacity audiences every time it was presented.

Doris Barry had been working as our press officer for some time. She was instrumental in organising Markova's return as our guest artist for the Theatre des Nations Festival at the Sarah Bernhardt Theatre in Paris. For the first time ever, because we were officially representing Britain, the British Council agreed to pay for our Paris-recruited orchestra. The Festival lasted four weeks. Opera, ballet and drama companies from all over the world were invited. The participants came from Peking, Stuttgart, Leipzig, Moscow, Stockholm, Italy, Canada, Korea, Morocco, Argentina, Switzerland,

Poland and the United States. Representing Britain, besides ourselves, were the Old Vic and the Glyndebourne Opera.

The Sarah Bernhardt Theatre belongs to the municipality of Paris and the first evening was a preview for the theatre directors and city officials. Our contract gave us the gross box-office takings and I was very keen that this time in Paris, we should make some money. Our programme included *Les Sylphides*, with Markova dancing the Prelude, *The Witch Boy*, which was receiving its Paris premiere, and *Graduation Ball*. Having provided a paper house for the municipality, I thought that would be an end of the complimentary tickets. Not at all.

After the premiere, I saw a long queue at the box office. Delighted that we should be attracting such good business, I mentioned it to A. M. Julien, Director of the Paris Opera, who was in charge of the Festival.

'Yes, when they come for complimentary tickets, you're a success in Paris,' he said.

'What do you mean, complimentary tickets?'

'The queue you see are mostly friends of friends. There is perhaps a city official with a mistress or boyfriend and when he or she demands complimentary tickets, it's in our interest to provide them. We only ever get such demands when a company is popular. You should be very happy.'

'But we provided them with a free performance. Isn't that enough?'

'Success is judged by the demand for comps after the preview.'

With a 1,200 seating capacity and as many as 400 tickets being provided free for every performance, I knew we would not be making any cash. I was right.

In England, *The Witch Boy* had only been presented in Manchester. As it was not to be danced in London until the following July, I invited the prominent London ballet critics to Paris for the premiere. There were thirteen of them. They stayed overnight and were invited to an excellent dinner party as guests of the company. Among them was the late A. V. Coton, whom Dolin once banned from the theatre for writing not about the ballets, but about the dancers' lives, which, it is true, are often far more interesting. Years later I took similar action with Coton's protégé, an untidy young man called Ted Mason, who always wore sandals. He wrote several uncharitable notices, and I asked him not to come to our performances. Coton intervened and Mason was allowed in. By that time, I'd decided it was better to let the critics get on with their job. An evil mention in a paper is better than no mention at all.

The critics invariably compared us to the Royal Ballet whose misguided no-star policy has ensured that none of their excellent dancers – all potential stars – are known anywhere outside London. We in Festival had to get as much publicity as possible. Everywhere we went, press coverage was imperative, as it improved our box-office takings. Festival Ballet were a company performing popular works and the dancers knew that if they did not appeal to their audiences, they would be out of work. Our audiences wanted magic and fantasy. They wanted escapism, to get away from the kitchen sink and the potato peelings, the monotonous world they lived in. That's what we tried to give them – good, enjoyable entertainment at prices they could afford.

Based in London, the critics had no appreciation of our aims or our difficulties. Festival performed an excellent service in the provinces and travelled abroad extensively, more than any other company. We had no subsidy and unlike the Royal, no permanent home. To mount new productions and maintain a high technical standard of dancing is incredibly difficult when a company is constantly touring. We managed it.

I think most ballet critics are frustrated dancers at heart. They are read by the fanatical minority of balletomanes and I do not think they have much effect on shaping the likes or dislikes of the general public. Many of our ballets such as *Vilia*, *Alice in Wonderland*, *The Snow Maiden* and *Peer Gynt* were panned by the critics. They all played to full houses at home and abroad.

For the Paris season we had been joined by Toni Lander and Flemming Flindt, who danced in *Napoli* and *Etudes*. Towards the end of *Etudes* one evening, Flindt's knee gave away and he was carried in agony to Markova's dressing room. Michael Hogan, still costumed for an earlier ballet, stepped in and danced Flindt's role for the remainder of *Etudes*.

The following day, Flindt had to be flown to London, where a specialist diagnosed torn ligaments in the knee. It was thought he might not be able to dance again. He was sent to the Orthopaedic Hospital in Aarhus, where a great healer of dancers' limbs, Professor Thomasen, operated on the knee.

In the autumn of 1959, when we were playing Copenhagen, the entire company had the pleasure of seeing Flindt dancing again in *Napoli* with the Royal Danish Ballet, and dancing better than ever. He was a very popular member of our company and when he finished his solo he was compelled to break a strict rule that existed at that time in his company, not to acknowledge applause. Our dancers clapped so hard that Flindt had to take a bow as the ballet could not continue. For committing this appalling offence, he had to buy beer for all the dancers in his company. Later, when he became Artistic Director of the Royal Danish Ballet, he ended this rule and allowed artists to take individual bows and curtain calls at the end of the performance.

CHAPTER 15

THREE GREAT GISELLES

Israel wanted to see Markova. Dolin persuaded her to accompany us on our second visit in 1958. We had been invited to take part in the country's tenth anniversary celebrations.

Arriving at Tel Aviv airport, the whole company were held up at customs. No one knew why. Markova and her sister, Doris, who had had their passports taken, sat and seethed with anger in the airport lounge. Everyone had heard of Markova, but no one had ever seen her in Israel. Apparently the officials were showing the passport of our prima ballerina around, just to prove that she was alive and well and with the company. Finally, Markova and Doris were allowed through the barrier, but Markova was told her passport had been 'mislaid'. She did get it back eventually. The Israelis regarded it as a document of historic importance. They displayed it in a private exhibition for all to see.

With Markova back, we had the Nutcracker pink carpet, 'Black Magic' and all the tiresome, temperamental outbursts that I had forgotten. In Tel Aviv, she danced two solos, *The Dying Swan* and Taglioni in *Pas de Quatre*. The audience recalled her again and again, hoping she would repeat *The Dying Swan*. She refused.

I explained to her that the public wanted to see her in something other than solo items. They wanted to see as much of her as they could.

'Why not dance *Les Sylphides*, or *Swan Lake*?' I suggested.

She refused.

At the Armond Theatre, an awful cinema in Haifa, there was one dressing-room under the stage which Benn Toff divided in two. Markova took one look at it and shrieked her disapproval and refused to appear. Up to the last moment she was refusing to go on in *The*

193

Dying Swan, but finally she began changing. A central staircase led to the dressing-room straight from the street. As Benn Toff rushed around trying to placate Markova and look after the rest of the company, two very old ladies smelling of lavender and moth balls and dressed in organza, appeared at the bottom of the stairway.

'We've come to pay our respects to Pavlova,' said one.

'She's not dancing tonight,' said Benn rather testily.

'She must be. You've advertised *The Dying Swan*. Pavlova always dances *The Dying Swan*. I met her in Paris. I was just saying to Ruth, she must be very old. I hope she remembers me. I'm eighty, and she was older than me when I saw her. I was very surprised to see she was still dancing. I find it difficult to stand.'

'It isn't Pavlova, it's Markova,' snapped Benn. 'At least, I hope she's dancing, but we can never depend on it,' said Benn, knowing that Markova must be overhearing the conversation.

'I thought she must be old. Can't depend on old dancers you know,' said the old lady, oblivious of Benn's remark.

'Could you get me her autograph?' asked the old lady's companion. 'It might be worth some money if I kept it for a while.'

'I've told you, it isn't Pavlova,' cried Benn desperately.

'If you haven't got Pavlova, how dare you advertise *The Dying Swan*. No one else can dance that solo, that's all there is to it. We will not stay if she isn't appearing.' They were still discussing Pavlova's Paris performance as they stumbled off up the stairs.

Just outside Haifa, we danced in an open-air stadium. Again the dressing-room accommodation was terrible. Again Markova threatened not to dance. She wouldn't even put her Nutcracker pink carpet down. The stadium seated 20,000 and was sold out. People were sitting in the aisles, even on the front of the stage. Markova argued with Dolin. She argued with Benn. How could a world-renowned ballerina be expected to dance on uneven boards? And the dressing-room was a disgrace.

'The corps de ballet haven't even got dressing-rooms,' said Benn. 'They're changing behind a screen.'

The lower slopes of the hills of Carmel, which overlooked the stadium, were thick with people who had come to watch the perfornance free. Other non-paying spectators included the inhabitants of the huge blocks of flats immediately outside the stadium. They brought their chairs out on the balconies to watch the ballet beneath a star-lit sky.

We removed the enthusiasts from the front of the stage and Markova – knowing full well that the evening was hers – danced *Giselle*, watched by the largest audience in the company's history.

The scene for act two of the ballet is Giselle's grave. When the cross marking the tomb was erected, many of the spectators on the balconies of the flats disappeared. I asked one of the officials why.

He laughed. 'Perhaps they feel a little guilty of watching the performance free. The flats have a large proportion of orthodox Jews. They might have felt a little easier,' he said pointing at the cross, 'if you'd put the Star of David up there.'

'The cross doesn't seem to have scared any of these away,' I said, pointing to the packed auditorium.

'No,' he said, 'They're paying, so they're staying.'

In Jerusalem, we were the first foreign company to appear in the Binyanei Ha'ooma Hall, one of the most modern theatres in Israel. We played to capacity. Then we went on to Ramat-Gan, the open-air arena where we were to give our final performance. *Giselle*, with Markova and Dolin. I don't think, in the last fifty years, that any artist in the world has received such acclaim as Markova did that night. Again and again she was recalled by name to the stage. Flowers were piled high all around her and a continuous hail of bouquets landed at her feet, finally carpeting the stage. This time she hadn't hired them. As I stood to one side, watching her, I thought that despite all the frustrating problems that surrounded Markova, it was all worth while.

Whilst in Jerusalem I was honoured by Mayor Gershom Agron at a ceremony at the Town Hall. I received the capital's emblem as a tribute to the company's participation in the tenth anniversary celebrations.

Nervi, in Northern Italy, is no joke in a heat-wave. It was here we were to premiere a new modern ballet, *Octetto*, choreographed by the Canadian dancer Paddy Stone to music arranged by Arthur Wilkinson. Stone was a choreographer from television and musicals making his debut with a classical ballet company. He worked the four couples dancing this ballet until they rebelled. I thought I would have a strike on my hands. Stone rehearsed them without rest hour after hour in a small hall, hotter than a furnace. He wanted the dancers to forget their classical training, something it is quite impossible for most dancers to do, and move in the uninhibited, free-style movement of contemporary dance.

By the time the premiere came, the dancers hated their choreographer. The ballet, however, was greeted with cheers and the enmity quickly forgotten. *Octetto* did have other problems. Everyone seemed to agree that the costumes, by Jack Notman, were not suitable and it was decided to have them redesigned by Tom Lingwood. I smoked another cigar and arranged a visit to one of my Shylocks.

At the end of the last performance in Nervi, I was honoured by the festival authorities, who presented me with a gold and onyx plaque. This award was made as a mark of appreciation of the company's outstanding success and contribution to the festival.

Markova continued as guest artist at our Festival Hall summer season, followed by Beryl Grey. She is a very tall ballerina, perhaps the only one who capitalised on her height and used it to display a superb line. But throughout her career she had difficulty finding a partner. We engaged the tall Caj Selling from Sweden. Miss Grey danced *Sylphides*, *Swan Lake*, *Giselle* and the *Don Quixote* and the Black Swan pas de deux. She was also seen in a solo called *Reverie* choreographed by her teacher, Audrey de Vos. The critics were rather cruel to Beryl. Commenting on the unfavourable notices, her husband, Dr S. G. Svenson, said to me backstage: 'Festival Ballet is the first company she's ever danced with where she's got bad notices. It must be the company.'

The life of Festival Ballet had fallen into a regular pattern. Provincial tours, European engagements and two London seasons at

he Festival Hall – *Nutcracker* at Christmas and our summer
season. My life too had fallen into a regular pattern – regular visits to
my Shylocks and the constant avoidance of the garnishee man.

The company had built up an audience in Spain and our seasons
at Barcelona's Gran Teatro de Liceo were always a great success.
On our 1959 visit, David Lichine choreographed a new work called
Vision of Chopin. Dolin was the consumptive pianist who sat at a
massive grand piano decorated with an enormous candelabra, pre-
tending to play Chopin's music. His main preoccupation during
rehearsals was to get the piano position so he could be seen to the
best possible advantage. He had lengthy discussions with the
indefatigable Benn Toff and the piano was tried in every conceivable position before Dolin was satisfied. On opening night, the
dim lighting made it impossible for Dolin to be seen at all. *Vision of
Chopin* was not the vision we all hoped it might be and after two or
three performances, the ballet was dropped from the repertoire.

Nevertheless, our season was seen by a record number of over
70,000 people. To mark this achievement, I was presented by the
Liceo management with a gold medal which now hangs on my
watch chain.

Our constant search for a typical English ballet had prompted
Dolin to persuade Noël Coward to create something lively and
British for the company. He joined us in Barcelona to begin rehear-
sals for his first and only excursion into the dance world, *London
Morning*, for which he wrote a detailed libretto and the music.

In Spain, where galas outnumber performances, Coward was
present for a gala commemorating the first appearance in the
Western world of Diaghilev's Ballets Russes.

'Where's your scenery?' he asked me after watching two pas de
deux. 'You should never play against tabs. It's so utilitarian and
without any atmosphere.'

'I can't provide scenery for galas,' I told him. 'It's impossible. I
have no money.'

He was horrified. He looked round the packed house for our
programme of ballets from the Diaghilev repertoire. 'You look so

successful, but then I should know better than anyone – the façade'
the thing.'

He, like everyone else, was startled by Serge Lifar's appearanc
in *L'Apres-midi d'un Faune*. It was the first and only time I had see
the faune with a corporation.

'Like a corpulent, rheumátic reptile on a block, my dear,' sai
the maestro.

It was customary to end gala performances with a defile in whic
the dancers were allowed to dress in their most glamorous costum
to take their bows. The dancers were all on permanent diets. Th
girls lived on steaks and salads, and when they could not affor
them, on black coffee. No one was more fastidious about keepin
slim than Jean-Pierre Alban. He hadn't eaten anything on the da
of the gala and Coward saw him just before the defile began. Jean
Pierre was dressed in a skin tight jersey, white leotard and tights
There was not a wrinkle to be seen anywhere. With stomach pulle
in to display his 19-inch waist, and cheeks sucked in to give hir
that haughty, model look, Jean-Pierre was hardly breathing.

Coward stopped in front of him and appraised the costume. 'S
pleased you've managed to slip into something loose and simple', h
said, without a flicker of a smile.

Jack Carter was the choreographer for *London Morning*. Se
outside the gates of Buckingham Palace, the ballet offered danc
opportunities for sight-seeing tourists, bowler-hatted businessmer
the traditional English policeman, a sailor on leave and, of course,
balletic changing of the guard. With decor by William Constabl
and costumes by Norman McDowell, the ballet came together ver
slowly. Coward charmed everyone and was on first-name terms wit
the dancers very quickly. His directions, however, were as detaile
and precise as those for a play and Carter found it difficult to fit step
around the libretto. Quite unused to the mad world of ballet, th
maestro began to have doubts whether the work would ever b
ready in time for its premiere.

Fortunately for me, Associated-Rediffusion, the London-base
television company, had agreed to finance the major part of th
production in exchange for their right to televise the ballet. A-I

also advertised *London Morning* prior to its presentation at the Festival Hall. RSM Brittain, the Sergeant Major with the stentorian voice who had spent a life-time terrifying officer cadets at Sandhurst, was engaged to show our 'guardsmen' how to march. It was a publicity gimmick, but it worked perfectly.

The critics were lukewarm about *London Morning*. So, the public flocked to see it. The ballet remained in the repertoire for three years and was a great success abroad.

The second half of the Festival Hall season brought three great Giselles – Markova with Vladimir Skouratoff, and Chauvire and Carla Fracci with Gilpin. Fracci was from La Scala, Milan, a frail, youthful girl whose aerial technique and wistful appearance were ideal for *Giselle*. Markova was still magnificent in the role and Chauvire was gentle and romantic, but the critics awarded Fracci the accolade. She had the touching innocence and vulnerability that were heart-breaking and brought a lump to the throat. Fracci's success in London had repercussions in Milan. She was promoted to prima ballerina.

Harald Lander created a new ballet, *Vita Eterna*. It turned out to be a non-starter. Then we went on to Dublin to premiere another catastrophe, Michael MacLiammoir's *The Enchanted Stream*. MacLiammoir worked with Dolin in the Christmas show, *Where the Rainbow Ends*. The ballet was based on Yeats's poem, 'Song of the Wandering Aengus', and MacLiammoir had designed the decor and costumes. Dolin was responsible for the choreography and the music was Debussy's *La mer*. The ballet can best be summed up in the words of the critic of the *Dublin Evening Mail*. Writing about the sets and costumes, he said: 'They are in the best vein of contemporary Irish "rural art". It cannot be said, however, that the invention and treatment of the ballet itself are likely to place this piece in the permanent repertoire.' He was right.

After touring Scandinavia and Italy, Festival made its first appearances in Yugoslavia, playing Lubljana, Zagreb and Belgrade with great success.

With the possibility of a three-month visit to South America in the offing, a tour which I had been negotiating for nearly six years, I thought the Christmas season at the Festival Hall would be an ideal time to have my troublesome gall-stones removed. I went into University College Hospital in January 1960. Being in hospital was a wonderful change for me. I just lay back in a room without a telephone. There was no need to hurry. I did not have to row with bank managers, placate temperamental artists, or hide behind pillars from the garnishee man. For the first time in my life, I had all the time in the world, and did not know what to do with it.

Edward MacLellan, who had taken care of the company's health, performed the operation. When I emerged, somewhat dreamily, from the anaesthetic, I found my wife sitting by my bedside.

'Julian, do you think you're strong enough to hear a telegram?'

I don't think I was, but imagining yet another catastrophe had befallen the company, I struggled out of my semi-consciousness and asked her to read it.

'Julian Braunsweg, under the artistic direction of Edward MacLellan. Would not fail to be great sucksess wiz publik. Love, everyone in Festival Ballet.'

'Great sucksess wiz publik' is one of several phrases I am always using. The company's spelling caught the right intonation. Arousing myself from my drug-induced torpor, I dictated a reply to Vera. 'Fantastic opening. Lost 60 stones during London Morning. Mac the Knife made deep impression. I was in stitches. Both doing well.'

CHAPTER 16

SOUTH AMERICAN SUCCESS

Festival Ballet had been negotiating a visit to South America for years. The stumbling block was the £30,000 needed to transport the company there. André Guerbilsky and his colleague Jean Clairjois were friends of mine. They had organised a number of tours to Latin America for Belgian and French companies. They arranged our tour by asking Shell and Rolls Royce, who were doing excellent business in Latin America, to join with the British Council and pay our transportation costs.

Our usual containers for scenery and costumes were too large to be loaded into the aircraft, so my secretary got the English Box Company to manufacture special fibre containers, made of the same material used for laundry boxes. Much of the scenery had to be modified and one of our major problems was of reducing the size and weight of the gates of Buckingham Palace, used in *London Morning*.

Our opening performance in Mexico City's Belles Artes Theatre was the first of any British ballet company to visit Latin America. It was a huge success and we were asked to give extra performances, not at the Belles Artes Theatre, but in the University Auditorium which seated 16,000.

In Caracas the humidity was appalling. 'There won't be any performance, Julian,' said our conductor who had been sent ahead to rehearse the orchestra.

'Is it the weather?'

'No, the musicians have not received their annual grant from the Municipality for 1960. It is still awaiting government approval, so they won't play.'

It was a Gilbertian situation, made even more bizarre by the intervention of the Mayor. He said he would willingly pay the musicians but needed the approval of the City Council. But they had no funds at all – so they could not give their approval. Knowing that this stalemate would go on *ad infinitum*, I began looking for gramophone records of the ballets we had in the repertoire. I was determined the company would perform and we would be paid by the theatre.

The British Ambassador, Sir John Walker, came up with the solution to the problem.

'Since the Mayor does not have any authority to pay the grant for 1960, he could exercise the authority he had for 1959.'

The Mayor was delighted. He promptly paid the orchestra for the first three months of 1960, and made a book-keeping entry saying he had overspent this amount in 1959. Rehearsals began, but then another problem – there were no dancers.

The company were to have made an inaugural flight from Mexico City to Caracas aboard a newly purchased DC 7. It developed an oil leak, then a military aircraft crashed on the runway, delaying the flight again. For the first and only time in Festival Ballet's history, I was compelled to cancel the opening performance.

In Caracas, the Government had built a white-elephant of a hotel called the Humbolt, perched 6,000 feet high on a mountain above the city and reached by funicular. It had been closed for some time, but it was re-opened specially for the company.

At first, the dancers were pleased to leave the humidity of Caracas, but as the cable car carried them to their hotel, they got colder and colder. From the Humbolt, nothing could be seen. The hotel was permanently enveloped in cloud. Every morning, the dancers put on their warmest clothes and then stripped as the funicular, descended to Caracas. To travel back and forth was a nuisance, so the dancers came down in the morning and stayed down. Inevitably they spent a great deal of money.

In Donizetti's *Lucia de Lammermoor*, there is a famous sextet where the six protagonists pour out their miseries. They are innumerable, and you know the singers are not happy. In the company we had three married couples. They were always pressing for more money or better conditions. The men had the ideas. Their wives did the talking. We named them the sextet from Lucia, or the Lucia Lot.

I thought the tour was going well. All the dancers were treated like visiting celebrities and invited out to a succession of luncheons, dinners, cocktail parties and receptions. They were entertained so lavishly that all of them began putting on weight. Almost overnight, the wispy spirits that frequented the moonlit glade in *Sylphide* changed into noticeably curvaceous girls and our Swans got a rounded, rotund look. The public did not notice and clapped and cheered everything.

Oxygen cylinders were needed in Caracas and Bogota. I used to see the corps de ballet and principals all inhaling the oxygen just before performances.

'Do you find it's good for you?' I asked Dianne Richards.

'Yes, marvellous for hang-overs,' she said.

One of the Lucia Lot came to see me in Caracas. 'We're going on strike unless we get more money. It's far too expensive for us to live here.'

'But you don't have to buy any food, or drink. You're always being entertained, all of you. When did you last buy a meal?'

'It's the cost of living. We need an increase in our touring allowance.'

Like Karsavina, all those years ago, the dancers saw full houses every night and were convinced that I was making a fortune. I explained the running costs and the overheads of the tour. The complainant was unconvinced.

As the Lucia Lot sowed seeds of discontent, Pamela Hart came to my defence. I overheard her at a meeting in one of the dressing-rooms.

'None of us knows or appreciates the organisation and operating costs of the company, and I do feel that we tend to take them for granted. I would like to remind you of some of the good things about Festival Ballet. We always get paid. No other company, not even the Royal Ballet with its enormous subsidies, tours abroad as much as we do. We are feted wherever we go and our tours are arranged by one man – Braunsweg. I do think we owe him some loyalty.

'The cost of living is high, but we're not spending any money on food. I think we should not press the claim. Anyway I don't want to have anything to do with it.'

Later that day, the sextet's representative said: 'You either increase our touring allowance, or we don't perform in Bogota.' I smoked another cigar and increased the allowance. The increases were covered by the sales of our souvenir programme which, I had hoped, might cover the cost of a new production.

In Lima, President Manuel Prado was so enthusiastic about the company, he told the British Ambassador that he would like to honour me for my contribution to Anglo-Peruvian relations. I tactfully suggested that Dolin was the Artistic Director of the company and I could not accept an honour unless he too received recognition for his work. British citizens cannot accept decorations without the approval of the Queen, so we had to send Her Majesty a telegram.

The investiture made me nervous. The Peruvian Foreign Minister, the British Ambassador's representative and a number of government ministers were present. We were given drinks and tiny sandwiches served on diminutive serviettes.

My name was called. As I went forward, I unconsciously tucked one of the serviettes holding a sandwich into my breast pocket. The President presented me with an enormous medal, the Commander of the Order of the Sun of Peru, the country's highest honour. Dolin was made an Officer of the Order. I thought he looked slightly green as we left the investiture. His medal was tiny.

In Santiago, the local impresario had absconded with all the box-office takings. The police and Robin Duke, the local representative of the British Council, spent days trying to trace the impresario, without success. Fortunately, in Chile the sins of the sons are laid at the door of their father. The impresario's father was a German national and the police threatened to deport him unless he repaid the missing money. He paid.

Robin Duke found himself playing impresario. He was responsible for our publicity, the hiring of an orchestra, rehearsal arrangements and a hundred and one other jobs.

At the Teatro Colon in Buenos Aires, we were invited to participate in a gala performance to commemorate the 100th anniversary of the founding of the Republic of Argentina. Three companies took part. The Marquis de Cuevas, the resident company from the Teatro Colon, and ourselves. Senor Frondisi, the President of Argentina, arranged the programme. We were to perform in the second half, after a champagne supper. Knowing that the audience's attention would not survive the champagne, I persuaded the President to restrict the interval and have the supper served after the performance.

The Marquis de Cuevas company opened with Lifar's *Noir et Blanc*. It was rapturously received. The resident company's modern work did not go well at all. Then Festival danced *Etudes*. We received a ten-minute ovation.

I was asked to allow *Etudes* to be televised. The dancers – led by the Lucia Lot – refused to perform for the TV cameras unless Equity approved. Equity said yes, providing the dancers received an extra fee. Our own budget did not run to it. The necessary cash was found by the British Embassy.

The ballet was danced before an invited audience. It included the ambassadors and diplomats from every country who maintained an embassy in Buenos Aires. Most of them were in parties of three or four, except the Israeli contingent. There were about a dozen of them, all in uniform. I supposed they must be a military mission and thought no more about it. A few weeks later Adolf Eichmann was spirited out of the country by a group of officers – the men who had watched *Etudes* – to stand trial in Israel for war crimes.

After the television programme, I was travelling to the theatre by taxi when the plump little driver asked me if I had seen 'Ballet Ingles'. I told him that I was responsible for the company being in Argentina. He stopped the cab, made me get out, and in a mixture of Spanish, French and German, gave me an enthusiastic step-by-step account of *Etudes*. He wanted to become a dancer and wondered if I would engage him. I was quite candid with him and told him he was too old, too fat and too late. When we arrived at the theatre I felt quite guilty when he refused to accept my fare.

The South American tour was a record. We had travelled 25,000 miles and presented four different programmes of bravura pas de deux and sixteen classical and modern works. In seventy-nine days we gave fifty-seven performances. On our return to London we were welcomed like conquering heroes and were deluged with telegrams of congratulations from everyone. There were best wishes from the British Commonwealth Society, the British Council, the Anglo-Argentina Society, the British-Mexican Society and the Anglo-Brazilian Society. We had done a magnificent job. We were the 'ambassadors of our country'. Fine-sounding words – but no money.

Nice was celebrating its *rattachement* with France and the creation of the Alpes-Maritimes region. Festival, together with the Marseille, Strasbourg and Nice companies, was invited to give three performances of ballets recounting the city's history. This might seem a rather costly celebration for the company – new ballets are always costly. But we had become closely identified with the Opera House in Monte Carlo, and I thought it would be an excellent goodwill gesture for us to make.

Ballets about history are invariably boring. Even the Russians cannot make them interesting. The French adore them. Usually they are static masques. They might be stupid, sentimental and unimaginative, but as long as they are well-dressed and proclaim the glory that was, or, as the French believe, still is, France – everything is permissible.

The programme opened at the Nice Opera House with the Marseille and Nice companies dancing a ballet recounting the foundation of the city by the Greeks. Festival followed with Francoise Adret's *Barbaresque*. Set to Henri Tomasis' music and dressed by Wahkevitch, the ballet recounted an incident in the early history of the city. *Catherine Segurano*, dealing with the Turks' siege of Cincaire, was performed by the Strasbourg company and we followed with Serge Lifar's *Bonaparte*, to music by Maris Thiriet and costumes by Andre Levasseur.

Bonaparte told the story of the young General's arrival in Nice in 1796. It was literally thrown together, so quickly in fact that we discovered three performances later that the fibre-glass horses on which the dancers made their entrance had no ears.

The Strasbourg company returned to dance *La Belle Epoque*, another episode in Napoleon's life, and then all four companies joined forces for the apotheosis.

After these performances, Festival danced for just over an hour in the Arenes de Cimiez outside Nice, and we were compelled to give a second performance to get our fee. The arena was packed. In the middle of *Barbaresque* it began to pour with rain. The stage became a skating rink and the dancers could hardly stand. The audience put on their plastic macs and put up their umbrellas. The orchestra were soaked but continued to play. The dancers were beginning to walk through the ballet. The audience remained. The performance stopped.

'We will not pay you,' said the manager to me. 'The programme only lasted fifty-eight minutes. You must perform at least an hour, regardless of the weather, to get the fee.'

The audience sat with umbrellas unfurled looking at an empty stage.

'We'll come back and give another performance,' I told the manager.

'Tomorrow night?'

'Tomorrow night.'

He went out into the deluge to make the announcement. The following night we got our fee.

Barbaresque was never seen again after the Nice performances. *Bonaparte* opened our 1960 summer season at the Festival Hall. It was quickly dropped.

Another more enduring acquisition was George Balanchine's *Bourree Fantasque*. I had met Balanchine in Scandinavia and asked him if he would choreograph a ballet for the company.

'I don't think your company is strong enough for a modern work, the kind of thing we dance in New York City Ballet,' he said. 'But why don't you take *Bourree Fantasque* into your repertoire? It's classical and has lots of humour. I think it would suit the company.'

Balanchine could not produce the ballet for us, so he sent his ballet mistress, Una Kai. She was pleased with the dancers and their quick response to her teaching. Set to Chabrier's music, *Bourree Fantasque* is a gentle send-up of classical ballet. It did suit the company. The critics, who for the most part dote on Balanchine, sang our praises. The public stayed away. In the provinces, no one had ever heard of the ballet. Our audiences were not sure whether to laugh at the subtle humour of the work, or regard it as a mistake. To get it accepted, it was necessary to present *Bourree* in a triple bill with popular favourites such as *Swan Lake*, *Sylphides*, *Prince Igor* or *Scheherazade*.

The summer season was enlivened by the appearance of two Hungarian guest artists, Gabriella Lakatos and Ferenc Havas, and Olga Ferri, prima ballerina of the Teatro Colon, Buenos Aires. The Hungarians danced a barbaric gypsy pas de deux and an athletic duet from the *Flames of Paris* by the Soviet choreographer, Vaganov. It was a stunning virtuoso show-piece which always got an encore. The season also included Jack Carter's *Grand pas des Fiancées*, a divertissement set to music Tchaikovsky wrote for *Swan Lake*, but omitted from the final orchestral score.

We earned some money that year from the BBC television production of *Graduation Ball*. It is difficult to film ballet for the small screen. The TV cameras often foreshorten the vision, making the sets look flat and overcrowded. Zoom lenses terrify the dancers. They are used to projecting on stage, and in close-up often appear to be gasping for their last breath. Fortunately for us, a former Royal Ballet dancer, Margaret Dale, was in charge of the production. With her special understanding of dancers' problems, the ballet was successfully transferred to the screen with all its high spirits and humour intact.

CHAPTER 17

MARKOVA ON MONDAYS

Duncan Harrison, a columnist from the *London Evening News*, telephoned me. 'I've heard John Gilpin is going to marry Sally Judd, one of the girls in your corps de ballet. Could you confirm it for me?'

I couldn't. The two dancers had been together on our South American tour, but the idea of them getting married came as something of a surprise. Gilpin was Dolin's protégé. I told Harrison that I would telephone Dolin at his villa in the South of France to see if I could get any information. Dolin told me that John and Sally were staying with him. I could tell he was quite surprised by my inquiry. I heard his asking John if he were getting married.

'Damn it, you could have let me know,' he said when John told him. The whole company were at the wedding a few months later. There was one notable exception – Dolin.

Nina Washington Stevens was a rich American lady who lived in the South of France. With her first husband, she had founded the Toledo Museum of Art. In her declining years she had retired to Monte Carlo, fallen in love with Dolin and bought him a villa near her own. He was a constant visitor, often flying from London to take care of her when she was ill. When she died, leaving him a considerable sum of money, Dolin continued to attend Gilpin's performances but showed less interest in the others. He was, however, still Artistic Director. I got quite angry with him when he once introduced me, quite absent-mindedly, as his manager. In return I played a trick on him. He had delegated the responsibility of casting the ballets to me. Every week I sent Duggie Abbot to him with the cast list, showing which artists would be dancing in the following week's programmes. Dolin gave his approval by signing his name across the sheet. When the next list was due, I included a formidable array of dance talent. If, by some magical means, the artists had even been brought together, it would have been an impresario's dream – and cost a fortune.

For *Sylphides*, I listed Pavlova, Nijinsky and Karsavina. Olga Spessittseva and Serge Lifar were to dance *Giselle*. Maria Taglioni, Carlotta Grisi, Fanny Cerrito and Lucille Grahn were scheduled to dance *The Pas de Quatre*. Other dancers such as Kchessinskaya, Lopokova, Sokolova, Baronova, Nijinska, Bolm, Massine and Woizikowsky were also scheduled to perform. Duggie took the list to Dolin. It came with his name scrawled across the bottom.

Just before the end of the season Dolin came to see me. 'I've had a very lucrative offer, Julian. I'm not going to turn it down. I've been invited by Toby Fine, the South African ballerina, to make a three-month tour of South Africa. I'm taking John and Belinda with me.'

I was appalled. With Gilpin and Wright gone, we would have to engage other dancers. We had three weeks' holiday before starting our provincial tour.

'Couldn't you do it in the holiday?' I asked.

'No.'

'But what am I to do? I can't postpone our tour to suit you.'

'That's entirely up to you.'

'We must work to earn our living. You know that. We must perform all the time, otherwise we have no money. What about the corps, the soloists, the company, what will happen to them?'

I argued and pleaded, but Dolin was adamant. He did not tell the company he was leaving, but the news quickly spread. The rumour was that without our Artistic Director and two principal dancers, Festival must be disbanded. Dolin, Gilpin and Wright left. So did Andre Prokovsky, Ben Stevenson, Anita Landa and a number of other soloists. Once they were gone an atmosphere of despondency and uncertainty descended which threatened our very existence.

I was determined we would continue. We had survived Markova's walk-out and we could survive without Dolin.

At the Royal Ballet School we engaged twenty dancers. Olga Ferri and Vladimir Skouratoff were retained as guest artists. I contacted Leon Woizikowsky, who was teaching in Warsaw. For fourteen years he had danced principal character roles with Diaghilev's company. As our Regisseur-General, he encouraged and reassured the dancers and rehearsed them for our provincial tour. It proved to be the most profitable in the company's history.

Belinda Wright returned for the *Nutcracker* Christmas season at the Festival Hall. Zsuzsa Kun from Budapest and Oleg Briansky, who had been working in America, were engaged as guest artists and the hall was filled for every performance.

The first time I met Vladimir Bourmeister, he was ill in bed in a Paris hotel. Bourmeister was the guiding spirit of the Stanislavsky and Nemirovitch-Danchenko Music Theatre in Moscow. It was an experimental theatre where Bourmeister had first attracted attention with a ballet based on Shakespeare's *The Merry Wives of Windsor*.

I had just seen his production of *Swan Lake* for the Paris Opera and was so impressed that I felt I must persuade him to do a ballet for Festival. For *Swan Lake* he had studied Tchaikovsky's original score, created new choreography for the first and fourth acts and revised the third, presenting all the divertissements as part of Von Rothbart's sorcery. In many ways, his version has become the definitive production of the ballet, copied by many companies throughout the world.

'I don't want to talk. I've got a chest complaint and I'm not feeling very well,' he said.

Ignoring his protestations, I began talking, explaining that I wanted him to do a ballet for Festival. I urged him to make some suggestions. My enthusiasm, and the fact that I was speaking his own language, made him forget his sickness. He suggested *Swan Lake* or *Sleeping Beauty*.

'I must have something new. Something Russian if possible.'

'Have you ever heard about Tchaikovsky's *Snow Maiden*?'

I could only think of the Rimsky-Korsakov opera.

'It's the same, it's the same,' cried Bourmeister, sitting up in bed.

'The plot's taken from Ostrovsky's play and tells the fairy story of the Snow Maiden. It's a lovely story. She renounces love to be safe from the rays of the sun. When she tries to live the life of a mortal, the merchant, Mizgir, falls in love with her. She returns his love. The sun melts her away. Mizgir commits suicide. It's a beautiful legend and Tchaikovsky's music is so danceable. He was the greatest composer for dancers.' He added, proudly, 'I'm a great nephew of his.'

Bourmeister had become quite excited. He was obviously keen to produce the ballet. He told me that the Kirov Ballet had presented *Snow Maiden*, but they had not used any of the original music, preferring some of Tchaikovsky's more popular pieces.

'The Bolshoi Ballet School did use the original music for a two-act production in Tchaikovsky's life-time. The score must be in the Bolshoi archives. If you can get that for me, I'll produce the ballet.'

Benn Toff was sent to Moscow to track down the missing score and negotiate contracts for Bourmeister, his wife and two Soviet artists who were to design the costumes and decor. Bourmeister, who was back in Moscow by then, introduced Benn to the Soviet officials and negotiations began. The score could not be found. The Russians talked and talked, but permission for Bourmeister and his colleagues to come to London was not given. Benn kept cabling me saying he was getting nowhere.

'Keep at it,' I cabled back.

After searching through hundreds of scores at the Bolshoi, Benn, helped by a Russian newspaper woman who wrote stories for the Western press, found the music. A few minutes before he was due to leave for London the Societ officials signed the contract for Bourmeister to produce the ballet.

In April, the Russian choreographer and his wife, Antonina Kroupenina, arrived in London to begin work. I invited them to stay with Vera and me. He was very excited to see our home, which is quite modest by any standards.

'It's a palace,' he said as he walked round. 'We live in a two-room flat, and we're privileged artists of the Soviet Union,' he said, laughing. His wife, who was devoted to her husband, did not share his enthusiasm and later, when we got to know Bourmeister well, disapproved of the comparisons he constantly made between East and West.

The score Benn Toff had found was not long enough for a three-act ballet. Bourmeister contacted Tchaikovsky's surviving relatives in Russia. They advised him what other music could be added to the existing score. The first two movements of the Symphony No. 1 in C Minor were used for act one. For act two, Francis Chagrin orchestrated from the Piano Sonata in G Major and the Invitation to the Trepak, one of Eighteen Pieces for Piano Solo, Opus 72.

The costumes and scenery were designed by Yuri Piminov and Genaddy Epishin who came to Britain shortly after the Bourmeisters. *The Snow Maiden* was the first ballet ever created for any Western company by Soviet artists.

I knew the production would be expensive. I applied to the Gulbenkian Foundation to see if they could provide us with a grant. The answer was 'No'. Our contract with the LCC stipulated that we must provide a new production every summer season. I appealed to the Council for financial help and they made a contribution. It was nowhere near enough to pay for the ballet, which cost something in the region of £15,000. So I went back to my Shylocks.

Vera and I watched Bourmeister fall in love, first with England and the company, and then with Europe. The dancers liked him. He was fifty-six, an intelligent, pleasant man with the good manners and breeding of the Russian aristocrats I had known in my youth.

We continued rehearsals for *Snow Maiden* while touring Europe. Bourmeister had never been to any of the places we visited, but his knowledge of paintings, sculpture and architecture was extensive. Arriving in a city, he knew exactly what should be seen and what works of art were on show at the local museum.

As the tour progressed, it was obvious that the costumes were not going to be ready in time for the sneak preview of *Snow Maiden* which we were to give in Florence. It was agreed that we could only present two acts of the ballet.

'I'll stage you the second act of *Swan Lake*,' said Bourmeister. 'Your version is horrible, quite horrible. You liked my Paris production. I don't want the Florentines to be disappointed. After all, they gave us Giotto's Campanile, the Baptistry doors, the Ponte Vecchio and David. We must at least try and make some gesture of appreciation.'

Bourmeister worked hard and re-produced his version of the second act of *Swan Lake*, with decor and costumes by his Russian colleagues. It was premiered in Lausanne and was very popular with the dancers and the public. I decided that if ever we staged the full four-act ballet, Bourmeister would be the man to do it.

Belinda Wright and Dianne Richards were to alternate in the title role of *Snow Maiden*. When we arrived in Florence, both dancers were ill. Bourmeister was unperturbed. He was busy wandering in and out of the museums and galleries as if he had known them all his life.

'I've read all about them. I've always wanted to visit Florence,' he told me. 'It's so marvellous to be able to tour like this, to see all the things you've always wanted to see.'

'Yes, but what about *Snow Maiden*?'

'You have a girl in the corps de ballet who will be just right for the part. She has lightness and delicacy of movement, she's a natural for the role.'

The girl was Gaye Fulton. Bourmeister worked with her and she danced in the two acts of the ballet we presented at the Florence Maggio Musicale. The part suited her. Overnight she was promoted from the corps de ballet to soloist.

Snow Maiden was a mixture of classical and character dancing. With Russian dancers, perhaps the character ensembles might have had more zest and spirit, but the ballet had a good scenario and was entertaining. When we presented it at Festival Hall, the critics did not care for it. Our audiences, however, enjoyed it. We were sold out for all performances and the ballet, later rearranged in two acts, remained in the repertoire for nearly three years.

It was time for Bourmeister and his wife to leave us. He had worked with the company for three months and was sad to go.

'You will come back,' I said to him when he and his wife were leaving for the airport. 'I'm planning for you to come back. I want you to do the whole of *Swan Lake* for us. All I need is the money. I'll get it somehow.'

He was clutching a silver tray presented to him by the company. He was crying. 'You only have to tell me when, and I'll be back. Don't forget now. I like London.' He paused and dabbed his eyes with a handkerchief. 'It would be truer to say, I love London.'

Markova was one of our six guest artists at the annual gala. She had no further engagements, and as Mondays are always bad days for ballet companies, I asked her to dance the *Dying Swan* every Monday. Her appearances drew the audiences we needed. *Swan Lake*, *Witch Boy* and *Graduation Ball* pulled in the mid-week audiences, and we played *Snow Maiden* on Friday and Saturday. This programme planning resulted in a good profit at the box office.

Our Christmas season at the Festival Hall saw the return of the prodigal son, John Gilpin. Dolin asked me if he too could return, as Artistic Director. I refused to have him back. During his year's absence, Gilpin had given hardly more than a dozen performances. He had danced with the Royal Ballet and appeared as Harlequin in Western Theatre Ballet's production of *Carnaval*. I have always regarded him as a great dancer. His speed, ballon and technique were remarkable. His style was aesthetic, rather than virile, and his line was as perfect and beautiful as many of the ballerinas he partnered. In some cases it was better.

I felt that I must try and involve him in the company's activities. He had excellent taste and I offered him the job of Artistic Director. Sensing his uncertainty, I suggested John Auld, a young Australian dancer with the company, should be his assistant.

Great dancing rarely equips anyone to run a company and Gilpin had little organising ability. He was a magnificent performer but could never visualise the artistic or box-office potential of any new work. Throughout his career with Festival, he often disappeared – sometimes for up to two weeks – regardless of whether he was scheduled to dance. These disappearances were known in the company as 'John's affairs of the heart'. We all got used to them. When he didn't turn up, his understudy went on. As Artistic

Director Gilpin failed to grasp the opportunity presented to him, but John Auld didn't. He absorbed everything he could about running the company and became an expert in programme planning.

In Vienna we premiered a new production of *Scheherazade*. In 1961, Massine was responsible for organising the Nervi Festival. He had mounted a number of productions, including *Scheherazade*. His administration proved so costly that Nervi could not afford another festival for two years. To recoup their losses, the municipality sold the *Scheherazade* costumes to me for £600. They were copied from the Bakst originals and were beautiful. But they did not fit any of our dancers.

The resident wardrobe at Vienna, staffed by a legion of workers, altered them in record time.

'How much do I owe you for the alterations?' I asked the director of the opera.

He looked surprised. 'There is no charge. That's what the wardrobe are paid to do.' It was the first time in running the company that I had ever got something for nothing. I had to have a drink and cigar to get over the shock.

When we arrived in Portugal, the Communist Party were considerate enough to publish the dates of their riots. Two of them coincided with our performances. The British Embassy advised us all to remain in our hotels. The performances were cancelled.

Former Regimental Sergeant Major Arthur Bunce was in charge of our wardrobe. He foolishly ignored the advice to remain indoors and was caught up in the demonstration in Lisbon.

In an attempt to arrest the rioters, the Portuguese police were patrolling the streets with armoured cars, spraying blue dye over the demonstrators. Bunce was covered in dye. He was arrested by the police and roughly handled. He spoke no Portuguese, did not have his passport with him and was given a hard time. The blue Bunce arrived at the hotel accompanied by two machine-gun-carrying officers who released him once he had been identified as a member of the company. The dye took some time to wear off and for quite a few days Bunce looked like one of the demons from *Walpurgis Night*.

India had just annexed the Portuguese enclave of Goa. The move was entirely contradictory to Nehru's life-long policy of non-aggression, but it was of little interest to the major Western powers. Portugal, however, interpreted Britain's disinterest as tacit approval of the invasion. Diplomatic relations between the two countries were distinctly strained.

The British Embassy in Lisbon found all its receptions being boycotted by the diplomatic representatives in the city. The diplomats feared that to patronise the parties might be taken as an indication of support for Britain. After our opening performance at Lisbon's San Carlos, the British Ambassador gave a party for the company. Every country with diplomatic representation in Lisbon attended.

Our final performance was attended by Dr Salazar, the Portuguese Prime Minister. On his suggestion, the director of the theatre presented me with a silver tray on behalf of the Government, to commemorate a successful visit.

At the quaint old Teatro Lirico in Palma de Majorca you had to shoo the chickens away from the stage door. As we had six weeks with no bookings, I was looking for engagements. Equity insisted that if we spent the time rehearsing, full salaries would have to be paid. Without any box-office takings, this was impossible. Hence the Teatro Lirico. We needed the money.

I flew to Tel Aviv to organise a third visit to Israel. On previous occasions, we had appeared for a fixed fee. This covered our expenses and made the visits financially worthwhile. On this occasion, I was obliged to accept a contract on a percentage basis – it was either that or nothing at all.

Just before we flew to Tel Aviv, Geoffrey Davidson, the Equity deputy, presented me with an ultimatum from the company. If I did not increase the salaries for our visit to Israel, the dancers would not board the plane. This demand added £1,500 to the company's operating costs. I reasoned, argued, but all to no avail. All I could do was to promise to pay the money in London, prior to the opening of our Festival Hall season.

Negotiating a contract for a fixed fee, an impresario knows

exactly how much he will receive and budgets accordingly. On a percentage basis, you are dependent on attendances and the honesty of the impresario or manager who gives you your cut. Financially the season in Israel was a disaster. We played one arena seating 25,000. When I got my percentage it seemed ludicrously small.

'How many people were there?' I asked the managing impresario.

'Only 1,500, I'm afraid.'

I did not believe him. First I consulted a solicitor, then the police. All I got were the stubs of 1,500 tickets.

In July, back in London, I had to find the £1,500 I had promised to pay the dancers. As I already owed a great deal of money to my Shylocks, it was impossible for me to borrow any more.

Vera's brother-in-law had left her a house in Israel.

'I'll sell it,' she said. 'We won't ever go and live there. We don't need it.'

The house was sold. The proceeds helped to pay the dancers' salaries.

CHAPTER 18

DON'T DEPEND ON GOD

———

The Marchioness of Blandford was chairman of the gala committee selling tickets for a performance at the Festival Hall in aid of the Royal College of Nursing. She had asked a notable millionaire London property developer to buy two tickets.

'How much are they?' he asked.

'You can give anything you like. It's a charity performance.'

'Yes, but if I were buying them for an ordinary performance, how much would they be?'

'Two guineas each.'

'I'll have two,' he said, and gave her four guineas.

Princess Margaret and Lord Snowdon were the patrons of the gala programme of *Swan Lake* act two, *Etudes* and a new ballet by Jack Carter, *Improvisations*. The programme note described it as 'A ballet for youth seeking the tenuous threads that lead to . . .'.

The critics knew exactly where – to *West Side Story*. Most of them compared the ballet somewhat unfavourably to the musical. 'Even the costumes and set looked as if they came from the touring version of the show,' said one. *Improvisations* was shelved, and replaced by that favourite old warhorse, *Scheherazade*.

At the gala I was so preoccupied with my financial problems that I made a monumental *faux pas*. Princess Margaret and Lord Snowden went back-stage to meet the company. Introducing them, I said: 'Company, I would like to introduce Princess Margaret and Lord Snow Maiden.' To my surprise, everyone laughed.

Our Festival Hall seasons were always financially successful, but with *Improvisions*, increased costs and an accumulation of debts, I had reached the end of the road. I could not raise any money to keep the company going.

You will wonder why I went on. Wouldn't it have been easier for me and my wife to let Festival Ballet go into liquidation? Why do any of us struggle at all? For money? That was never one of my accomplishments – all I ever did was lose a fortune. For success? I had kept Festival Ballet going for sixteen years altogether, fourteen without a subsidy, so there was an element of success. For self-aggrandisement? Yes, I admit to a little conceit. What I enjoyed was giving the public the kind of entertainment they wanted at prices they could afford. Festival Ballet was my life, the dancers were the family. There comes a time in your life when you cannot imagine living it in any other way. That's why Vera and I went on. Every obstacle had to be surmounted. The company was the thing, and yet when I told people I hadn't any money, they thought I was joking.

On 8 September 1962, I issued a press statement. London Festival Ballet was to go into voluntary liquidation. A new company was formed to carry on the management – London Festival Ballet Enterprises Ltd., a wholly-owned subsidiary of a non-profit-making organisation, London Festival Ballet Trust Ltd.

The Governors of the Trust were the Marchioness of Blandford, Lady Douglas of Kirtleside, the Hon. Mrs Osborn King, Mrs Terence Kennedy, Sir Frank Tait, Edward MacLellan, Harry Lee Danziger, Leonard Matthews, Mike Davis, Edward Delany and Gerry Weiss.

In this way, we avoided bankruptcy and, being non-profit-making, became eligible for financial aid from any philanthropic organisation willing to give us support. That was, of course, if we could persuade them we were worthy of it. The LCC were the first to come to our aid with a grant of £30,000. The money enabled us to settle some debts and present our usual *Nutcracker* season at the Festival Hall at Christmas. The Council emphasised, however, that they could not go on shouldering the heavy financial burden of running Festival Ballet indefinitely. They said some recognition of the company's achievements by the Arts Council was long overdue. A small grant from the Council would be sufficient in the way of official recognition and might attract financial backing from other sources. At that time, as far as ballet was concerned, the Arts Council were amateurs dabbling in a professional world. The only person on the policy-making executive committee connected with ballet was Hugh Willatt, Chairman of the Mercury Theatre Trust, the Ballet Rambert.

We applied for a grant from the Arts Council. We were refused. The Council said their existing budget could not support another ballet company – they were already maintaining the Royal and Ballet Rambert. However, they did encourage me to believe that sympathetic consideration would be given to Festival Ballet in planning the Council's budget for 1963 to 1966.

My hopes were raised. But in May, I received a letter from the Arts Council which read: 'I now have to inform you that a comprehensive assessment of our future responsibilities for this period [1963 to 1966], both in general and in the particular field of ballet, shows that we cannot afford to add a major additional ballet commitment to those which are at present in our estimates.'

At this point, the LCC came forward with the ludicrous idea that Festival Ballet should be merged with Ballet Rambert. Such an amalgamation, the Council reasoned, would enable the LCC to join forces with the Arts Council in supporting one major ballet company on a grander and more secure financial footing. I agreed to go along with this idea, although I knew it was just not feasible. Rambert were a small, dedicated troupe, presenting small-scale ballets, attempting new experimental works, and encouraging the development of dancers and choreographers. Festival had seventy dancers. We presented the classics at popular prices. The subsidy received by Rambert from the Arts Council equalled their box-office takings. The LCC grant to Festival was one-third of our box-office takings.

During the discussions that followed the LCC's suggestion, several things became crystal clear. The Arts Council were highly critical of our policy and had no interest in Festival Ballet. Their sole concern was to keep the name of Rambert alive.

When the news of the proposed merger was made known to the

press, Hugh Jenkins, at that time Assistant General Secretary of British Actors' Equity, wrote to the *Observer* saying it was

> most unwelcome news. . . . Ever since the company became non-profit-making and thus qualified itself to receive financial assistance from public funds, the LCC has been concerned, in that the Arts Council has refused to find any money at all. It becomes virtually impossible for a local authority continuously to finance a company which is constantly refused the cachet of Arts Council aid.

The Arts Council does assist the Ballet Rambert and its argument is that it cannot afford to support a third major company in addition to its existing commitments to the Royal Ballet and the Ballet Rambert. This is not a very convincing argument.

Whatever case may be made out for a monopoly elsewhere, surely everyone is opposed to it in any sphere of the arts; and to merge two disparate organisations as these two companies is impossible, except in terms of one of them disappearing. It seems that it is Festival Ballet which will go; this would be a great pity, because Festival Ballet has established its own persona and its own public.

The press were full of the possible disappearance of Festival in favour of an enlarged Ballet Rambert. I felt the Arts Council were unsympathetic to the company and particularly to myself. I had a nagging suspicion that I should never have sought the Council's aid, I felt a premonition of disaster. This premonition proved correct. The intervention of the Council in Festival's affairs eventually was to end my association with the company I had created.

Lord Robens had always taken an interest in Festival Ballet. I decided to ask his advice. With Sir Ashley Clarke, former British Ambassador to Rome, Lorraine Phillips, the company's printer, and Gerry Weiss, secretary of Festival Ballet Trust, I met the Coal Board Chief.

He listened to our problems and then gave us this advice.

'Keep them talking. You have everything to gain by keeping

the talks going on,' he said. 'The longer the discussions continue, the better it will be for you. If you present your case well, I'm sure you have a good chance of achieving success. It wouldn't be possible for Rambert to take you over – it's the mouse swallowing the elephant.'

Unfortunately, we had no chance of contributing to the discussions. They were conducted between representatives of the LCC and the Arts Council. I was never consulted, neither was Dame Marie Rambert. And of course, I was very busy – I had a ballet company to run.

Nicholas Beriosoff had told me that I should go to Basle to see a company created by Vaslav Orlikowsky, a firebrand Russian emigré from Kiev.

'He might agree to do a ballet for you. Be careful though, he has a habit of losing his temper and breaking chairs.'

Orlikowsky was in his forties, bright and lively and full of ideas. I told him I was looking for a new ballet.

'*Fountains of Bakchiserai*, that's a marvellous ballet,' he said immediately.

'Something new, perhaps Russian, but something new,' I insisted.

'Have you ever thought of *Peer Gynt* as a ballet? Good music. I've already choreographed a version for our company here and I have the score. The score won't cost you anything.'

When I was much younger, I had seen a magnificent production of the Ibsen play in Norway. As Orlikowsky outlined his idea of the story, I became quite enthusiastic.

The LCC put up £10,000 but when it was finally produced, *Peer Gynt* cost nearer £15,000. Tilly Marks, of Marks and Spencer, came to our aid with a gift of £4,000.

After a tour of Italy, Orlikowsky joined us in Torquay. There were difficulties. Orlikowsky spoke only Russian, so Vassilie Trunoff worked as his interpreter.

'*Peer Gynt*. I'm certainly not going to dance to that awful Greig music,' said John Gilpin. 'Cafe music, that's what it is.'

'No matter,' said the choreographer when he had our Artistic

Director's statement translated, 'I'll get Karl Musil to dance the title role.'

The Russian lifts Orlikowsky devised were unfamiliar and difficult. The ballet progressed very slowly and everything had to be translated, even the choreographer's screams and shouts. However, when Orlikowsky began to break a few chairs, the company did respond to his discipline.

'I want to dance Peer,' said Gilpin, after watching Karl Musil dance the leading role at the dress rehearsal.

The ballet was first presented in Monte Carlo on 13 April 1963. The decor was by Edward Delany, the costumes by Yvonne Lloyd. Marilyn Burr danced Ingrid, Irina Borowska was the Green Lady, Olga Ferri, Anitra, Irene Skorik, a guest from Paris, Solveig, and Gilpin danced Peer. The press were very complimentary.

In Rome, the ballet was to be presented at one performance – a gala at the Opera House to celebrate the opening of the capital's new Hilton Hotel. The Hilton management cancelled the evening. The Pope had died.

We were stranded. I contacted our Italian lawyers.

'How can you behave in such an undignified way at a time like this?' said one of the Hilton officials. 'In such circumstances you shouldn't go to lawyers for help, you should pray to God.'

I knew I would have to wait a long time before God got the company to its next engagement. Under threat of litigation, the Hilton gave us half our fee. The LCC sent funds to Genoa, an advance on our Festival Hall takings, and we were able to continue our European tour.

At the Festival Hall that summer we played for eight weeks. The thirty-two performances of *Peer Gynt* were sold out. The remaining programmes included *Coppelia, Scheherazade, Spectre de la Rose, Etudes, Napoli, Prince Igor, Witch Boy, Swan Lake*, Act two, and *Bourée Fantasque*.

The merger discussions dragged on and on without getting anywhere. In 1964, Robert Helpmann, the ballet representative of the Equity Council, suggested that Michael Benthall, a man with

33. *London Morning*
Schoolgirls tease the Buckingham Palace Guards.

The finale.

34.

The Snowmaiden – A desig
conference (l to r) Vladim
Bourmeister, Mme Lilynn
Oleg Briansky, Mme Bou
meister and Julian Braun
weg.

Julian Braunsweg and Anton Dolin with the Peruvian Foreign Minister afte
being invested with the Order of the Sun of Peru.

35. *Bourrée Fantasque.*

Bonaparte à Nice.

36. 13th Anniversary Gala – Front row l to r: Aubrey Bowman, Irina Borowsk
Royes Fernandez, Toni Lander, Kirsten Petersen, Milorad Miskovitch, Maril
Burr, David Adams. Extreme right: Alicia Markova, Julian Braunsweg.

Peer Gynt – Vassilie Trunoff, Marilyn Burr, Jeffrey Kovel.

37. Brussels 1963 (l to r) Marilyn Burr, Irina Borowska, Karl Musil, Julian Braunsweg, Prince of Liege, Princess Paola and Prince's ADC.

Vaslav Orlikowsky and Julian Braunsweg.

38.
John Truscott, designer of the 19 production of *Swan Lake*.

Swan Lake (Act III).

39. *Swan Lake* (Act III) – Janet Lewis as the Queen Mother wearing the production's costliest costume.

40. (l to r): Lucette Aldous, Galina Samtsova, Carmen Mathe, Irina Borowsk
Zsuzsa Kun – five ballerinas who danced the Swan Queen in the 1965 produc
tion of *Swan Lake*.

41. Galina Samtsova.

42. Irina Borowska.

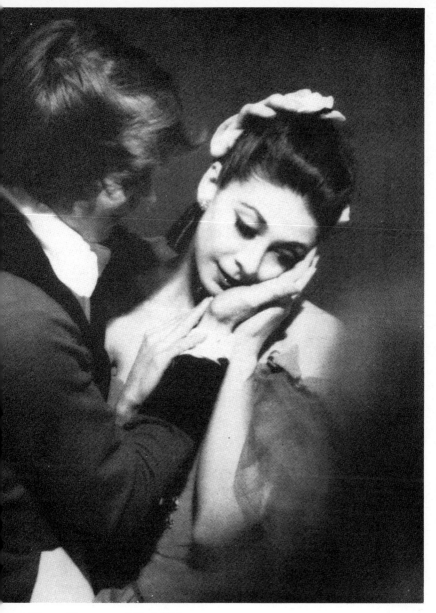

43. Margot Fonteyn and Rudolf Nureyev.

44.
John Field rehearsing
Doreen Wells.

Margot Fonteyn and
Rudolf Nureyev.

45. The Royal Ballet – *The Dream*.

The Royal Ballet – *Les Sylphides*.

46. Liliana Cosi on stage at La Scala, Milan.

Eva Evdokimova and Cyril Atanassoff.

47.
Bronislava Nijinska.

Rudolf Nureyev in *La Sylphide*.

48. Rudolf Nureyev.

considerable experience in the theatre, would make an excellent Artistic Director for the company. His appointment, Helpmann argued, might make the Arts Council more sympathetic to our needs. The salary Benthall asked was reasonable, but at that moment, not one we could afford. Helpmann thought the idea of a merger quite ridiculous, and decided it was high time for showdown with the LCC. He went to see the Council's leader, Sir Isaac Hayward.

'Do you mean you won't go on supporting Festival if the Arts Council continue to refuse to?' he asked Sir Isaac.

'The answer is the same as before,' Sir Isaac said. 'We are very willing to go on, but Festival is an important company, doing important work not only in London, but in Europe and even further afield. As a borough council, our commitment should really only be concerned with London. We think it is highly desirable for some recognition, however modest, to be given by the Arts Council.'

For the first time since the merger discussions had begun, Dame Marie Rambert and I were invited to take part. At the meeting were Sir William Fiske, Nigel Abercrombie, Secretary General of the Arts Council, Hugh Willatt, Chairman of the Mercury Theatre Trust (Ballet Rambert), William Abernethy and Victor Mischon of the LCC.

Dame Marie is an extremely energetic and dynamic person who has done more for British ballet than any other woman. She comes from my birth-place, Warsaw, and I thought that might give us a common bond – but it didn't. She had obviously been told that she was to take over Festival Ballet and presumed the meeting was a mere formality to finalise details.

'I don't want popular ballets in my repertoire,' said this very determined little person as she turned back and forth addressing the meeting. 'I don't mind enlarging my company by some thirty or more dancers. I presume, however, that if I agree, we will receive the grant Festival gets from the LCC, as well as the money we now get from the Arts Council.'

'Dame Marie, you've been deliberately misinformed,' I told her. 'When the LCC proposed the merger, they did not envisage the disappearance of Festival Ballet. I think that is the way the Arts

Council may have interpreted it, but it is entirely at variance with the original concept. You seem to have got the impression that the whole thing is a *fait accompli* – that you will be taking over my company. I assure you you won't. I'm opposed to any such merger.'

This statement brought a hail of criticism from the Arts Council representative who accused me of deliberately sabotaging the negotiations. After a good deal of acrimonious discussion the meeting broke up. Eventually it was decided to establish a committee – there's nothing like a good committee even if it doesn't accomplish anything – to consider policies, programmes and budgets of the two companies. Called The Two Ballets Trust, the idea was that it would make recommendations to the LCC and Arts Council on what grants should be made and keep an eye on expenses. This led us to believe that the Arts Council might one day favour us with a grant. They never did.

The Secretary General of the Arts Council, Nigel Abercrombie, and the Council's Musical Director, John Denison, chose Alfred Edwin Francis as the independent chairman of the Trust. Representatives of the LCC, the Arts Council, Festival Ballet and Ballet Rambert were nominated to serve on the Trust's committee.

Francis began his career as a musician – 'I played the piano and blew a few instruments,' is the way he describes it. He had helped to found the Liverpool Ballet Club in the early thirties, and knew Ninette de Valois, Sir Frederick Ashton and Dame Marie Rambert well. Francis had also worked as administrator at the Old Vic, and was on the board of Donald Albery's theatre management company, Donmar Production Limited. Abercrombie and Denison knew of his work and admired him as a capable and efficient administrator.

Shortly after his appointment, Francis realised there was no possibility of merging the two companies. There was no valid reason for The Two Ballets Trust to continue. Nevertheless it did so without holding any meetings for over a year, achieving absolutely nothing.

The LCC, now renamed the Greater London Council, had seconded one of their officials, D. G. Ball, to act as the Trust's secretary. Winding up the Trust in December 1966, and commenting on its useless existence, Ball said: 'The whole idea behind the Trust was to get closer contact between the two ballet companies, but the scheme never really got off the ground because the two managements' policies were probably incompatible.

'As it is, with the grants being made almost as they were before the Trust existed, people feel it isn't worth continuing.'

Some of the 'people' had never been asked. Members of the committee complained that they had never been consulted or informed about what was happening. They had not even attended a meeting. 'Nobody ever asked me to do anything and I was never even told whom I should contact,' said Lady Douglas of Kirtleside.

So after all the talk, Festival still received a grant from the GLC, and nothing from the Arts Council.

CHAPTER 19

SWAN LAKE
WITHOUT BOURMEISTER

———

The Festival Hall was closed for extensive rebuilding in 1963/64. I was anxious to present our usual season of *Nutcracker* somewhere in London – but where?

Tom Arnold, the impresario, was arranging for a number of Soviet dancers to appear at the Albert Hall.

'It might be possible for us to have a joint season, with them appearing with your company,' he suggested.

For many years I had been trying to persuade dancers from the Bolshoi and Kirov companies to be our guest artists. The invitations went regularly to the Soviet Minister of Culture. They were always ignored.

Arnold was presenting the Albert Hall season and Victor Hochhauser was arranging for the Russian dancers to appear in Britain. I signed a contract, but took the precaution of engaging Zsuzsa Kun and Viktor Fulop from Budapest, Doris Laine from Helsinki, Karl Musil from Vienna and Anna-Marie and David Holmes from Canada. The diminutive Lucette Aldous had joined us from the Rambert company and proved to be an excellent partner for Gilpin. Festival boasted a formidable array of talented dancers.

Hochhauser went to Moscow to conclude the arrangements. I was told that the eighteen artists would not be appearing with us, but dancing a series of divertissements as part of a complete programme.

The Soviet dancers included Natalia Makarova, who defected to the West in 1970, Marina Kondratieva, Irina Kolpakova, Svetlana Adyrkhaeva, Semenov and Maris Liepa. When the season opened, they danced their pas de deux and we presented the second act of

Nutcracker. At matinees we danced ballets from our repertoire. Orlikowsky, who was now completely accepted by the company, produced *Walpurgis Night*, setting a large cast dancing furiously. We also presented *Symphonette*, a Latin American ballet Malcolm Goddard had originally created for television.

Kolpakova and Adyrkhaeva came to see me shortly after the season began. 'Would it be possible for us to dance in *Nutcracker*?' asked Kolpakova. 'We would both like to, and I think our version would fit nicely into yours.'

I told them that that had been my original intention and I would be delighted to see them in the ballet. Both gave a number of performances partnered respectively by Aleksei Zakalinski and Vadim Budarin.

When Orlikowsky first pointed out Galina Samtsova to me at one of the company's classes, she was sitting down in practise costume and I did not like what I saw.

'Her legs are the wrong shape,' I said.

'Not when she dances. She is fantastic,' said Orlikowsky.

Trained at the Kiev Ballet School, Samtsova had married a Canadian and danced with the Canadian National Ballet. Orlikowsky had seen her and offered her the leading role in his new production of *Cinderella* in Paris. She was a great success in the ballet and later, appearing in the International Festival of Dance in the French capital, was nominated the best dancer and awarded the 'Etoile d'Or'.

She began class. As it progressed I was astounded by her extraordinary technique. She had expressive head and arms and accomplished the most difficult steps easily. She also had that wonderful Russian lyrical quality.

'You must take her into the company. She is the finest Soviet dancer outside Russia,' said Orlikowsky.

Samtsova was a modest, quiet, unassuming girl, with a pleasant sense of humour. She did not have ideally shaped legs, but Orlikowsky showed her how to use them and once in the company, she quickly moved from soloist to ballerina roles. Ultimately she became the star of Festival Ballet.

Trade Fairs were a craze of the British Government to increase exports. We were asked to provide entertainment for one being held in Barcelona and we opened a box office at our London offices. We presented *Peer Gynt*. Anton Dolin returned briefly to mount a new production of *Giselle*, and David Adams, a Canadian recruit from the Royal Ballet, choreographed *Suite No. 3* to Tchaikovsky.

In Lisbon I earned the displeasure of the Portuguese President, Dr Salazar. We had nineteen principal dancers with the company – David Adams, Lucette Aldous, Irina Borowska, Marilyn Burr, Eugene Collins, John Gilpin, Anna-Marie Holmes, David Holmes, Nora Kovach, Doris Laine, Barry McGrath, Carmen Mathe, Genia Melikova, Karl Musil, Istvan Rabovsky, Dianne Richards, Galina Samtsova, Ben Stevenson and Vassilie Trunoff. All had to appear in the farewell gala performance.

In arranging the programme, I decided the best way to display them all was to stage a number of pas de deux, demonstrating each dancer's virtuosity and style.

Anna-Marie and her husband, David Holmes, had studied with the Kirov Company in Leningrad. They were talented in a spectacular, virtuoso way and Anna-Marie could have been a great dancer with a little more discipline. As in most husband-and-wife dancing teams, David Holmes was the dominant partner. Two of their pas de deux were *Spring Waters* and *Corsair*, which they danced with all the spectacular abandon they had learned from the Kirov teachers. In the first half of the gala, watched by Dr Salazar, they danced *Spring Waters*. They were applauded and applauded. The audience would not stop. The theatre director came back-stage.

'Dr Salazar would like to see the Holmeses in the second half of the programme.'

As this would cause trouble with the other artists, I said the first thing that came into my head: 'They haven't anything else they can dance. They haven't got another pas de deux, and the programme is already running late.'

The director disappeared, only to reappear a few minutes later.

'Dr Salazar says he will see them dance *Spring Waters* again.'

I explained to the director that this would be impossible.

'I would like to please the President, but they are tired. Anyway, my life would be intolerable if I allowed them to dance again. You know all about professional jealousies, I'm sure.'

The director left. He returned a few minutes later looking very stern.

'You have earned the President's displeasure. In fact, he is very angry indeed.'

When we left, I did not get my usual silver tray.

The Holmes quickly heard of Salazar's request and were angry because I had not allowed them to repeat their pas de deux. Some months later, just before starting a provincial tour of Britain, David Holmes produced a doctor's certificate saying his wife needed a rest. We began the tour and I received a postcard from the Holmeses. They were dancing with the Kirov and were writing to reassure me that they would be returning to the company. I contacted Equity who assured me that this was a breach of contract.

The Holmeses returned, bringing with them an enormous tin of caviar which they presented ceremoniously to Vera and me. We gave a party for some members of the company. We ate the caviar. I fired the Holmeses.

With the Festival Hall still closed for the summer, I negotiated a contract for the company to appear in the Arena di Verona with a full-length production of *Swan Lake*. Orlikowsky had been chosen to mount this open-air production which had scenery and costumes by Attilio Colonnello.

The arena seated 20,000, and everything in the ballet was designed to look its best on the mammoth stage. The orchestra were supplemented with musicians from La Scala and La Fenice in Venice. They numbered 350. Orlikowsky engaged 400 extra dancers and supers for the two White Acts and the ballroom scene in Act three. His choreography was extended to enable the dancers to cover the enormous distances on stage. As there were no curtains, it was decided to reverse the stage lighting to dazzle the audience, thus concealing the scene changes. It proved very effective.

Everything was going smoothly, or as smoothly as you can

expect anything to go with a new production, when the arena management got cold feet about presenting a complete evening of ballet. It was their first attempt. To keep the opera-loving Italians happy, they decided to stage *Cavalleria Rusticana* as a curtain raiser to the four-act *Swan-Lake*.

'The audience won't stay,' I protested. 'If you begin a performance at 8.30 p.m. you cannot expect an audience to continue sitting in the open air watching ballet until two in the morning. They'll be bored, and they'll also be frozen to death.'

The management were adamant. Opera always brought in the customers in Italy, so *Cavalleria Rusticana* would bring them in. If they didn't stay for *Swan Lake*, they would have already paid for their tickets, and it didn't really matter.

On opening night, it was found that the management had oversold 2,000 un-numbered gallery seats. As the audience lit their candles to read their programmes, pandemonium broke out in the gallery. The 2,000 were looking for their seats. They were all occupied. No one rows as volubly or as effectively as the Italians and the first fifteen minutes of *Cavalleria Rusticana* were drowned in violent screams, yells, shouts and fights in the auditorium. The singers on stage stopped singing. More benches were brought in hurriedly. Everything was sorted out amicably and the performance began again.

My fears that the audience would not stay for the whole of *Swan Lake* were unjustified. The ballet was seen by over 100,000 people and the box office took 100,000,000 lire. As the Swan Queen, Samtsova attained her ballerina status, and Lucette Aldous too was acclaimed. Orlikowsky had choreographed the pas de trois for Aldous, Carmen Mathe and Alain Dubreuil. I thought Aldous would be lost on the huge stage, but in her solo, her meteoric dancing, her magnificent elevation and speedy turns proved to be one of the highlights of the evening.

The company refused to dance in Santander unless I gave them a bonus. Our long stay in Verona – four weeks' rehearsal and only five performances of *Swan Lake* – had virtually been a holiday. The journey to Santander, our next engagement, took sixteen hours, the dancers arriving early in the morning. They refused to perform the same evening unless I paid a seventh of their salaries. There were the usual telephone calls to Equity in London. I smoked a cigar, had a drink and paid out the dancers' demands.

For our fourth season in Paris we received a fixed fee of £5,000 for the week, and managed to break even.

I was quite unprepared for my reception at the Festival Hall. Mr T. E. Bean, the manager, told me that he had already accepted a booking for the Bolshoi Ballet for the 1965 summer season.

'There was a certain amount of doubt about the company's future. We could not be left without an attraction to compete with the Proms. Victor Hochhauser is presenting the Bolshoi company, but we may be able to offer you a two-week season when they finish.'

The GLC's action was extraordinary. On the one hand they were subsidising the company. On the other they were threatening our very existence by not allowing us to appear at our traditional London home – the Festival Hall.

The costs of presenting a season at the Hall are very high. It was impossible to make a profit on a two-week engagement. Bean, who appreciated the absurdity of the situation, asked Hochhauser to release the last week of his season. It was fifteen years since I had had any dealings with Hochhauser. The atmosphere was friendly and cordial when we met. He asked me if I would help him stage the Bolshoi season at the Festival Hall.

'I apologise for our past differences,' he said. 'They were rather unfortunate, but I won because I had a very clever lawyer, you know.' he joked, 'Let's forgive and forget.'

I don't carry grudges. To me every day is a new one. The ballet world is very small. It's like a merry-go-round, you work with everyone three times over if you stay in the business. Our discussions went well. His contract with the Soviet Ministry of Culture was for fifty-six dancers from the Bolshoi company, so he could not really advertise them as the Bolshoi Ballet. They would not be performing full-length works and would be appearing at the Festival Hall with little or no decor. He considered the possibility of releasing

233

another week of his season enabling Festival to play a four-week engagement.

'I'll discuss the matter with the Russians and let you know the outcome before Christmas,' he said.

I asked him to see if at the same time he could negotiate a Russian tour for Festival Ballet.

'If we could be in Russia while the Soviet dancers are over here, it would be ideal for us,' I told him.

Hochhauser had excellent connections with the Russians who are renowned for protracted negotiations. Even when they reach agreement, they invariably change their minds at the last moment.

'There's another favour I would like you to do for me. Bourmeister staged the second act of *Swan Lake* for us. I promised him that if I ever reproduced the whole ballet, I would let him do it for us. He promised to come. When you're in Moscow, could you contact him and tell him I'm planning to stage the ballet next year?'

The discussion ended with promises all round. We would get Bourmeister, a four-week season at the Festival Hall and possibly a tour of the Soviet Union. In return, we were to help Hochhauser stage his season at the Festival Hall.

Hochhauser returned from Russia, in November 1964. I tried to contact him without success. When advertisements appeared in the national press announcing the Bolshoi Ballet Company as the summer attraction at the Festival Hall, I realised that all my plans had come to nothing.

With the Festival Hall still closed, we presented our Christmas season of *Nutcracker* at the Rank Organisation's New Victoria cinema. We grossed about 20 per cent less than our customary box-office takings at the Festival Hall, but the Rank Organisation were very happy with their profit. When they told me that the company would be welcome to return any time, I negotiated a six-week summer season. They promised to redecorate the cinema, enlarge and rake the stage and install modern lighting facilities to provide a suitable theatre for ballet.

I had decided to stage a full-length version of *Swan Lake* because this classic and ballets such as *The Sleeping Beauty* are what the public want to see. Everyone wants new ballets. The critics, organisations supporting the arts, but new works that stay the course of time are rare. Modern choreographers are largely preoccupied with the miseries of life, but what gets polite applause from the ballet elite in London, will more likely be given the bird in Newcastle where audiences want to be entertained. Few of today's choreographers have any sense of humour. If they made their audiences laugh, their works would have a better chance of acceptance. Festival depended on the classics, they brought in the customers. We mounted many new works, but nothing succeeded like *Swan Lake*.

I telephoned Bourmeister in Moscow, only to be told that he could not be contacted. I went on telephoning him. He was never available. I wrote letters. They were unanswered.

Robin Duke of the British Council took me to the Soviet Embassy and introduced me to an official there. I explained that I wanted to get in touch with Bourmeister and hoped that permission would be given for him to come to London to mount *Swan Lake*. The official agreed in principle. He would contact Bourmeister. Everything would be arranged. There would be no problem. A week later I went back to the Embassy.

'Will Bourmeister be able to come?' I asked the official.

'*Niet*,' was his reply, and I could get no more out of him.

Although the Soviet authorities allowed the Bolshoi dancers to appear at the Festival Hall, I am convinced that they were still angry about Rudolf Nureyev's defection in 1961. Bourmeister's pro-Western feelings would not have gone unnoticed when he returned to Moscow. He had stated quite openly that he liked the Western way of life. The Russians were obviously afraid that he might choose to remain in the West. He remained incommunicado until the day he died.

I went to the Paris Opera, where Bourmeister's *Swan Lake* had been staged. Leonie Mail had appeared as the Queen in the ballet, and knew it well. Unfortunately she did not know it well enough to reproduce it in its entirety, although she did come to London to give us some help. The Bourmeister *Swan Lake* had never been notated. If it had there would have been no problem. Ever since that time I fully support the growing practice – particularly by the Royal Ballet – to notate and film all works.

Nureyev had just staged his version of the ballet in Vienna. I asked him to help us. David Webster, the General Administrator of Covent Garden, gave permission. Nureyev's designer, Nicholas Georgiadis, looked at the New Victoria stage and said it was quite unsuitable for his conception of the ballet. Time was running out. I was committed to stage *Swan Lake* at the New Victoria. The contract had been signed. I asked Orlikowsky to produce the ballet.

A young Australian, John Truscott, had won praise for his costumes and decor for the musical *Camelot* at Drury Lane. I asked him to design *Swan Lake* and we agreed on a budget of £20,000. Truscott had originally been an actor in Melbourne. He had assisted Kenneth Rowell on one or two productions and showed quite a flair for the job. He was asked to design *Camelot* in Australia and when Jack Hilton decided to stage the musical in London, Truscott came to Britain to redesign the show.

The British Council were sponsoring our second visit to South America. The Council insisted that we have a British ballet in the repertoire, but we could not find one. Ninette de Valois gave permission for *The Haunted Ballroom* to be mounted for the tour. I hadn't seen the de Valois ballet for over twenty years. Although it satisfied the British Council's demands, it was too old-fashioned for our South American audiences. With Aldous and Desmond Kelly dancing the roles Markova and Helpmann created, *The Haunted Ballroom* proved to be a dead duck.

Carmen Mathe had joined Festival Ballet in 1962. Born in Dundee, she had danced with the Marquis de Cuevas, American Ballet Theatre and New York City Ballet before coming to us. It was in South America she established herself as a first-class dancer. She was given the ballerina role in *Etudes* and was terrified. At the dress rehearsal she was awful, falling about and very shaky.

'You are doing very well,' I told her, knowing that the performance was going to be a disaster.

Her first night was only slightly better than the rehearsal.

'You are doing marvellously,' I said.

Each time she danced the role, she improved, and I paid her a compliment. Ten days later she was throwing off her difficult variation with all the panache and style in the world.

CHAPTER 20

HOW I LOST FESTIVAL BALLET

———

Benn Toff left the company in South America, returning to London to start work on *Swan Lake*. Orlikowsky joined us on our Swiss tour to begin rehearsals. Truscott did not begin work until April, which gave him three months before opening night.

When we returned to London in May, I went to see the designer in his Maida Vale flat.

'There is too much to do,' he told me. 'I don't think we can get the whole thing finished in time. We'll have to employ more people. That will cost more money.'

'How much?'

'It might be in the region of £26,000.'

I was worried about costs. Aware of the need for economy, Harry Lee Danziger, one of the directors of the Festival Ballet Trust, arranged for the *Swan Lake* scenery to be painted in Elstree Studios without charge. However, the Two Ballets Trust rumbled along, achieving nothing and making no contribution in the way of finance or advice. We were still entirely dependent on the generosity of the GLC, who had promised us £104,000 for 1965. Of this amount, £50,000 had already been spent.

Truscott explained that there was much more work than he had imagined. 'I don't know if we can get the extra money,' I said. 'We've already had half of our grant from the GLC and we won't be getting any more until next March.'

'If you can't, then I'm afraid I will not be able to continue the production,' he said. 'The *Swan Lake* I have conceived will look magnificent. Time is short and without more money we'll never get it done.'

I went to see Alfred Francis, Chairman of the Two Ballets Trust.

238

'I warned you he would be an expensive designer,' he said. 'But then, have you ever heard of a theatrical production that hasn't exceeded the budget? Providing it is a good production, I think the extra money must be regarded as an investment. I'll see what I can do to help.'

Truscott was told to go ahead.

Unfortunately, John Gilpin's ideas differed from those of Orlikowsky. Consequently some of the other dancers were not giving the choreographer their full support. Orlikowsky, like everyone else, was working very hard. There were displays of temperament from everyone and everybody. The number of broken chairs increased daily. My cigar and whisky consumption had reached an all-time record.

There were also disagreements between Orlikowsky and Truscott. The choreographer had arranged for entrances for some of the dances from one side of the stage; for his costumes to look their most effective, Truscott insisted the entrances should be made from the opposite side. Gilpin agreed.

'I'm the choreographer, he's the designer. He'll have to work to what I've set,' said Orlikowsky angrily.

Gilpin told Truscott not to worry – he would change the entrances.

The designer came to the theatre one day with the most magnificent, heavily embroidered gold costume for the Queen. It was so heavy that I doubted whether the dancer would be able to move in it.

'It's fantastic, but how much does something like that cost?' I asked Truscott.

'Around £500,' he replied.

Every new costume produced a drama. Several times Truscott threatened to leave. The costs soared, but, as Benn Toff put it, 'You must confess, he's a fantastic designer.'

Benn was working eighteen hours a day on the production. Two weeks before opening night he collapsed and went into hospital suffering from nervous exhaustion. Gerry Weiss, the company's financial adviser, was also away ill. Orlikowsky walked out. 'I've had enough rows. I've done my job. If anyone thinks he can do better, then they can get on with it.'

Swan Lake, as Orlikowsky produced it, was a mixture of his own choreography, Agrippina Vaganova's Leningrad production he remembered from his youth, and Bourmeister. When Orlikowsky left, some of his choreography was changed and this resulted in the disparate styles on opening night. Joyce Graeme was responsible for the mise-en-scène. For the first time in British ballet, the story of the German legend was developed logically and dramatically. As in the Russian version, a jester was the master of ceremonies in all the court scenes.

In the Prologue, behind a gauze drop, a princess was seen on the banks of the lake, gathering flowers. Von Rothbart, disguised as an owl, appeared from his lair, enveloping the girl in his powerful wings. At the same time, a white swan, with a crown on its head, appeared on the lake. This introduction added greater poignancy to the story. Throughout the ballet the dances flowed from this action, rather than being staged as divertissements.

The second act remained much as Bourmeister had choreographed it for the company in 1961, but Orlikowsky did introduce one dramatic touch. As Odette bade Siegfried farewell and bourreed backwards to resume her life under Von Rothbart's spell, a white feather fluttered from her crown, Siegfried picked it up and, in the third act ballroom scene, presented it to the beguiling Odile as a sign of his devotion.

The national dances in the ballroom scene were presented as part of the magician's magic. In the Spanish dance, for one girl and four boys, Odile replaced the girl to dazzle and mesmerise the prince.

In Act one, Truscott used gauzes which parted to reveal a vast sweep of castle wall vanishing into the distance, the foreground thronged with peasants dressed in pinks and various shades of brown. But his conception of the ballet was best in the ballroom scene, which had a marvellous perspective, with glittering chandeliers and walls hung with rich, heavy drapes of dull reds and browns creating an atmosphere of foreboding and doom. As the magician introduced each variation, the elaborately embroidered costumes were startling in their beauty and contrasted magnificently with their gloomy setting. The superb creations were paraded as in a fashion show – the heavy scarlet, fur-trimmed costumes of the Mazurka dancers, the cool greys of the Neapolitans and the dramatic purples and blacks of the Spaniards.

A great deal of money had been spent on the intricate embroidery decorating the costumes. Unfortunately, on the stage, its beautiful detail was completely lost. Truscott had stylised his lake-side trees and rocks which looked vaguely oriental. The swans wore powder-puff wigs which, I must confess, I didn't care for. But the designer's main error was in creating the production specifically for the New Victoria stage, making no allowance for touring requirements.

Samtsova and Gilpin danced on opening night with Neils Kehlet, the nimble, high-jumping spinner from the Royal Danish Ballet as the jester. This role was later danced by Max Natiez and a new recruit from Switzerland, Peter Heubi. Other Swan Queens were Irina Borowska, Zsuzsa Kun, Lucette Aldous and Carmen Mathe, while Siegfried was danced by Karl Musil, David Adams, Ben Stevenson and Bruce Marks, a guest artist from America.

Unfortunately the critics had had enough of *Swan Lake*. The Royal Ballet had just produced their fourth version of it. Though I wrote to David Webster asking him not to include it in their repertoire while we were playing the New Victoria, Covent Garden still presented it in competition with our version. At the Festival Hall, the Bolshoi were presenting the second act in badly designed costumes and with no scenery at all.

Our notices were mixed. Everyone agreed that the company had never looked so good or danced so well. Truscott's costumes and scenery came in for a good deal of praise, but some critics said the choreography was unmusical and stodgy.

A number of European and American impresarios had seen the new production. I was offered contracts for Monte Carlo and tours of America, Canada, Italy, Mexico, Scandinavia and Spain.

I had signed a contract for a month's season at the New Victoria and our houses were good. In the hope that we might recoup the cost of the production, I asked the Rank Organisation for a two-week extension. But at the end of four weeks we had no advance bookings. The Rank Organisation released me from the contract, but I still had to pay the theatre rental and the artists' salaries. Our production had been seen by 54,000 people and over £42,000 had been taken at the box-office. This amount had barely covered our overheads. *Swan Lake* had cost £40,000. That was also the extent of our debts. Before the season ended, I appealed to the GLC to help us. The Council agreed to give us half this amount if the remainder could be raised from the Arts Council or any other source. I went back to my Shylocks, without success.

On 17 August 1965, I wrote to Alfred Francis, explaining that an announcement must be made immediately about the company's future. I also gave him a list of our future bookings and financial prospects – two weeks in Torquay at a guaranteed fee of £2,500 a week; Belfast at a guaranteed fee of £6,000; the Christmas season at the Festival Hall with an estimated profit of £10,000; and finally a tour of Italy with a guaranteed contract of £20,000 profit.

Three days later, Francis replied. 'The situation in which the Festival Ballet now finds itself is so serious that everything must first depend on the decisions of the benefactors, and it is only realistic to anticipate that some of them may be hard decisions.

'Considerable efforts were made by various representatives concerned before I left London and any results should be known on my return early in September. Meanwhile, there is nothing I can usefully add.'

I was puzzled by the letter. Who were the 'benefactors' Francis referred to? I knew only of one – the GLC.

When the season at the New Victoria ended, I stood in the foyer while the company held a meeting inside the theatre at Equity's instigation. Peter Brownlee, the company manager, announced the possibility of the company being disbanded. Gilpin and Aldous suggested that Festival should be taken over by Rambert. Vassilie Trunoff got up and said that whatever happened, Braunsweg must go. There were endless discussions, but the dancers knew that nothing could be done without the agreement of the GLC.

Irina Borowska, Dianne Richards and Bruce Marks came out of the theatre. They were all in tears.

'I'm disgusted by their behaviour,' said Irina.

'It's all so unfair,' said Dianne.

Bruce Marks looked sadly at me. 'The thing that's so unfair is that not one of them, not one, had a good word to say about you, Julian.'

Three days later the newspapers carried a story. Lord Goodman, Chairman of the Arts Council, had persuaded two or three private benefactors to contribute £20,000 to match the GLC grant to save Festival Ballet from breaking up. There was one condition attached to the £20,000 – a change in the company's management – me.

My solicitor, Victor Mischcon, gave his advice.

'The GLC won't provide any more than £20,000. If you can't raise an equal amount, then the company can only be saved by Goodman's intervention.'

He could see I was upset. 'You're over sixty-five, Julian,' he went on. 'You'll be retiring soon anyway. Why do you want to go on struggling with a ballet company? Take my advice, resign. It will be much easier for you and the company will be able to continue.'

Festival Ballet without Braunsweg? A flock without a shepherd, a child without its mother! The idea was inconceivable. What angered me most of all was the way the Arts Council was proposing to take over the company.

On 26 August, the GLC discussed the company's future. I was not invited to this meeting, but I had written a long *aide-mémoire* to the Council explaining the events that had led to our financial crisis. Immediately the meeting ended, Gerry Weiss took a telephone call in my office from Sir William Hart, Clerk to the GLC. Sir William said that while the Council had every sympathy with me, the decision on Festival Ballet's future was no longer in their hands. It depended entirely on the Arts Council who said that the unnamed benefactors would withhold their £20,000 if I remained in control of the company.

It is difficult for me to piece together evidence of how the company was taken over since I was never directly involved in the negotiations. What I believe happened was that somehow it was decided that I must go. But there was no way of getting rid of me. I was the proprietor of Festival Ballet. The only way to get me out was to make my dismissal a condition of the benefactors' gift. It worked.

At that time it was stated that the benefactors wished to remain anonymous. Later, it transpired that there were not two or three benefactors. There was only one. She was Coral Samuel, President of the Union of Jewish Women and wife of the property millionaire, Basil Samuel. Coral Samuel was a devotee of opera, music and ballet, and a keen supporter of Festival. She had followed the company's fortunes since we first began and knew of the struggles we had to keep going. She thought it would be a tragedy if all the hard work that had gone into creating the company was wasted for the want of £20,000. She asked her husband to provide the money. She made the gift unconditionally – there were no strings attached.

Some time later, Lord Goodman told Benn Toff that there had to be a change of management because Festival Ballet did not produce any new works. In 1971, with grants from the GLC and Arts Council totalling £325,000, Festival mounted three 'new' ballets for their 21st birthday celebrations. They were *Petrouchka*, *Le Beau Danube* and *Giselle*. They were the first ballets I presented when Festival Ballet began in 1950.

Early in these back-stage negotiations, which I knew nothing about at the time, Alfred Francis had contacted Donald Albery, Chairman of Donmar Productions Ltd. He suggested that Albery should take over Festival Ballet. Albery was owner of Wyndham's theatres, and had launched many successful plays and musicals in the West End of London. He had managed Sadler's Wells Ballet when they made their home at his New Theatre during the war. He was a successful West End manager with a ready-made management company capable of administering Festival. But he had no experience of touring a ballet company abroad and had no connections with European managements – an important factor in the success of Festival's continental tours.

On 3 September, the press announced that Albery had been called in to save the company from financial collapse. Albery had agreed to work without a fee. He was to have a completely free hand in administering Festival Ballet and would only be accountable to Lord Goodman; the GLC were to give him £54,000 plus £40,000 to meet the company's debts and Donmar Productions were to get £20,000 in the first year of operations for managing Festival.

Albery took over one of the most renowned ballet companies in the world, with seventy dancers, a repertoire of forty ballets, including a new £40,000 production of *Swan Lake* and contracts for six months. Who could fail to succeed with such assets?

On 10 September, at a meeting at County Hall, I together with other members of the London Festival Ballet Trust, was told by Sir William Hart that we must all resign. The GLC were to pay a debt of £1,500 I had incurred on behalf of the company and I was to remain on half salary for a six months' bridging period as a consultant impresario. I might also be eligible for a pension! Above all I wanted Festival Ballet to continue. My resignation was announced. Not one dancer came to bid me good-bye.

Shortly after the County Hall meeting, Albery's accountant, Richard Blake, and a companion who was not introduced, came to our offices in Holborn and asked to see the books. I explained to Blake that our accountant, Walter Templeton, was out. He was looking for another job, I discovered later. Eventually he returned and gave Blake the books.

Vera came to the office for a few days. She always thought that food is the solution to every crisis and one morning came up from Kew with a basketful of her favourite Maid of Honour cakes. By that time, members of Albery's staff had been in and out checking various things. In the afternoon I was on the telephone talking to Andre Prokovsky when suddenly the line went dead. One of Albery's assistants explained that they were running the company now! The atmosphere in the office was tense, but eventually we were left to ourselves to pack up and leave. I gathered my personal possessions. Beatrice Meyer and Reg Cooper, my two secretaries, packed their

CHAPTER 21

CONSULTANT IMPRESARIO

London Dance Theatre was a modest company of fifteen dancers managed by Norman McDowell and Jack Carter. The company performed modern ballets and, being without any financial support had been in and out of existence for two years. However, they did have the support of the critics. At one point when the company were facing a financial crisis, as they did quite frequently, the ballet writers, led by Peter Williams who donated £100, contributed to a fund to save the company. It was a gesture unique in ballet history.

The first mistake of the new Festival Ballet was to absorb London Dance Theatre, appoint McDowell as Artistic Director, and Carter as resident choreographer. They engaged a number of LDT's dancers and bought two ballets, Carter's *Four Seasons* and Charrat's *La Repetition de Phaedre*, for Festival's repertoire.

McDowell and Carter promptly imposed LDT's policy on Festival. All Orlikowsky's ballets were abandoned. McDowell, who was also a designer, busily began redesigning the ballets while Carter began rechoreographing them. *Swan Lake* and *Nutcracker* both came in for overhauls. The *Swan Lake* costumes were stripped of their embroidery. The third act was completely redressed. The production was now muted and subdued. Truscott, who was still credited as the designer, promptly had his name removed from all posters and programmes. Poor Benois went on being credited for the *Nutcracker* costumes. He could not protest. He was dead.

The company did not respond to McDowell. He had formerly been a corps de ballet dancer with Festival and there was a feeling of uncertainty about his capacity to handle the difficult job of Artistic Director.

The contract I had negotiated for Venice called for Festival to perform Orlikowsky's *Walpurgis Night* in the La Fenice production of Gounod's *Faust*. By the time the company got there, the ballet the Fenice's impresario had seen in London no longer existed. Shortly afterward, the Adams/McDowell version of the ballet was dropped from the repertoire, together with *Four Seasons* and *La Repetition de Phaedre*.

As 'consultant impresario', I sat at home, twiddling my thumbs and did not hear from anyone until one day in November, when Donald Albery telephoned to invite me to lunch.

'I haven't been able to get any bookings for next spring and wondered if you would be willing to help?'

I told him I would consider it.

'Don't,' said Vera. 'Forget them.'

'You've got to help,' said Gerry Weiss who was still helping the company himself. 'They've got no contracts at all. If they don't get a European tour they may have to close down.'

Running the company for so long, I knew the operating costs backwards. Working to my old budgets I obtained contracts for a five-and-a-half week tour of Spain and Portugal. With Vera, I went to Venice to tell Albery of the plans I had made. I found the company's strength had grown from seventy dancers to ninety. Revolution was in the air. Some of the dancers seemed to want McDowell to leave the company.

Anton Dolin was in Venice at the same time.

'You must come and see Peggy Guggenheim's Museum,' he said. 'She's a great friend of mine and she's got the most fabulous collection of modern pictures.'

Irina Borowska, Karl Musil, Vera and I were entertained to tea by the millionairess at her grand palazzo. After being given a catalogue we toured the galleries hung with paintings by such artists as Picasso, Max Ernst, Salvador Dali, Miro, Robert Delaunay, Chirico, Paolozzi, Kokoschka and Francis Bacon.

'I must autograph your catalogues,' said Mrs Guggenheim as we were leaving. She wrote a suitable message in each one.

The doorman moved forward.

'That will be two thousand lire.'

'What for?' I asked.

'The catalogue, sir.'

I was so surprised, I paid. Irina Borowska and Karl Musil did the same.

'I'm certainly not paying,' said Dolin as he walked out.

Festival Ballet received generous fees for the tour I arranged for them in Spain and Portugal. With ninety dancers, whose salaries and touring allowances had been increased, and the transportation costs, there was no profit.

Albery said: 'I'd like you to act as the company's impresario for future engagements abroad.'

'Sorry,' I said, 'I can't sell the company to European impresarios any more. You don't have a policy. Your running costs are high. How can you make a profit?'

I had been approached by three ballet companies to arrange tours for them in Europe. I chose to promote Orlikowsky's Vienna State Opera Ballet in Italy and Spain during July and August of 1966.

This company, completely different in style and repertoire to London's Festival Ballet, was after sixteen years with my own company a novelty for me. The Vienna company had two excellent Balanchine ballets in the touring repertoire – *Serenade* and *The Four Temperaments*. These works together with their typically Viennese ballets – in particular Orlikowsky's Donauwalzer, which he choreographed to celebrate the 100th anniversary of the first performance of Strauss' Blue Danube waltz – made for two interesting and contrasting programmes.

The discontent in the company continued. McDowell was replaced as Artistic Director by Carter. Later, Albery took over the job. Albery thought Carter's new three-act romantic ballet, *La Jolie Fille de Gand*, would parallel the Royal Ballet's superb and successful *La Fille Mal Gardée*. It didn't, even with its title changed to *Beatrix* so as not to alienate a public presumably unacquainted with French.

Carter used only three of the company's twelve principal dancers and this caused problems with the dancers. Some of them left, including Lucette Aldous who joined the Royal Ballet. The scenery and costumes for *Beatrix* were designed by Henry Bardon and David Walker, who thought in terms of presentation at the Festival Hall. Without extensive alteration and rebuilding, the production could not be toured. After a few performances in the provinces, *Beatrix* vanished, never to be seen again.

However, there were many good old ballets added to the repertoire. Lifar's *Noir et Blanc* proved a spectacular showpiece. A divertissement from Petipa's *Paquita* made a fine setting for Samtsova. The company also performed Balanchine's romantic and enduring *Night Shadow* and John Taras' *Design with Strings*.

At the end of 1967, a new Festival Ballet Trust was formed to supervise the finances and future plans of the company. Sir Max Raine was appointed Chairman, with Sir Louis Gluckstein, W. L. Abernethy and Leslie Freeman representing the GLC, and Nigel Abercrombie, John Cruft and David Reynolds – a former corps de ballet dancer with Festival Ballet – representing the Arts Council. Other Governors were Lord Fiske, the Hon. John Sainsbury, Gerry Weiss, Alfred Francis, Beryl Grey, Laurence Harbottle and Humphrey Burton.

Albery demanded that his grant for the forthcoming year be increased to £240,000. The Trust formed a sub-committee to consider this request. Albery never met the members of the sub-committee. He did, however, meet the Trust on 18 March 1968. Immediately afterwards he resigned. In a press statement, Albery said that he had no time for committees. 'Before, I was directly responsible to the authorities and when I had to deal with only Lord Goodman or the head of the GLC, I could get a quick answer and expeditious decisions. Now I have to do a lot of committee work that does not get us any further.'

From September 1965 to September 1967, the GLC and the Arts

Council had given Festival Ballet over £500,000. At the end of 1967, the company had a deficit of £181,000.

CHAPTER 22

FONTEYN, NUREYEV AND THE ROYAL BALLET

———

I began juggling again. I arranged for Orlikowsky's Vienna State Opera Ballet to tour Spain and Italy for six weeks. It was the company's first venture outside their own country for ten years. As we were leaving Madrid, Leon Ura, the Spanish Government's Festival Director, congratulated me on the company. 'Who are you bringing next year?' he asked.

'What about the Royal Ballet?' I joked.

'We'd have the Royal Ballet. But only with Nureyev and Fonteyn.'

The Royal Ballet's touring company were free. David Webster, the General Administrator of Covent Garden, was keen for them to visit Portugal where they had not appeared for twelve years. I had always cornered the Portuguese market for Festival Ballet.

The Portuguese impresario Constantino Varela-Cid of Lisbon's Teatro Nacional de San Carlos came to London for discussions. There was one major obstacle. Webster could not pay the travelling expenses for the eighty members of the company to visit Lisbon and return to London. I suggested that he should pay the fares one way. Once the company were in Lisbon I would arrange a two-month tour of European Festivals in Spain, Italy, France and Switzerland and then bring them back to London.

The touring company had been built and developed by John Field, a former principal of the Sadler's Wells Ballet. Zest, youth and enthusiasm were its main characteristics. The company performed ballets from the Covent Garden repertoire and had works specially commissioned for them. The dancers, drawn largely from the Royal Ballet School, spent their lives constantly touring the provinces, usually giving one season at Covent Garden every year. Despite their youth, they were a troupe of hardy professionals and maintained a high artistic standard.

Doreen Wells, Lucette Aldous, Elizabeth Anderton and Shirley Grahame were among the company's ballerinas, while David Wall was the young white hope of the Royal Ballet. Two of the outstanding character dancers were Ronald Emblen and Johaar Mosaval. The ballet master was my old friend from *A Bullet in the Ballet*, Henry Legerton.

Nureyev and Fonteyn agreed to dance as guest artists with the company and I began six months of hectic negotiations with festival managements all over Europe.

Fonteyn's technique has never been her greatest asset but she has distilled her art and in her dancing the virtuoso passages are secondary to her characterisation. Her face and ability to project emotion have been her fortune. At the age of forty-nine she was past her prime. Her performances varied but – she *is* a star. Audiences watching her suspend their critical faculties. They have heard of the great ballerina and are convinced that they are witnessing a great performance. Fonteyn's reputation is sacrosanct. Making a partner of the youthful Rudolf Nureyev has ensured that her reign as prima ballerina at Covent Garden will continue for as long as she chooses. Her name is world famous. Coupled with Nureyev's it can fill any theatre in the world. The two stars are an impresario's delight. Nevertheless, Fonteyn is a shrewd businesswoman and my negotiations with her, although, friendly, have never been easy.

Many years ago, Ernest Fleischman, a South African impresario, came to see Festival Ballet in London.

'I'd like to take the company to South Africa. But what I'd like even better would be Fonteyn as guest artist. Is there any chance of that being arranged?'

Fonteyn had danced with us a number of times. Yes, she would be delighted to visit South Africa with the company. I introduced the impresario to Fonteyn and heard no more. Fonteyn could not be reached, she was on holiday. I got a letter from Fleischman.

Fonteyn had been engaged for South Africa – without Festival Ballet.

The Dutch National Ballet were appearing in Zurich. I was asked to persuade Nureyev and Fonteyn to dance one performance of *Giselle* with the company. I arranged the deal with Nureyev, who said he would talk to Fonteyn.

In the meantime, the Opernhaus in Zurich prematurely advertised the programme. The performance was immediately sold out. Fonteyn said she could not possibly dance that night as she had television commitments. Noelle Pontois of the Paris Opera agreed to substitute. I sent her the contract. She found she was expecting a baby. The Dutch company was annoyed. I went back to Fonteyn and offered to increase her fee from 1,600 dollars for a single performance to 2,500 dollars and she agreed to dance for me.

On the European tour not I but the festival authorities in the country where they performed would be responsible for paying Nureyev and Fonteyn. Dollars are always the favoured currency in international dance negotiations – they are easily convertible. Of the forty-nine scheduled performances, Nureyev and Fonteyn were to appear in thirty-five.

Before the tour began there were arguments about the repertoire. Fonteyn wanted to dance one ballet, Nureyev didn't. Fonteyn changed her mind. Nureyev changed his. The festival managements became hysterical. They were constantly having to change their advertisements. The repertoire was finally decided. It included Peter Wright's new production of *Giselle*, Nureyev's *Raymonda*, Act two, Alfred Rodrigues' *Blood Wedding*, and Sir Frederick Ashton's *The Dream*, *Monotones* and *Marguerite and Armand*, the *La Dame aux Camelias* ballet he had created specially for Fonteyn and Nureyev.

The two conductors for the touring company were Yuval Zaliouk and Stewart Kershaw. Fonteyn demanded a third conductor for her performances – Ashley Lawrence, who had worked with the touring company before joining the Berlin State Opera. Lawrence has great expertise and an even greater understanding of dancers' problems and has become acknowledged as one of the finest ballet conductors in the Western world. But his engagement as conductor for Nureyev and Fonteyn performances did not endear him to his colleagues. They rehearsed the orchestra and thought it unfair for them not to conduct the star performances as well. Kershaw was particularly angry about it and at one point threatened to leave.

The tour opened in Bordeaux in the middle of the French revolution, 1968 vintage, the student riots. The performances were cancelled and the dancers confined to their hotels.

Blood Wedding is an excellent ballet based on Garcia Lorca's play, *Bodas de Sangre*. Years before, it had been performed in Spain by the Sadler's Wells Theatre Ballet and had been a resounding flop. The ballet is a dramatic tale of love, passion and symbolism. But the way Rodrigues, a South African, had interpreted the Spanish story was unacceptable to the Spaniards. No one had thought to tell me this at the Opera House.

In Lisbon the programmes were a resounding success – a success which continued throughout the tour. The exception was *Blood Wedding*. It was given the bird. John Field thought it might get a similar reception in Spain. He replaced it with Kenneth MacMillan's *Concerto*.

Lorca was born in Granada. He was killed by design or misunderstanding by the Franco regime in 1936. Granada regarded the playright as their hero and insisted that *Blood Wedding* had been promised, *Blood Wedding* had been advertised and *Blood Wedding* would be performed. There were two days of exasperating telephone calls. The Granada management were adamant and I could not persuade them otherwise. By a fortunate chance one of the lorries carrying scenery and costumes from France to Spain was in a collision with another vehicle. I successfully appealed to Granada to be magnanimous and accept *Concerto* as the *Blood Wedding* costumes had been damaged beyond repair.

Nureyev had once been duped by an impresario who did not pay him his salary. Naturally he was on his guard. He and Fonteyn insisted that before each performance, I pay their secretary, Joan Thring, their fees in dollars. After ten performances the artists became slightly more confident and Joan failed to appear. I had to sleep in great discomfort with bundles of dollars stuffed beneath my pillow.

Marguerite and Armand is one of those lush romantic ballets which Ashton does so well. He created the role of the consumptive courtesan for Fonteyn, who looks ravishing in her Cecil Beaton costumes. As the passionate Armand, Nureyev has all the intensity and devotion required for the role. Fonteyn decided the ballet was unsuitable for open-air performances. There were arguments.

'If it's included in the repertoire, I will leave the tour,' she threatened. The ballet was replaced by *Les Sylphides*.

Used to touring, the company's young dancers adapted to every changing situation, overcame every difficulty and were really marvellous. But just before they were to fly from Oporto to Granada, Nureyev came to see me. 'I don't like flying charter. It makes me nervous. I get very worried when people walk up and down the aisle and they always do when everyone knows one another. Margot and I don't like travelling with the company.'

Joan Thring said that she would accompany the two dancers on a scheduled flight to Lisbon and then hire a three-seater biplane to fly them to a military airfield in Granada. I objected to her demand for £140 to hire the plane.

'You'd better let Margot do what she likes . . .'

I paid the money and smoked a cigar.

Their journey to Granada turned out to be a nightmare. When the trio arrived in Lisbon, the pilot for their midget plane could not be found. Eventually they persuaded someone to fly them to Seville and then had to make an exhausting seven-hour drive to Granada by road. For the rest of the tour they insisted on travelling by scheduled airlines. There was one exception when the Bolivian tin millionaire, Antenor Patino, flew them in his private jet from Amsterdam to Geneva. He wanted them there on time – they were guests of honour at a party he was giving.

The Royal Ballet opened in Granada. For the newsmen it was an occasion to be exploited and the photographers were anxious to take as many pictures as possible – particularly of Nureyev and

Fonteyn. The two dancers declined to have a photo-call during their rehearsals for *Giselle*. In order to placate the angry photographers, facilities were provided for them to take pictures during the performance from the orchestra pit. There was one condition. No flash-bulbs were to be used.

Giselle began. Don Carlos, the Pretender to the Spanish Throne, Princess Sophia, his wife, the British Ambassador and the Spanish nobility from Madrid were in the packed auditorium. The photographers began taking pictures.

Half-way through the first act, Fonteyn stopped dancing and stormed down to the orchestra pit. Staring angrily at the photographers, who with professional aplomb continued to take pictures, she shouted: 'Get out. I will not go on with the performance unless you leave. You are not supposed to be taking pictures.' As she was speaking in English and they were Spanish, they had no idea what she was saying.

I was amazed at Fonteyn's behaviour. In the ballet everything can go wrong. The scenery can fall down – it did in Spain; holes can appear in the stage – they did in Lyons; dancers can fall flat on their bottoms – they did in Spain; but the show must go on. When Fonteyn was dancing *Sleeping Beauty* at the New Theatre in London during the war, a bomb fell quite close to the theatre just as she made her entrance as Aurora. The explosion was shattering but she continued to dance. The frightened audience, taking heart from her courage, remained to watch her.

Nureyev walked down to the photographers and gave them a piece of his mind. If the Spaniards had understood him they would have lynched him. The embarrassed corps de ballet quietly left the stage while the stars continued to argue. Officials asked the photographers to leave.

'Start from the waltz,' Nureyev called, as he and Fonteyn moved back to their positions. The orchestra struck up, the corps de ballet made their entrance and the performance continued.

However, Fonteyn had made a major mistake. She had stepped out of her character of the gentle, vulnerable, peasant maid who dies for love. The make-believe spell, so essential in ballet, had been broken. With all her artistry, it was impossible for her to re-establish the characterisation for the audience. The next day, she, Nureyev and the company were attacked by the press. The story of Fonteyn's temperamental behaviour made front-page news in London and New York.

To try and combat the prejudice gathering momentum against the Royal Ballet, John Field called a press conference. A smiling Fonteyn explained that she did not approve of unposed ballet pictures as they invariably showed a leg, arm or foot out of position. Aesthetically they were not pleasing or flattering. She was right, but she had antagonised the press and they did not deal kindly with her.

Reporters were everywhere, looking for a scandal. When one cornered me in the hotel lobby I couldn't decide what to say. Should I tell the truth and say how appalled I was by Fonteyn's behaviour? Should I pretend I didn't understand the language? Or just say I had nothing at all to do with it? However, all the reporter said was: 'I'd like to talk to you about your job as impresario, Dr Braunsweg, if you can spare me a few minutes.' I talked to him and I got an excellent press.

The stars' temperamental behaviour continued. The lighting was bad, the scenery was wrong, the hotels were awful. All reporters and photographers were banned.

In Nervi I paid dearly for the Royal Ballet's lack of co-operation with the festival management who, naturally enough, wanted to publicise the company and the two stars. Photo-calls were not allowed. A suggestion that two minutes of *Giselle* should be televised for news purposes was flatly rejected. And by the time John Field finally relented, the photographers and television crew had disappeared.

'We are deducting a million lire from your fee, Dr Braunsweg,' said Mario Porcile, the representative for the festival when I went to collect the company's pay.

'But why?'

'You have shown a distinct lack of co-operation. You refused to allow the photographers in and refused to have a few minutes of

Giselle televised. Generally, we feel that the company has been unco-operative.'

I had every sympathy with Signor Porcile, but my sympathies were not worth a million lire. I beat him down to 500,000.

In Monte Carlo, the company gave three performances. The agent, Youly Algaroff, booked Nureyev and Fonteyn for the first and last performance and Nureyev by himself for the second. I warned Algaroff that people would obviously come to see two stars rather than one, but he said he couldn't afford the fees.

'The house is half empty,' Nureyev said to me before the curtain went up on his performance.

'Do you know the difference between a pessimist and an optimist?' I asked him.

'What?'

'A pessimist says the theatre is half empty. The optimist, like me, always says the house is half full.'

There was one delightful interlude. After one of the Monte Carlo performances, Nureyev invited the whole company to his villa high on the Grand Corniche. He and Fonteyn were host and hostess at a lavish party, which was regarded as one of the highlights of the tour.

But trouble was not confined to the stars. The conductors had never been happy with the arrangements for the tour and Stewart Kershaw's discontent erupted in Amsterdam, where he had gone ahead to rehearse the orchestra in readiness for a Fonteyn performance. The hotel into which the company had been booked (and which accommodates all visiting ballet companies) was considered reasonable. Kershaw did not agree. He sent a strongly worded telegram to John Field saying it was a terrible place and that the company should find somewhere else to stay. Unfortunately he gave the telegram to the head porter at the hotel to despatch.

When I arrived, the irate manager was waiting in the foyer.

'How dare a member of your company describe my hotel as cheap and shoddy,' he shouted at me. 'I demand an apology now or you can all get out straight away.'

Some of the dancers, convinced that the name of the hotel sounded like a youth hostel, had already cancelled their reservations. I apologised profusely to the manager and explained that it was all due to artistic temperament and that there was a lot of it about. Hotel accommodation was a recurring problem. When the company left London, reservations had been made throughout the tour for twenty-nine double rooms and fifteen singles. Whether the scandals, the heat or artistic temperament affected the dancers I'll never know. But by the time we got to Spain, my representative there, Felicitas Keller, was having to travel ahead of the company to change the reservations to seventeen doubles and twenty-seven singles.

In Madrid, the Festivales de Espana reserved the right to televise thirty minutes of *Giselle* for their news programme. An agreement had been reached with John Tooley, Assistant General Administrator at Covent Garden. I would pay the corps de ballet, and Nureyev and Fonteyn would give their services free.

Fonteyn looked at the packed auditorium at the open-air Chopera del Parque del Retiro and said she could not dance unless she were paid an extra fee for the television screening. There were frantic telephone calls to Tooley in London, who pointed out that Fonteyn had already agreed. Meanwhile, John Field told Doreen Wells to be ready to replace Fonteyn. The situation was resolved by the television camera team not appearing. They had been called out to cover an appearance by General Franco. I thanked God for Franco.

Nureyev was being a shade difficult too and John Field was getting the backwash of temperamental displays which culminated in a scandal after a performance of *The Dream*. Nureyev, who was dancing Oberon, made a late entrance and collided mid-air with Johaar Mosaval, who was dancing Puck. Mosaval lay on the stage completely winded. Being a trouper, he staggered to his feet and tried to continue the performance.

After curtain calls, Field momentarily lost his sang-froid and in true, bluff, Yorkshire fashion, took Nureyev to task in front of the whole company.

'It's one thing for you to keep making detrimental remarks about the company, but it's quite another thing to try to kill one of our dancers. If you don't like us then you can go. We've got other dancers who dance just as well as you do. I'm fed up with all these tantrums.'

Throughout the tour in Spain we were accompanied by Manuel Castellanos, from the Festivales de Espana. We called him Our Man from the Ministry. He overheard the row.

'But he can't go. It would be a catastrophe. We would have to cancel the performances.'

'It's just a display of artistic temperament,' I reassured him.

Nureyev stayed and the displays of artistic temperament continued. In Barcelona the company were booked to appear in the beautiful garden setting of the Cascada del Parque de la Cuidadela. The authorities changed the venue to a bullring. When I arrived I found there was no stage, no dressing-rooms and no wardrobe accommodation. The place was filthy. Moreover, the publicity was abominable. I complained bitterly to Our Man from the Ministry, who rushed around trying to get the portable stage erected in time. When John Field arrived he was even more depressed than I was.

When Fonteyn saw the seating capacity of the bullring, she was angry and upset and refused to dance unless she received a higher fee.

'She is not going to dance,' said Joan Thring. 'She's reserved a seat on the plane back to London tonight.'

Our Man from the Ministry, who was now quite used to the mad English and a demented Russian, grinned amiably. 'If she tries to leave and thereby disrupts our festival I can have her arrested,' he said.

That afternoon I had a telephone call from Fonteyn.

'Everyone is taking advantage of me,' she complained. 'I think you must be in league with the authorities. You must have agreed to stage the ballet in this awful bullring. There are far more seats. When I last appeared in Barcelona, I got a much higher fee.'

'That isn't so. I arranged the contract and you got exactly what you're getting now.'

She continued to complain about her three performances in Barcelona. I realised that we were getting nowhere. For her to be arrested would certainly give us excellent publicity but would be disastrous at the box office. I decided it would be better if she danced.

'The festival authorities are paying your fee and they will not pay any more. Would you be happier if I made a gesture and gave you say 200 extra dollars for each performance?'

She agreed to accept the extra 600 dollars and danced that night, talking and laughing with the company and even volunteering to meet the press.

The 25,000 arena, however, was only half full.

In the street next day, Nureyev, whether in a moment of anger or with an eye to the possible publicity, angrily pushed a photographer out of the way who was attempting to snap him. Another newsman was on hand to take a picture of the incident, which was splashed across all the newspapers. The subsequent Nureyev/Fonteyn performances were all packed.

Nureyev asked Field to replace Mosaval in *The Dream*. Field refused. Nureyev said he would not dance in the ballet at all, but promised to dance the *Nutcracker* pas de deux with Lucette Aldous as an extra item in the programme.

When he had danced the pas de deux in Granada, he had accidentally dropped Aldous on the stage. When she was asked to dance with Nureyev again, she said she was ill. Unfortunately Nureyev was in the hotel foyer when Lucette bounded out to sunbathe, swinging her beach-bag and looking the picture of health.

Nureyev was furious. 'I won't dance with this company any more. I'm finished with them, finished altogether.' He rushed off to do battle with John Field. I reached for a cigar.

Aldous quickly recovered and danced with him. This time he didn't drop her.

At the end of the Barcelona season I sat with John Field on a skip back-stage – both very relieved that the visit was almost over.

'There are only six more days of the tour – three in Bilbao and three in Santander. Do you think we could keep the scandals down to one a day? Three a day is too much for me.'

He laughed, but the last six days were scandal-free.

I heaved a sigh of relief when the company ended its tour in

Santander. Everyone else also seemed happy. Fonteyn met Vera and I in the hotel foyer in Bilbao. Kissing us both warmly, she apologised for her outbursts, explaining that after the stress and emotional strain of thirty-two performances one should not take too seriously anything said in the heat of the moment. The last programme of the tour included *Giselle* and without question it was the finest performance in this role that I have ever seen Fonteyn give – she was truly magnificent and it gave me great pleasure to tell her so.

Our Man from the Ministry was at Bilbao Airport to see us off. I felt he was rather disappointed at not having been able to arrest anyone after all.

CHAPTER 23

MY FINAL SCANDAL

———

Kathleen Crofton's career in the ballet goes back to the days of Pavlova. She is a gentle, well-spoken English lady in her sixties, with delicate features and hair looped in the traditional ballerina style. When taking ballet class she whistles melodies through her teeth.

After dancing with the Pavlova company, she worked with such artists as Laurent Novikoff at the Chicago Civic Opera Ballet, Nijinska, Olga Spessivtseva and Anatole Vilzac. In the Markova–Dolin Ballet before the war she understudied Markova. In 1950 she opened her own dance studio in London.

In 1966, Markova was trying to establish the Metropolitan Opera Ballet in New York. She invited Katie, as she is universally known in the ballet world, to help her. A year later, when the project failed, Katie went to Buffalo, in up-state New York and opened a ballet centre. Backed by Franz T. Stone, a prominent Buffalo businessman, she formed her own company with students from the centre. They appeared in Buffalo and had made a brief tour of North America.

Katie thought the youngsters had potential and could be built up to a permanent troupe based on Buffalo, touring North America and further afield. What was needed to establish them on a permanent basis was a European tour.

I had seen them dance Nijinska's *Les Biches* and Lichine's *Graduation Ball* and I liked their youth, bubbling vivacity and enthusiasm. They had something reminiscent of Festival Ballet in its early years. And several people I had worked with before were associated with the company. Markova had mounted *Carnaval* for them and the two principal dancers were Anna-Marie and David

Holmes, the two who had won the admiration of Dr Salazar in Portugal. The principal choreographer was Nijinska, whom I had toured with in the thirties with Poland's National Ballet. She had revived her *Chopin Piano Concerto*, an abstract ballet she created for the Polish company, for the youthful Americans.

In my discussions with Katie it was decided to change the name of the company to the American Classical Ballet. They were known originally as New York State's Niagara Frontier Ballet Company – a cumbersome title which made them sound like a troupe of touring Red Indians.

In Europe, I could not get one booking for the American Classical Ballet.

'They're unknown. They have no established stars,' said one young agent in Paris.

'Nijinska has been working with them. In fact, she is responsible for the company's repertoire.'

'Nijinska?' He looked puzzled. 'I've heard of Nijinsky – famous racehorse. But who's Nijinska?'

I realised that I was dealing with a different generation.

Some time before in Basle, I had watched Nureyev and Fonteyn dance the final pas de deux from Bournonville's romantic ballet, *La Sylphide*. As the supernatural being who falls in love with the mortal, Fonteyn was the personification of romantic love. As James, the Scottish youth who deserts his fiancee on the eve of his wedding to pursue the Sylph into the forest, Nureyev was quite a surprise. He acted out the role. The audience shared his enchantment with his ethereal partner and enjoyed the way he projected happiness and delight in his dancing.

Afterwards I asked him why he did not dance in the full-length ballet. 'You seem ideally suited for the role.'

'I would very much like to,' he replied, 'but nobody wants to revive it.'

Remembering this conversation, I asked Nureyev if he would dance with a young, unknown American company if they revived *La Sylphide* specially for him. He was interested.

Fonteyn's comment was: 'It's a jump ballet, and I can't jump any more.'

Nureyev had danced with Liliana Cosi, prima ballerina of La Scala, Milan. She agreed to partner him in *La Sylphide*, which was revived by Hans Brenaa of the Royal Danish Ballet.

With Nureyev and Cosi as the stars I was able to arrange a five-week European tour for the American Classical Ballet.

And so began an episode which, in all my fifty years of juggling in every kind of situation, has no parallel. The troubles Katie and I experienced once we arrived in Europe did not come directly from the dancers, but were instigated by the stage staff who almost succeeded in wrecking the tour. It is a situation which must be unique in the history of the theatre.

Katie had recruited her stage and managerial staff in Buffalo. The general manager of the American Classical Ballet was Russell R. Rokahr, who remained in Buffalo to administer to our needs and provide us with money. The company manager who came on the tour was Marie Tinsley, a girl in her late twenties with arresting blue eyes, pale complexion, long black hair and a passion for midi-length black dresses.

The stage director, Malcolm Waters, or Taffy as he was called, was married to one of the company's soloists, Wendy Barker. He chose E. O. Larsen – nicknamed Skip – as stage manager. Skip became the boyfriend of one of the newly recruited ballerinas, Michelle Lees. John Green was appointed chief electrician and Vernon Jeffrey, master carpenter. Jeffrey and Marie Tinsley – who both dressed in rather unconventional clothes, as did the rest of the stage crew – became fast friends.

The troubles began even before the company left home. In Buffalo the Holmeses were annoyed that the tour did not include Portugal where, it will be remembered, they had an influential admirer. They were also furious about the engagement of Nureyev and Cosi.

The Holmeses had some influence with the younger dancers, but Katie was the company's Artistic Director. The two dancers had differences with Katie, Markova and Hans Brenaa and were eventually asked to leave. They did, and some of their friends, including Jeanne Armin, one of the principals, left as well.

I replaced them with Eva Evdokimova, a frail beauty with an aerial technique from the Deutsches Opernhaus, Berlin, Cyril Atanassoff, a brilliant technician from the Paris Opera and Peter Mallek, a talented premier danseur from the Vienna State Opera Ballet.

When the company arrived in London in June 1971 to begin rehearsals, more trouble was in store. The dancers stuck rigidly to the rules laid down in their contracts by the American Guild of Musical Artists – insisting on the very letter of the law. The dancers were not happy with their hotels. Later, when rehearsal rooms could not be found in central London, they refused to make the half-hour journey to Barnes. The Holmeses too were in London trying to recruit dancers from the company for a visit to Portugal.

Nureyev had matured since his tour with me three years earlier. He was much more easy-going and co-operative. He knew the company were slightly apprehensive about making their debut in Europe and he went out of his way to encourage all the dancers. And despite their grumbles, they were young talented girls and boys whose enthusiasm and determination to succeed compensated for their inexperience.

The repertoire included *La Sylphide, Carnaval, Graduation Ball, Chopin Piano Concerto, Les Biches, Aurora's Wedding* and *Tyrolean Fantasy*. Other show pieces were the pas de deux from Act two of *Giselle, Flower Festival at Genzano, Don Quixote* and *The Black Swan*.

The first European performance of the American Classical Ballet was given in Lausanne on 25 June 1971 and everything went well. The kilted Nureyev did not appear in *La Sylphide* until the second night when he whispered words of encouragement to the dancers and inspired them to give an outstanding performance. He entirely fulfilled the promise he had shown when I had seen him dance the pas de deux from the ballet. As the Sylph, Cosi was superb, masking her formidable technique with a characterisation sometimes wistful, sometimes wilful, but entirely in keeping with the traditions of the romantic ballet. I thought everything was set for a successful tour.

I was to secure Nureyev's fees from each theatre where he appeared, but the company, and all the other guest artists, received their salaries and travelling expenses from Tinsley, the money being sent by Franz Stone from Buffalo.

In Frankfurt, one of the company's conductors, David Taylor, went to see Tinsley for his salary.

'We've no money to pay,' she told him.

The dancers' salaries had been paid and Katie immediately paid Taylor's salary from her own pocket.

As Tinsley obviously needed help in administering the company I sent for Beatrice Meyer, my secretary in London. She remained with the company, dealing with travel arrangements and hotels for the rest of the tour.

The stage staff too were being awkward. The *La Sylphide* set was erected in such a way that there was absolutely no room to dance. The lighting was appalling and sometimes the spots were directed behind the set. Nureyev complained bitterly.

'We must open the set out more,' Katie suggested to Taffy. 'We need more room to dance. And could we have brighter lighting please? The set is too dark.'

'Hans Brenaa gave it his OK in Lausanne. He approved it like that,' said Taffy. So the set was left as it was.

In the first act of *La Sylphide*, Nureyev sits asleep in a big chair dreaming of the Sylph who materialises at the window. In Lausanne, he got a big round of applause when the curtain went up. In subsequent performances, the lighting was so bad that he could not even be seen. *Aurora's Wedding* should be a brilliantly lit palace scene, a glittering setting for a series of brilliant divertissements. Instead, it was dim and drab and the Bluebirds vanished under their blue lighting.

Evdokimova danced *La Sylphide* with Nureyev in Böblingen. She was a frail, ethereal Sylph, giving the role a spiritual interpretation. Like Cosi, she was well received. Nureyev who was commuting back and forth to London where he was dancing at Covent Garden, had had no time to rehearse *Flower Festival of Genzano* with Evdokimova. In the second programme, he had nothing to dance except the grand pas de deux in *Aurora's Wedding*.

In Freiburg the audience were very angry. They had paid high prices to see as much of Nureyev as they could. One pas de deux was not enough. The press were highly critical, not of the company but of Nureyev for not giving value for money.

In Düsseldorf he was booed. We were booked to appear in a new hall. When I had seen it originally, it was still being built. When we arrived, it had been turned into an ice rink. After endless arguments, a portable stage was erected over the ice and proper theatre seating was installed. The dancers danced – but their feet were frozen. The opening night Nureyev danced *Aurora's Wedding* only. The audience hissed, booed and cat-called.

'If we'd been performing in a proper theatre, it wouldn't have happened,' he said. One good thing, the news of the anti-Nureyev demonstration attracted a capacity audience for the second performance of *Carnaval* and *La Sylphide*. This time, Nureyev and Cosi were cheered.

David Taylor was ill. Cosi telephoned an Italian conductor, de Mori, to deputise. After the performance, Katie, André Guerbilsky, an old impresario friend of mine who was helping us, and I, accompanied de Mori to the theatre restaurant to collect the conductor's fee.

'We have no money,' Tinsley told us. Katie, André and I looked at her in amazement. The Italian was ready to explode. To save any further embarrassment, I quickly offered to pay him his fee.

At Zürich's Kongresshaus, the stage was not deep enough. I asked Eynar Grabowsky, the agent there, to extend the stage, which he did. Nureyev jumped and went straight through the extension. Grabowsky had apparently been told that the extension could be made of either old or new wood. New wood would be 200 dollars more than old. Naturally he chose the old.

Nureyev took the whole thing quite calmly. He told the company that they would have to keep to the back of the stage and although the performance was cramped, it went off quite well. He continued to complain about the lack of space in *La Sylphide* and the abominable lighting. In Nice, after getting no satisfaction from the stage staff about the lighting, Nureyev began removing the gels from the spotlights himself.

'Leave them alone. What the hell are you doing?' asked the stage manager. Nureyev went on removing the gels.

'You don't know anything at all about lighting, you're just a dancer.' He leaned forward and punched Nureyev.

Hitherto the stage staff had refused to take orders from anyone. They now tried to terrorise Nureyev, and to some extent succeeded. With Katie, they were completely unco-operative.

We were dancing in the Arene des Cimiez. The stage had rippled with the heat and the surface was so bad that it tore the dancer's shoes. The company travelled a linoleum for such emergencies. We asked Tinsley to have it put down.

'It's gone to Madrid,' she said.

Nureyev and Cosi, who had been rehearsing, said that something must be done about the surface before the performance began. André Guerbilsky searched through the scenery and found the linoleum. Katie asked Taffy to lay it.

'It will be worse than useless. It will just curl up,' said Taffy.

'You can put some weights on it. Anyway, do try, the surface is so awful.'

On the darkened stage, one of the French stage crew noticed something glistening. The lights were turned on and a broken Coca-Cola bottle was found just where Nureyev made his entrance. After picking up the broken pieces, the French crew checked the whole stage to ensure everything was all right.

When Atanassoff asked Tinsley for his salary he got the usual reply. 'We have no money.' Katie advanced the money.

I felt that things had gone far enough. Arriving in Madrid, I invited Katie, André, Taffy and Tinsley to dinner. I thought Katie should be given the opportunity of resolving the unbearable situation that had arisen with the stage crew.

Taffy was amicable. Tinsley sat quietly throughout the meal.

Finally Katie plucked up enough courage to broach the subject everyone was waiting for.

'Taffy, I'm very worried about the stage staff and the way you all react to Nureyev. If it weren't for him, none of us would be here. He's the reason for us being able to make this tour of Europe. And we've had such trouble with the sets and lighting.'

'What do you want then?'

'Well, more room for the dancers to dance. And brighter sets.'

'Everything will be all right,' Taffy assured us.

At the Teatro de la Zarzuela, *La Sylphide* had been set as usual with no room to dance. The stage was vast. At rehearsal, Nureyev and Cosi found the stage impossible for other reasons. It had an appalling slippery surface. The linoleum had not arrived from Nice. Katie talked to the theatre's director, Federico Orduna. 'Isn't there anything you could do to make the surface better?' she asked.

'We could spray it with plastic paint. That's worked before,' he suggested.

Our stage hands were taking their siesta. The Spanish stage staff struck the set and began covering the stage with thick, grey plastic paint. Hours later, when the job was nearing completion, Taffy appeared and asked who had ordered the set to be taken down.

'I did, something had to be done,' Katie explained, 'otherwise there would have been no performance tonight. The linoleum has not arrived and I hear it is not due until after the performance.'

The Spaniards finished painting. Taffy and his crew began erecting the set again, watched by Nureyev and Cosi.

'Take it out. Please do open up the stage, there's lots of room. It is a ballet performance you know, and the dancers must have room to dance,' pleaded Katie.

'It's amateur to have it the way you want,' Taffy replied.

Katie's patience snapped. She was tired of arguments, tired of the unco-operativeness of the stage hands and exhausted with the strain of the tour.

'If you don't want to do it the way I want, then I'll ask the Spanish crew,' she said with a determination that surprised me.

Taffy and his crew walked off stage. Orduna called the Spanish crew who, with Nureyev, Jimmy Starbuck and Katie supervising, quickly began work. They set the stage correctly. Taffy and his men returned and attempted to help, but by then the job was done.

Katie asked Taffy to see her in the director's office that night, together with the ballet master, Jimmy Starbuck.

Taffy arrived.

'We've managed to arrange a lighting rehearsal tomorrow evening. You can have the stage at six o'clock,' said Jimmy to break the ice.

'You'll be having it without me. I won't be there. You've made us look like fools in front of the Spanish stage staff. We looked like idiots, amateurs. Nureyev is a dancer, he doesn't know anything about stage management, neither do you.'

'I'm very sorry, but if that's what you think, then I suppose that's it. What about the others?'

'They'll have to answer for themselves.'

'Would you be kind enough to ask them to come and see me, please?'

The next person through the door was Wendy Barker.

'Where Taffy goes, I go. I'm leaving.'

Vernon Jeffrey, John Green and Skip all said they were leaving immediately. Unexpectedly, Tinsley appeared. She was rarely seen at the theatre.

'As the stage staff have been fired, I'm leaving too,' she said. 'I'll prepare tomorrow's pay-roll and then I'm off.'

'The stage staff were not fired, they walked out,' said Katie.

The following morning Michelle Lees, Jerry Ives and Larry Dill, the company's AGMA representative, said that as various clauses in their contracts – such as the posting of casting lists and rehearsal times – had been contravened, they were resigning immediately.

They signed documents releasing the company from paying their salaries after 20 July. Lees and Skip went for a holiday to Paris.

When Katie saw Tinsley she did not have to explain that the dancers had left. Tinsley knew.

'You must not pay them, or the stage staff after the 20th.'

'I'll have to check that with AGMA,' said Tinsley.

'Those are my orders.'

'I don't take orders from you. Mr Rokahr is my boss,' she replied.

No one ever knew whether the departing dancers or the stage staff were paid after the 20th, not even Stone.

Lees and Ives were the principal dancers in *Chopin Piano Concerto* which was to be performed that night. It was impossible to present another ballet. The scenery and costumes had been despatched to Santander.

Katie was in a state of collapse. She considered resigning there and then and going home. As she entered her hotel, she met Liliana Cosi, on her way to do a television performance.

'What's the matter?'

Katie told her story.

'Oh, who will dance *Chopin Piano Concerto*?' Cosi did not wait for Katie's reply. 'Would you like me to do it? I've got to do the television, but then I'll go back to the theatre and Jimmy can teach it to me. Mallek can partner me, he knows it. Everything is going to be fine – don't worry,' she said as she rushed out of the hotel.

And it was. The Spanish stage staff worked most efficiently. Cosi learned the role in two hours and was marvellous in it. Mallek put back all the difficult steps in his variation that had had to be taken out for Ives. Ives had also danced the travesty role of the Mistress in *Graduation Ball*. Jimmy Starbuck deputised. When the General picked him up in a passionate embrace, he squeezed him so hard he cracked two of Jimmy's ribs. But he continued to work throughout the rest of the tour.

We did not have Our Man from the Ministry, but I was called to the Festivales de Espana and asked if I would like the dancers who had left and the stage crew arrested. They were threatening to interrupt the festival and we were no longer maintaining our contract with the theatre. We were four dancers short as well as the stage hands. I said that it was entirely an internal dispute, and as the company were better off without them, to arrest the defaulters would only create a scandal we could not afford.

By now there was a hot line between Madrid and Stone in Buffalo and the AGMA office in New York. Katie asked Stone to send Tinsley a telegram saying that her resignation was accepted and asking her to turn over the accounts.

'You'd better have them audited before she gives them to you,' said Stone.

Katie found a firm of accountants, but the accounts were never made available. The cable accepting Tinsley's resignation did not arrive. The situation was intolerable. Stone was asked to fly to Madrid and straighten things out. He arrived, listened to Katie, listened to Tinsley, listened to Taffy. He ordained that Katie was in charge of the company, Tinsley would continue to pay salaries and Taffy would go on holiday and rejoin the company at the end of the tour to send the scenery and costumes back to America.

Stone departed. The situation was ridiculous. Without having any money, Katie was powerless.

Nureyev had pulled a muscle in his left leg and was in agony. He was due to dance at a UNICEF charity gala which had been sold out. Orduna accompanied him to hospital in the afternoon where he was given pain-killing injections and ultra-violet ray treatment. But he was in such pain that when he put the leg to the floor he screamed. It had not improved by the evening.

'If I don't appear, they're sure to say that I haven't been paid. Something like that. No one ever believes that I might be injured,' he said miserably.

'I'll get a doctor's certificate. We'll register it with the police and then everyone will be satisfied,' said Orduna, rushing off.

'Everyone except the audience,' said Nureyev.

When Nureyev turned up at the theatre at ten o'clock, the Minister of Tourism, Sanchez Bella, and his Sub-Director, Antolin de Santiago y Juarez, were there.

The audience too were arriving, among them the two renowned Spanish dancers Antonio and Pilar Lopez.

Nureyev was still in pain. 'I will have to dance. Perhaps if I do *Aurora's Wedding*, the last ballet in the programme, my leg will feel better.'

The performance began with *Carnaval*. Over the theatre tannoy system the stage manager made an announcement.

'There is an amendment to the programme. The performance will continue with Evdokimova and Atanassoff in *Flower Festival in Genzano*.' This was the pas de deux Nureyev should have danced. Pandemonium broke out. The audience stood up, banged their seats, shouted, screamed and threw things on the stage.

'We want Nureyev. We've paid for Nureyev. We want Nureyev,' they bellowed.

Nureyev, obviously frightened, heard all the hullabaloo on the tannoy.

'Take the curtain up, start the ballet,' shouted Orduna.

Amid the screams and shouts the curtain rose on Evdokimova and Atanassoff. The screaming changed to booing and grew to such a pitch that the orchestra could not be heard. Evdokimova danced her gentle, charming Bournonville steps, while Atanassoff turned like a top.

'We want Nureyev, we want Nureyev,' screamed the audience. Things were thrown on the stage, the audience began to climb on the stage. After three minutes the curtain came down with the dancers still dancing.

'I'll make an announcement,' said Senor Bella.

Switching on the tannoy, the Minister said: 'Nureyev has been injured. He cannot dance, but has agreed to perform in the final ballet of the programme, *Aurora's Wedding*.'

The booing continued, the audience began clattering their seats, and its was obvious that they were not going to stop.

Nureyev, with his leg heavily bandaged, was standing in the wings.

'I'll dance, I'll dance,' he said. White-faced and anxious, he took Atanassoff's place. The curtain rose again to the booing audience. As soon as they saw Nureyev's bandaged leg they were silent. The pas de deux began. Nureyev was unsteady partnering, but managed. In his variation it was as if he couldn't bear to put the injured leg to the ground. The coda finished with him obviously in pain. The audience cheered. Back stage he was moaning in agony.

In *Aurora's Wedding* he partnered Cosi. The pain-killing injection in the interval proved ineffective. His partnering was more assured and when it came to his variation, he took off in the air and seemed to remain permanently off the ground. His turns were taken at a tremendous pace, the music getting faster and faster to keep up with him. He literally flew through his solo. The coda too was taken at a fantastic speed. The audience gave him an ovation. He staggered off stage after his final bow and collapsed in his dressing-room, crying with pain.

'You're a genius, that's what you are, a genius,' I told him.

He looked at me sadly. 'You can only be a genius once in your life. Never again.'

Tinsley was supposed to be at the theatre to pay salaries. She did not come. Glassman, one of the principals, who acted as spokesman for the dancers, told Katie that Tinsley and Jeffrey had gone to London.

'Gone to London, But why?'

'The money for salaries has been sent to London. Marie's gone to collect it.'

On the hot line from Buffalo, Rokahr told Katie that Tinsley was under the impression, an impression entirely unfounded, that it was impossible to obtain dollars or sterling in Madrid.

Glassman telephoned the Hilton in London, where Tinsley was supposed to be staying. She was not there. I lent Katie the money to pay off the stage staff in Madrid and the guest artists' hotel bills.

The hot line to Buffalo got even hotter. Katie insisted that Tinsley come to Spain to pay the company.

'Oh yes, Marie is leaving by car. It won't take her long to get to Madrid, it's only a few hundred miles,' said Rokahr.

But Tinsley didn't arrive. By this time the company had moved on to its final engagement in Santander.

Taffy, looking brown and fit after his holiday, told Jimmy that Tinsley would not be coming back to Spain. She would remain in London to pay the company when they returned there. The fact that some of the company were not returning to London hadn't been taken into account.

Hurok had sent his representative to see the company. He turned out to be my old friend from Reinhardt days, Simon Semenoff.

'If the dancers are not paid by midnight tonight, they will not finish the performance. They will walk off stage,' Glassman told Katie. There were telephone calls and cables to AGMA. The union had had a sum of money deposited with them to guarantee salaries. They told the dancers that they should perform and assured them that money had been sent by Stone. Some of the dancers remained loyal to Katie and did not approve of Glassman's ultimatum. Others were ready to strike.

'Marie is coming to Santander by private plane. She hasn't been able to get on one of the planes to Bilbao, so she's chartered her own,' Glassman told Katie.

'Presumably she and Jeffrey will be flying at Mr Stone's expense?' said Katie. 'But when will she arrive?'

'She'll be here as soon as possible.'

Everyone was uncertain about whether the company would strike. Fortunately they didn't. Nureyev was relieved, Katie was relieved, and so was I. I thought we might all be arrested.

Semenoff saw two performances and was pleased with *La Sylphide*, *Graduation Ball* and *Chopin Piano Concerto*. He was even more delighted with the guest artists and told Katie that with them appearing from time to time, the company might have a future in America.

There was another cable to Glassman from Tinsley. She and Jeffrey were in Bordeaux. They would arrive in Santander the following morning at 10 a.m. The company were due to leave for Bilbao, a three-and-a-half-hour drive away, to catch their plane for London at 9.30 a.m. Katie asked Glassman to remain in Santander, collect the pay for the artists who were remaining there and then fly with Tinsley to Bilbao and pay the rest of the company.

Everything worked according to plan. In Bilbao, some of the company went on to join the Holmeses, who were giving a season independently in Portugal. Others went on holiday, the remainder returned home via London. Tinsley and Jeffrey flew back to London, where Katie was on the brink of a nervous breakdown.

So ended the tour which in preparation had cost Stone over half a million dollars. Nureyev had worked like a Trojan. So had Cosi. Nothing was too much for her and frequently, when Evdokimova was dancing the principal role, she offered to do corps de ballet work. All the guest artists had set an example to the company who, it must be remembered, had had no experience of the rigours of professional touring. Some of the young members of the corps de ballet, despite the annoyance of not being paid on time and the call for strike action, had remained loyal to Katie. For all of them, the tour was a chastening experience. For the first time ever, they realised that dancing in the ballet is not a glamorous, elegant life of parties and adulation. It's just plain hard work needing a lot of guts, determination and sweat.

As for me, well, I'm back at Kew with Vera, contemplating the last scandal and calculating whether it has been a profit or a loss. I'm not immune to all the passions and temperaments that are part and parcel of the ballet world. But over the years, I've noticed that my skin has become decidedly thicker and, in some ways, I've become as egocentric as the dancers I deal with. Thick-skinned egocentric! Not attractive characteristics but very necessary if you are to survive with Swan Queens, Sleeping Beauties, sylphs and fairies.

Inevitably I look backwards and perhaps I'm a little bitter. But then I think I have every reason to be. One of the most emotionally disturbing events for me in 1971 was not the tour I have just described, but my brief re-appearance with Festival Ballet. Beryl Grey, the company's Artistic Director, invited me to attend the 21st Birthday Gala at the London Coliseum on 19 April 1971 and suggested, for old times' sake, I should take a bow with the company.

When the final curtain came down and the cheering and hand-shaking was all over, I turned round to see what artists remained from my old company. Of the seventy dancers on stage, there were only eight from the old Festival Ballet. Of the twelve British principals who had led the company in my day, only one remained. In the six years since I had been forced to resign the new administrators had not produced one British soloist or principal, not one British choreographer, not one British musician and not one British ballet. After seeing the company dance that night, I knew it was no longer the Festival Ballet I had created. As I walked out of the theatre, I could not help feeling that my sixteen years of hard work and juggling had been a complete waste of time.

Retirement is not a word I know in any language. So I must continue to juggle, for without juggling – and cigars and whisky – life would be inconceivable. Impresarios are pedlars of dreams. We traffic in a world of escapism and make-believe and hope we'll make a profit. In the ballet world, one rarely does. Dancers live in a make-believe world where competition is keen, talent often overlooked and neurosis is rife. It is a world in which I'm very much at home.

So next time you go to the ballet, remember, all is not what it seems. Odette may be suing the company, Siegfried may have just been punched by someone back-stage and the swans may all be threatening strike action!

Kew Gardens *September, 1971*

APPENDIXES

Festival Ballet Guest Artists: 1949–1965

AMIEL Josette
ASHBRIDGE Bryan
AUDRAN Edmund

BELITA
BLAIR David

CHARRAT Janine
CHAUVIRE Yvette
CLAVIER Josette
COLLINS Eugene

DANILOVA Alexandra

ELVIN Violetta

FERNANDEZ Royes
FONTEYN Margot
FRACCI Carla
FULOP Victor

GILMOUR Sally
GRAEME Joyce

GRANTZEVA Tatiana
GREY Beryl

HAVAS Ferenc

JONES Marilyn
JOVANOVITCH Militza

KEHLET Niels
KOVACH Nora
KUN Zsuzsa

LAINE Doris
LAKATOS Gabriella
LICHINE David

MARCHAND Colette
MARKS Bruce
MASSINE Leonide
MELIKOVA Genia
MISKOVITCH Milorad

PALLEY Xenia
PETERSEN Kirsten
PISTONI Mario
PLANK Melinda
POURNY Serge

RABOVSKY Istvan
RIABOUCHINKSA
   Tatiana

SELLING Caj
SHEARER Moira
SKIBINE George
SKORIK Irene
SLAVENSKA Mia
SVETLOVA Marina
SOMBERT Claire
SOMES Michael

TALLCHIEF Majorie
TCHERINA Ludmilla
TOUMANOVA Tamara

Guest Artists who subsequently became members of the company appear in the following list.

Festival Ballet Dancers: 1949–1965

ADAMS David
ADRIAANS Hilmar
ALBAN Jean-Pierre
ALDERTON Jennifer
ALDOUS Lucette
ANDERSON Graeme
ANDRE Jennifer
AROVA Sonia

BAINBRIDGE Lynda
BATHURST Jill
BARRY Wendy
BAPTIE Ivan
BECKETT Keith
BELL Karin
BENTLEY Patricia
BENTON Nicholas
BERDICHEVSKY Igal
BERIOSOFF Nicholas
BEVAN Pixie
BISHOPP Angela
BLAIR Gabrielle
BOROWSKA Irina
BOSMAN Petrus
BOSWORTH Gillian
BOUDET Michel
BRADLEY Sally
BRADY Dellice
BRIANSKY Oleg
BROWNLEE Peter
BURGESS Walter
BURKE Anthony
BRUNNER Wolfgang
BURR Marilyn

CARTWRIGHT David
CAZALET Peter
CHESELKA Anna

CLAIRE Susan
CLIFFORD Mel
LE COMTE Denise
COMELIN Jean-Paul
CORSER Geoffrey
CROWTHER Leslie
CURTIS Roslyn
COULSON Mary
COWARD Hazel
COX Elizabeth

DALE Daphne
DARRELL Peter
DRAGADZE Ivan
DAVEL Hendrik
DAVIDSON Geoffrey
DAVIS Dalton
DEW Mary
DEY Sheila
DONALDSON Gail
DOLIN Anton
DUBREUIL Alain
DUCHESNE Mary
DUKE Valerie
DUNCAN Clare
DUNCAN Roma

ELESMORE Diane
EMBLEN Ronald
EVANS Lesley

FERRI Olga
FITZWILLIAM Neil
FLETCHER Tony
FLINDT Flemming
FOSTER Susan
FRANKLYN Shelagh
FULTON Gaye

GAREYA Paula
GAYLE David
GILBERT Terry
GILCHRIST Douglas
GILL William
GILLESPIE Kenn
GILPIN John
GODDARD Malcolm
GODFREY Louis
GOHAR Alexis
GOVILOFF Georges
GRACE Maretta
GREENHALGH June

HAMILTON June
HARMAN Audrey
HART Pamela
HAYLES Patricia
HEARNE Bridget
HEUBI Peter
HILL Douglas
HINTON Paula
HOGAN Michael
HOLDEN Ann
HOLMES Anna-Marie
HOLMES David
HUGHES Christine
HUTCHINSON Christine

JOPE Christine
JUDD Sally

KARRAS Vicki
KATIN Christina
KEDGE Janet
KELLY Desmond
KINSEY Rose
KINSON Janet
KIRSHNER Patricia

284

KNOX Moya
KOVAL Jeffrey
KRASSOVSKA Natalie

LAMB Susan
LAMBERT Gillian
LANDA Anita
LANDER Toni
LAW Gale
LEIGH Monica
LEPAGE Roger
LEWIS Gloria
LEWIS Janet
LEWIS Raymond
LEYLAND Jennifer
LINDSAY Joan
VON LOGGENBURG
  Dudley
LONG David
LONG Geraldine
LONG John
LOOKER Gwenn
LYNDON Joyce

MACDONALD Rodney
MAIDWELL Keith
MANNECHEZ Jacqueline
MANSFIELD Ken
MARKOVA Alicia
MARTIN Christina
MARTIN Len
MARTIN-VISCOUNT
  William
MARTYNNE Ken
MATHE Carmen
MAULE Michael
MCALPINE Donald
MCDOWELL Norman
MCGRATH Barry
MELVILLE Kenneth
MELVIN Sheila
METLISS Maurice
MIKLOSY Margot

MILLAIRE Andree
MINTY Jeannette
MORRELL Anne
MOTTRAM Simon
MOULDS Priscilla
MULLER Margit
MUNRO Mary
MUSIL Karl

NATIEZ Max
NEL Gerard
NICHOLLS Edward
NISBET Joanne
NOVA Estella

O'CONAIRE Deirdre
OLENA Yvonne
OLUP Robert
ORTON Stella
OVERTON Janet

PERRIE William
PERROTTET Philippe
PETTINGER Eve
POLAJENKO Nicholai
POOLE Julia
PORTER Phyllida
POTTER Joan
PROKOVSKY Andre

REYNOLDS David
RESSIGA Louis
RHYS Alun
RICHARDS Dianne
ROBERTSON James
ROSENBERG Derek
ROSSANA Noel
ROWSE Anne
RUSSELL Sylvia

SALAVISA Jorges
SAMTSOVA Galina
SANDERS Carolyn
SANDERS Valerie
SAROVA Suzanne

SCHEEPERS Martin
SCHULLER Stephen
SCOTT Brian
SCOTT David
SEPTIMUS Rikki
SIDIMUS Joysanne
SIVYER Eugenia
SKOURATOFF Vladimir
SMITH Graeme
SMITH Jack
SMITH Janet
SHANE Gillian
SHIELDS David
SLATER Jean
STARR Helen
STEVENSON Ben
STIRLING Cristina
SUDELL Kenneth
SUREN Anne
SUTCLIFFE Jeremy
SWANE Dawn
SWEET Arthur
SYMONDS Angela

TELFORD Nona
TOOMBS Rosemary
TRUNOFF Vassilie

VANDERNOOT Jane
VARADY Imre
VAUGHAN Amanda
VERNON Rosalie
VOREMBERG Reuven
VERDY Violette

WAKS Jon
WARD Leon
WARD Rozanne
WARWICK Stephen
WATSON Chris
WEBB Geoffrey
WESLEY Isobel
WEST Wendy
WESTERMAN Diane

Festival Ballet Staff: 1949–1965

Musicians
BALKWILL Bryan
BEATON Colin
BOWMAN Aubrey
CORBETT Geoffrey
DOWNING Edna
ELLIOTT Donald
HERBERT Kenneth
LUCAS Leighton
MORGAN Alan
REID William
RORKE Peter
ROSS-RUSSELL Noel
SHERRELL Harold
STRAVINSKY Igor
  (Guest)
ZELLER Robert (Guest)

Wardrobe
BUNCE Arthur
DAVIES Sheila
FORD Deirdre
GLEESON Marjorie
GUY Geoffrey
HAWKER Edna
KENNAN Sidney
LINTOTT Elizabeth
ROWSELL Grace
STEWART Jane
STROWBRIDGE Edith
TINSLEY Nita
WATSON Stephen

Press Representatives
BARRY Doris
BUIST Michael
Messrs CLARK-NELSON
FROSTICK Michael
GRATTON Fred
ROLLO Duncan
WILLIAMS Peter
WORDSWORTH Audrey
WORDSWORTH William

Regisseurs
BERIOSOFF Nicholas
GRIGORIEFF Serge
TCHERNICHEVA Lubov
WOIZIKOWSKY Leon

Stage Direction
TOFF Benn

Company Manager
ABBOT Douglas W.
BROWNLEE Peter

Ballet Master/Mistress
BAKER Eileen
DICKSON Charles
GRAF Fritz
WARD Eileen
TRUNOFF Vassilie

Stage Management
BERRILL John
COLESHILL Alan
COOMBER Denis
CURTIS Alan
DUFF James
ELLIOTT Don
EVANS Peter
FARRELL Peter
FRYER Michael
GILPIN Anthony
GORDON Peter
HOGAN James
JAMES Joe
LOVE Bryan
MOHR David
SMITH James
SUDELL Ken
WRIGGLESWORTH
  Peter

Secretariat
COOPER Gwen
COOPER Reg
DIXON Shirley
FROSTICK Angela
KEET John
MEYER Beatrice
PALMER Iris
SESTA Hilary
TEMPLETON Walter
TUBB Dicksie

Festival Ballet Repertoire: 1949–1965

Year	Ballet	Choreographer	Composer	Designer
1949	Chopiniana	Markova/Dolin/Cone	Chopin	after lithograph
	Vestris	Celli	Rossini	
	Dying Swan	Fokine	Saint-Saens	
	Italian Suite	Dolin	Cimarosa	
	Blue Mountain Ballads	Saddler	Bowles	Kirsta
	Les Sylphides	Fokine	Chopin	
	Bolero	Dolin	Ravel	
	Autumn Song	Nijinska	Tchaikovsky	
	Hymn to the Sun		Rimsky-Korsakoff	
	Don Quixote Grand Pas de Deux		Minkus	
	Rondalla Aragonesa	Ricarda	Granados	
	Swan Lake (Act two)	Cone after Petipa/Ivanov	Tchaikovsky	Kirsta
	Tarentella	Cone	Rossini/Britten	
	Valse des Fleurs } The Nutcracker	Cone	Tchaikovsky	
	Grand Pas de Deux }	Markova/Dolin after Ivanov		
1950	Fiesta	Ricarda	Mariani	Hubbard
	The Nutcracker (Act two)	Cone after Petipa	Tchaikovsky	Hilliard/Schogel/Kirsta
	Capriccioso (Italiana)	Dolin/Cone	Rossini/Britten and Cimarosa	Kirsta
	Petrouchka	Fokine (Beriosoff)	Stravinsky	after Benois
	Le Beau Danube	Massine	J. Strauss	after Guys

Year	Title	Choreographer	Composer	Designer
	Giselle	Coralli/Dolin	Adam	Stevenson
	Le Spectre de la Rose	Fokine (Dolin/Karsavina)	Weber (Berlioz)	after Bakst
	Harlequinade	Lichine/Petipa	Drigo	Watts
1951	*The Blue Bird* Pas de Deux	Petipa	Tchaikovsky	Manya/Lillyne
	The Pas de Quatre	Dolin	Pugni	after Chalon
	Symphonic Impressions	Lichine	Bizet	Stevenson
	The Black Swan Grand Pas de Deux	Petipa	Tchaikovsky	
	Prince Igor	Fokine/Beriosoff	Borodin	Roerich
1952	*Concerto Grosso en Ballet*	Lichine	Vivaldi	Lingwood
	Scheherazade	Fokine/Beriosoff	Rimsky-Korsakoff	after Bakst
	Pas de Reve	Dolin	Bruch	Stevenson
	Vision of Marguerite	Ashton	Liszt	Bailey
	Symphony for Fun	Charnley	Gillis	Lingwood
	Concerto Pas de Deux	Charrat	Greig	
	Harlequinade (New Prod.)	Darrell	Drigo	Adams (pseudonym for Kenneth MacMillan)
1953	*Vilia*	Page	Lehar	Wakevitch
	Alice in Wonderland	Charnley	Horovitz	Rowell
	Concerto	Lambrinos	Greig	Reymundo
	The Laurel Crown	Lambrinos	Hobson	Gaylen
	Moszkowski Waltz	Vaganov	Moszkowski	
1954	*La Esmeralda*	Beriosoff	Pugni	N. Benois
	Napoli	Lander after Bournonville	Paulli/Helsted/Gade	Lancaster
	The Scarf Pas de Deux			
1955	*Grand Pas Classique*	Gsovsky	Auber	
	Mlle Fifi	Solov	la Jarte	Wade
	Etudes	Lander	Czerny/Riisager	

Year	Ballet	Choreographer	Composer	Designer
1955 (cont.)	Grand Adagio (*Sleeping Beauty*)	Petipa	Tchaikovsky	
	Shemakhan	Schwezoff	Rimsky-Korsakoff	
	Room for Three	Lester	Gillis	
	The Swan of Tuonela	Audran	Sibelius	
1956	*Sylvia* Pas de Deux	Ashton	Delibes	
	Gift of the Magi	Semenoff	Lucas Foss	Raoul Pene de Bois
	Les Deux Errants	Brunner	Russo	Snyder
	Homage to a Princess	Charnley	Kenton	Levasseur
	Petrouchka (New Prod.)	Fokine (Grigorieff/Tchernicheva)	Stravinsky	Kirsta after Benois
	Scheherazade (New Prod.)	Fokine (Grigorieff/Tchernicheva)	Rimsky-Korsakoff	after Bakst
	Prince Igor	Fokine (Grigorieff/Tchernicheva)	Borodin	after Roerich
	Coppelia	Lander	Delibes	Maillart
	Duetto Pas de Deux	Gsovsky	Donizetti	
	The Rose Adagio (*Sleeping Beauty*)	Petipa	Tchaikovsky	
1957	*Concerti*	Lichine	Vivaldi and Marcello	
	Graduation Ball	Lichine	J. Strauss	Benois
	Annabel Lee	Skibine	Schiffman	
	Variations for Four	Dolin	Keogh	Lingwood
	The Witch Boy	Carter	Salzedo	McDowell
	The Nutcracker (New Prod.) in its entirety	Lichine	Tchaikovsky	Benois

1958 Octetto	Stone	Various arr. Wilkinson	Notman (subsequently Lingwood)
Reverie	de Vos	Liszt	
Poeme	Goube	Damasse	
Romeo and Juliet	Br003 Brian Briansky	Tchaikovsky	Levasseur
The Seasons Pas de Deux	Rodrigues	Glazounoff	
1959 *Aurora Pas de Trois*	Petipa	Tchaikovsky	
Vision of Chopin	Lichine	Chopin	
Prelude a l'apres midi d'un Faune	Nijinsky/Lifar	Debussy	
London Morning	Carter	Coward	McDowell/Constable
Tyrolean Pas de Deux	Markova	Rossini	
Piece d'Occasion	Cranko	Delibes	Toms
Vita Eterna	Lander	Dvorak	Wakhevitch
The Enchanted Stream	Dolin	Debussy	MacLiammoir
1960 *Pas de Deux Royal*	Brunner	Vogkt	
Bonaparte a Nice	Lifar	Thiriet	Levasseur
Barbaresque	Andret	Constant	Wakhevitch
Bourree Fantasque	Balanchine	Chabrier	
Aubade	Lifar/Skouratoff	Poulenc	
Flammes de Paris Pas de Deux	Vaganov	Asaffiev	
Hungarian Gipsy Pas de Deux	Harongozo	Kenesei	
Grand Pas des Fiancees	Carter		McDowell
1961 *Swan Lake (Act two)* (New Prod.)	Bourmeister after Ivanov	Tchaikovsky	Delany
The Snow Maiden	Bourmeister	Tchaikovsky	Epishin and Pimenov
Flower Festival in Genzano	Bournonville	Helsted, Paulli	
Adagio	Briansky	Albinoni	Sonnabend
1962 *Le Spectre de la Rose* (New Prod.)	Fokine/Karsavina	Weber (Berlioz)	Delany

291

Year	Ballet	Choreographer	Composer	Designer
1962 (cont.)	*Prelude*	Charrat	Bach	
	Promenade a Deux	Beriosoff	Rossini/Britten	Espada
	Improvisations	Carter	Copland	McDowell
	Prelude a l'apres midi d'un Faune	Nijinsky/Markova	Debussy	
	Raymonda Pas de Deux	Balanchine	Glazounoff	
1963	*The Ballet Peer Gynt*	Orlikowsky	Greig	Lloyd and Delany
	Symphonette	Goddard	Gould	McDowell
	Le Corsair Pas de Deux	Petipa	Pugni	
	Wedding Song Pas de Deux	MacDonald	Delius	
	Spring Waters Pas de Deux	Messerer	Rachmaninoff	
1964	*Walpurgis Night*	Orlikowsky	Gounod	Reiter
	Tchaikovsky Suite No. 3	Adams	Tchaikovsky	Clifford
	Ballade de Chopin	Charrat	Chopin	
	Saffron Knot Pas de Deux	Asmus	Wagner	Karinska
	Swan Lake (Full-length – Verona)	Orlikowsky	Tchaikovsky	Colonello
1965	*The Haunted Ballroom*	de Valois	Toye	Voytek
	Swan Lake (New Full-length production – London)	Orlikowsky/Bourmeister	Tchaikovsky	Truscott

Festival Ballet Itinerary: 1949–1965

UNITED KINGDOM
Aberdeen
Bath
Belfast
Birmingham
Blackpool
Bolton
Bournemouth
Bradford
Brighton
Bristol
Brixton
Cardiff
Coventry
Doncaster
Eastbourne
Edinburgh
Edmonton
Exeter
Glasgow
Golders Green
Hanley
Harrogate
Hull
Ipswich
Llangollen
Leeds
Leicester
Liverpool
London
Manchester
Newcastle
Norwich
Nottingham
Oxford
Plymouth
Sheffield
Slough

Southampton
Southend-on-Sea
Southsea
Stockton-on-Tees
Stratford-upon-Avon
Streatham
Sunderland
Sutton
Torquay
Wimbledon
Wolverhampton
Woolwich

EUROPE
AUSTRIA
Vienna

BELGIUM
Antwerp
Brussels
Ostende

DENMARK
Aarhus
Copenhagen

EIRE
Dublin

FRANCE
Bordeaux
Cannes
Grenoble
Lyon
Marseilles
Nice
Paris
Vichy

GERMANY
Cologne

Dusseldorf
Frankfurt
Freiburg
Giessen
Hamburg
Landau
Munich
Stuttgart
Wiesbaden

HUNGARY
Budapest

ITALY
Bolognia
Breschia
Catania
Ferrara
Florence
Genoa
Mantova
Milan
Modena
Naples
Reggio Emelia
Rome
Trieste
Turin
Venice
Verona

MONACO
Monte Carlo

NETHERLANDS
Amsterdam
Haarlam
Rotterdam
The Hague

EUROPE (contd.)

NORWAY
  Oslo

POLAND
  Lodz
  Warsaw

PORTUGAL
  Braga
  Lisbon
  Oporto

RUMANIA
  Bucharest

SPAIN
  Barcelona
  Bilbao
  Madrid
  Palma di Majorca
  Santander
  San Sebastian
  Saragossa

SWEDEN
  Malmo
  Stockholm

SWITZERLAND
  Basle
  Biel
  Geneva
  Interlaken
  Lausanne
  Schaffhausen
  Zürich

YUGOSLAVIA
  Belgrade
  Ljubljana
  Zagreb

MIDDLE EAST

ISRAEL
  Beersheba
  Bethsham

Haifa
Jerusalem
Natania
Petah Tikuah
Ramat-Gan
Tel Aviv

NORTH AMERICA AND MEXICO

CANADA
  Montreal
  Ottawa
  Quebec
  Toronto
  Vancouver
  Winnipeg

MEXICO
  Mexico City

UNITED STATES
  Atlanta
  Augusta
  Bakersfield
  Baltimore
  Berkeley
  Birmingham
  Bloomington
  Boston
  Brooklyn
  Buffalo
  Chicago
  Cincinnati
  Cleveland
  Columbia
  Columbus
  Davenport
  Des Moines
  Detroit
  East Lancing
  Edmonton
  El Paso
  Fresno
  Greenboro

Houston
Huntingdon
Kansas City
Knoxville
Lafayette
Minneapolis
New York
Nottingham
Omaha
Philadelphia
Pittsburg
Portland
Richmond
Rochester
Sacremento
St. Louis
San Antonio
San Diego
San Francisco
Seattle
Spartanburg
Spokane
Washington
Youngstown

SOUTH AMERICA

ARGENTINA
  Buenos Aires

BRAZIL
  Rio de Janeiro
  Sao Paulo

CHILE
  Santiago

COLOMBIA
  Bogota

PERU
  Lima

URUGUAY
  Montevideo

VENEZUELA
  Caracas

NOTE ON THE ILLUSTRATIONS

The Author and Publishers would like to thank the following photographers for allowing them to reproduce their work:

Baron (Plate No. 15 *The Pas de Quatre*). Anthony Crickmay (No. 16 Benn Toff at the Royal Festival Hall; No. 36 *Peer Gynt*; No. 37 Vaslav Orlikowsky and Julian Braunsweg). Mike Davis (No. 3; No. 9; No. 10 Yvette Chauvire and Anton Dolin; No. 15 *Scheherazade*; No. 17 *Symphony for Fun*; No. 18 Pamela Hart; No. 19 *Harlequinade*; No. 23 *Etudes*; No. 24 Tamara Toumanova; No. 27; No. 28; No. 29; No. 30 *The Witch Boy*; No. 31 Leon Woizikowsky; No. 32 Noël Coward with Julian Braunsweg etc.; No. 33; No. 35 *Bourrée Fantasque*; No. 38 John Truscott; No. 39; No. 40; No. 41; No. 43; No. 46 Eva Evdokimova and Cyril Atanassoff). Dominic (No. 45). Guttenberg Ltd (No. 38 *Swan Lake* Act III). Douglas Jeffrey (No. 36 13th Anniversary Gala). Louis Klementaski (No. 21 *Esmeralda*). Serge Lido (No. 20 Oleg Briansky; No. 47 *La Sylphide*). Duncan Melvin (No. 20 *Vilia*). Photo Pic (No. 31 Charlie Chaplin and Natalie Krassovska). Rouston Rogers (No. 8; No. 12 Leonide Massine). Ken Ross-Mackenzie (No. 16 *Vision of Marguerite*). Paul Wilson (No. 10 Alicia Markova and Anton Dolin; No. 19 *Alice in Wonderland*; No. 22 *Napoli*; No. 32 Noël Coward and the Guards). Reg Wilson (No. 44 John Field and Doreen Wells).

Grateful acknowledgement is also made to the following:

Cyril Beaumont for loaning the valuable photographs of Tamara Karsavina and Serge Diaghilev with Serge Nouvel from his personal collection and the Radio Times Hulton Picture Library for the loan of the photographs of Michel Fokine and Vera Fokina.

The beautiful colour photos of Margot Fonteyn and Nureyev and of John Gilpin in *Peer Gynt* which appear on the jacket are both by Mike Davis.